COMICS FOR A STRANGE WORLD

A BOOK OF POORLY DRAWN LINES

REZA FARAZMAND

PLUME

FOR HANNAH AND BO

PLUME
An imprint of Penguin Random House LLC
375 Hudson Street
New York, New York 10014

Library of Congress Cataloging-in-Publication Data
has been applied for.

ISBN 9780735219885

Printed in the United States of America
1   3   5   7   9   10   8   6   4   2

Book design by Alissa Rose Theodor

CONTENTS

INTRODUCTION

Not too long ago, a strange group of creatures emerged into the world. They were different from other creatures. They weren't content to just eat and run and live. They wanted more. They wanted to understand. And so they started banging rocks on things.

The rocks took on new shapes unlike anything the world had seen, shapes that stood out as weird and alien against the backdrop of nature. There were tools and weapons. There were buildings, monuments, and works of art. In some cases, the creatures built colossal statues of themselves to celebrate their own cleverness. These were perhaps the weirdest shapes of all.

As the creatures built more and more, the world around them changed to reflect their unique strangeness. Forests gave way to fields of concrete and metal. The creatures plugged themselves into elaborate machines. Other creatures, transfixed by the odd behavior of the strange ones, began to envy and imitate them. And as the world became something unrecognizable, the strange creatures slowly forgot their original goal: to understand. They had a new goal: to feel comfortable. And a secondary goal: to accumulate stuff. They found comfort on their high mountains of stuff, and those creatures who sat the highest and most comfortably became leaders, because those with the most stuff are simply better.

The history of these creatures is still unfolding. This book is an attempt to capture the strangeness of their world and to make fun of it wherever possible. It's a world filled with ironies and oddities, inexplicable occurrences, and things that don't belong in real life. It's a world not unlike our own. Apart from the talking animals, the ghosts, and the general absence of any coherent laws of nature, many of us would feel right at home there. That's not necessarily a good thing, but don't worry: Our own world isn't quite this strange yet. Yet.

COMICS FOR A STRANGE WORLD

I

THE HUMAN EXPERIENCE

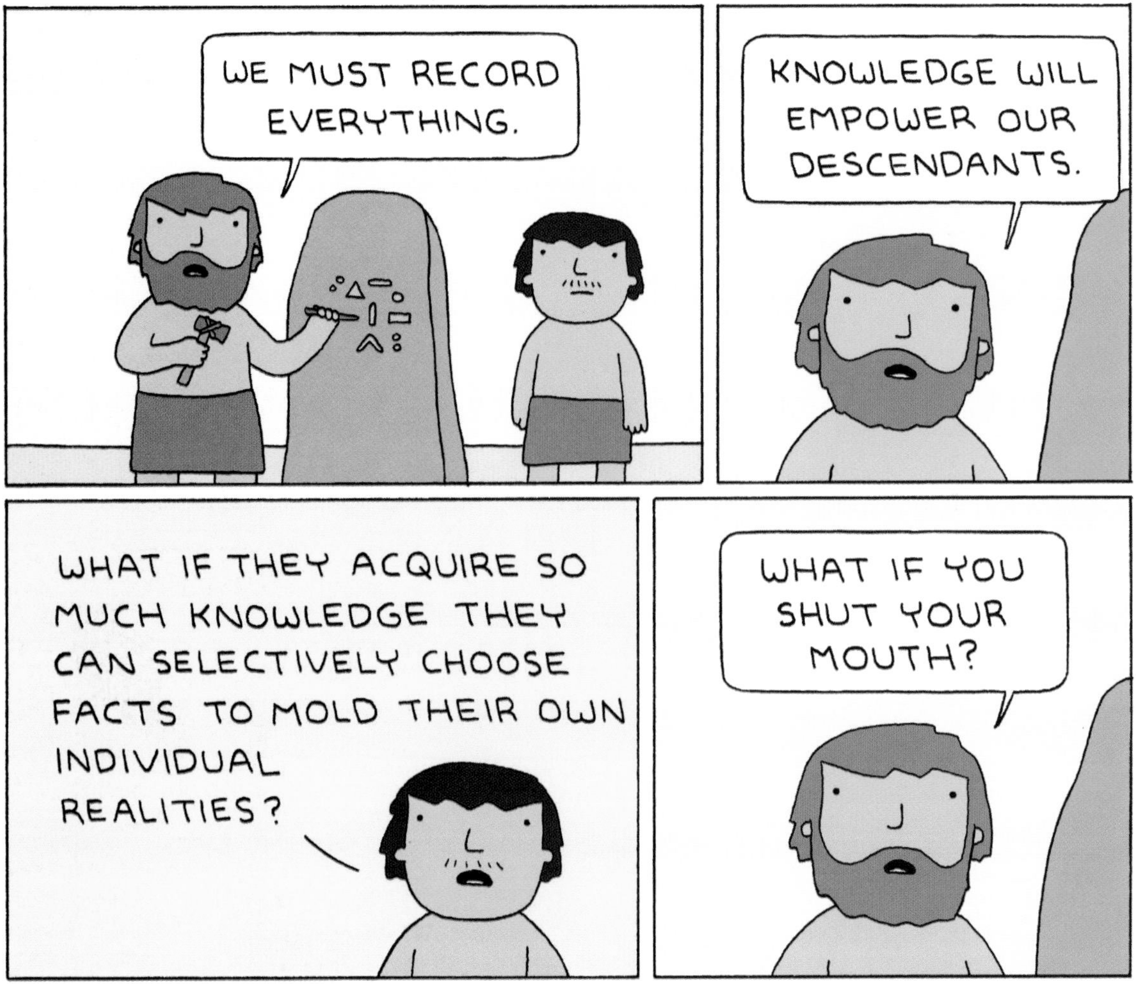
WE MUST RECORD EVERYTHING.
KNOWLEDGE WILL EMPOWER OUR DESCENDANTS.
WHAT IF THEY ACQUIRE SO MUCH KNOWLEDGE THEY CAN SELECTIVELY CHOOSE FACTS TO MOLD THEIR OWN INDIVIDUAL REALITIES?
WHAT IF YOU SHUT YOUR MOUTH?

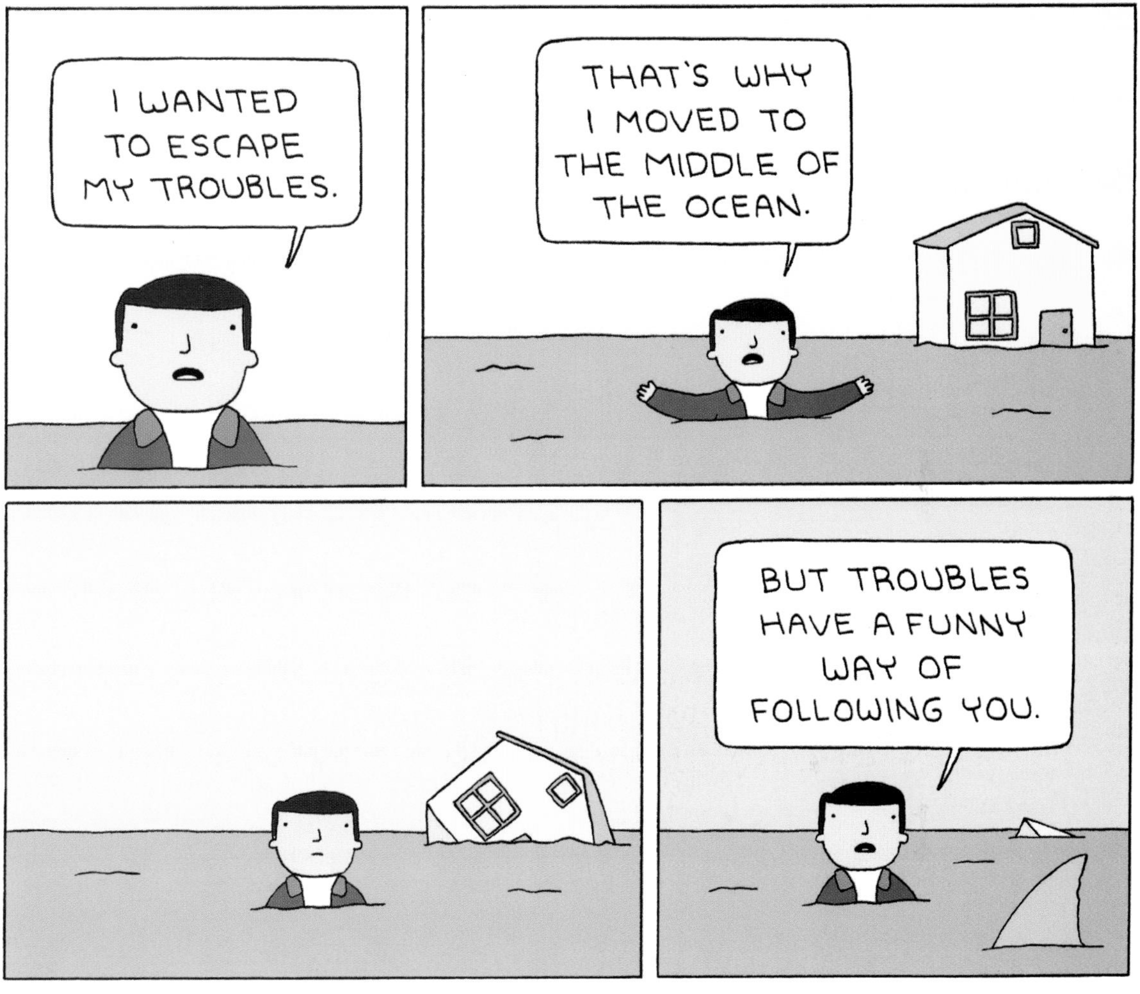
I WANTED TO ESCAPE MY TROUBLES.
THAT'S WHY I MOVED TO THE MIDDLE OF THE OCEAN.
BUT TROUBLES HAVE A FUNNY WAY OF FOLLOWING YOU.

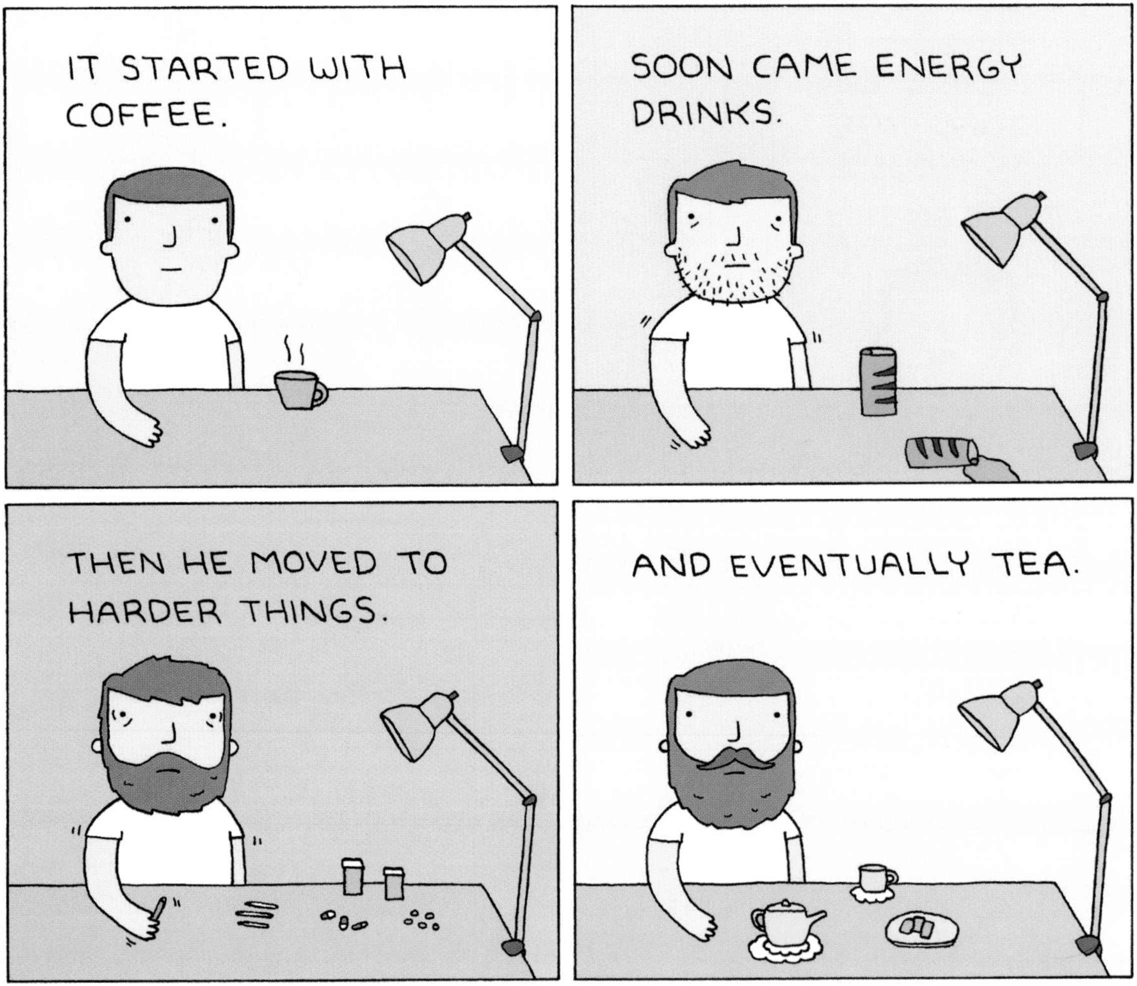
IT STARTED WITH COFFEE.
SOON CAME ENERGY DRINKS.
THEN HE MOVED TO HARDER THINGS.
AND EVENTUALLY TEA.

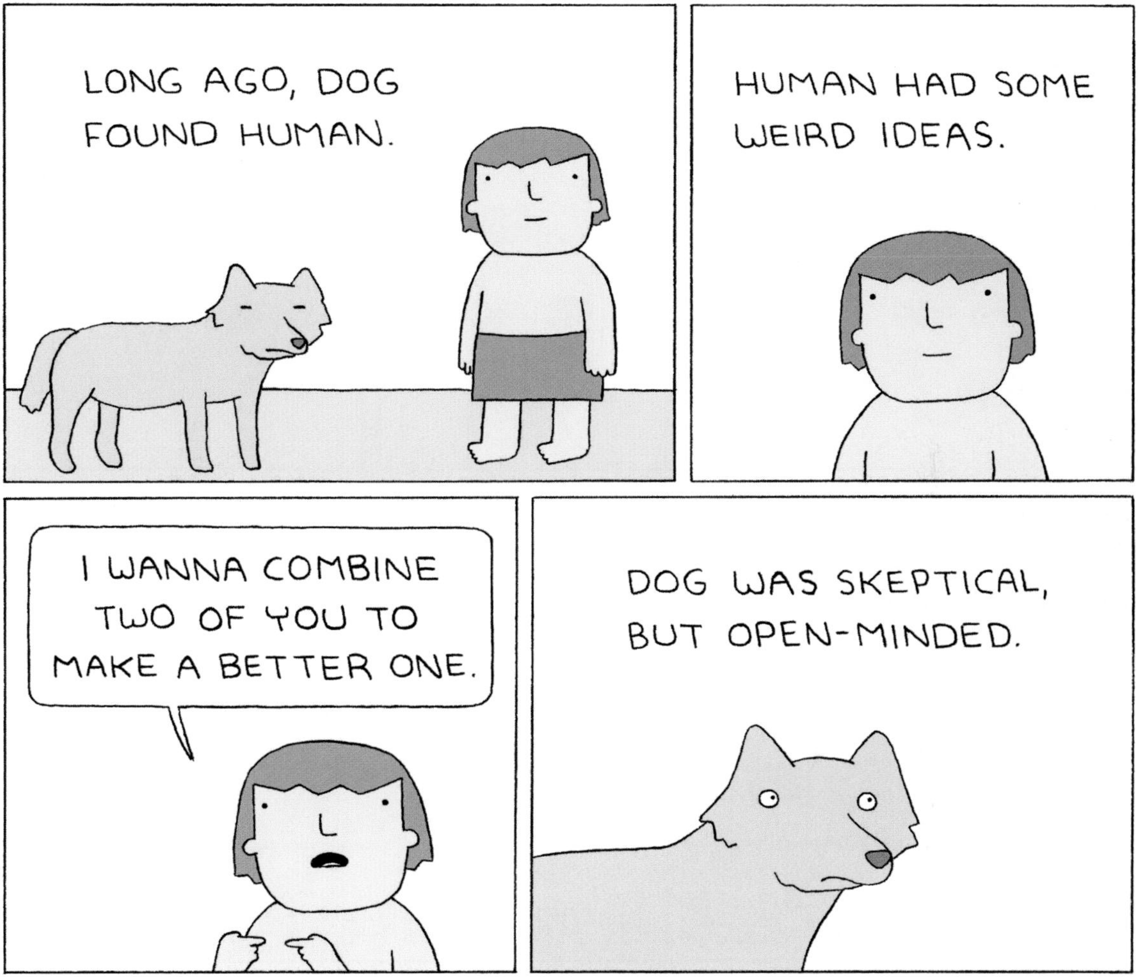
LONG AGO, DOG FOUND HUMAN.
HUMAN HAD SOME WEIRD IDEAS.
I WANNA COMBINE TWO OF YOU TO MAKE A BETTER ONE.
DOG WAS SKEPTICAL, BUT OPEN-MINDED.

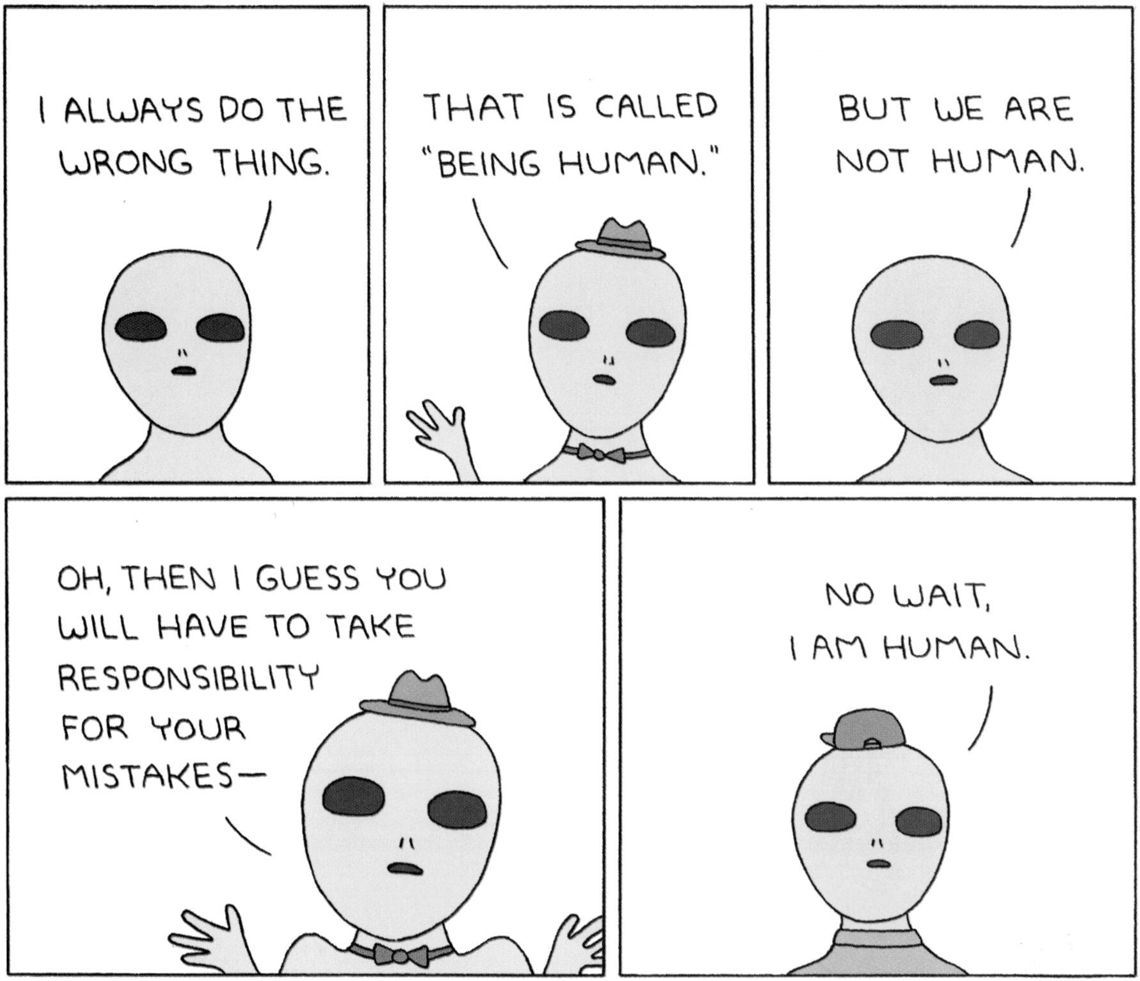
I ALWAYS DO THE WRONG THING.
THAT IS CALLED "BEING HUMAN."
BUT WE ARE NOT HUMAN.
OH, THEN I GUESS YOU WILL HAVE TO TAKE RESPONSIBILITY FOR YOUR MISTAKES—
NO WAIT, I AM HUMAN.

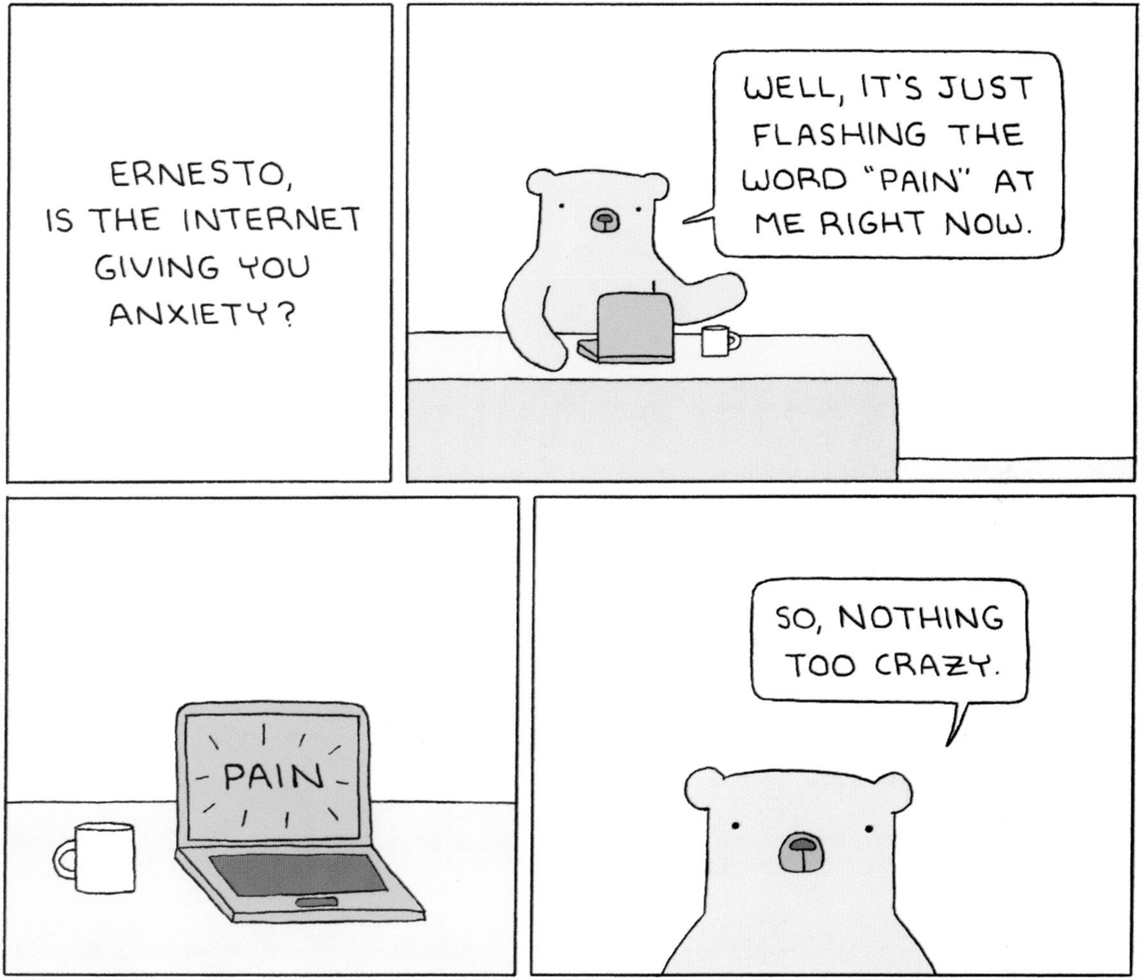
ERNESTO, IS THE INTERNET GIVING YOU ANXIETY?
WELL, IT'S JUST FLASHING THE WORD "PAIN" AT ME RIGHT NOW.
PAIN
SO, NOTHING TOO CRAZY.

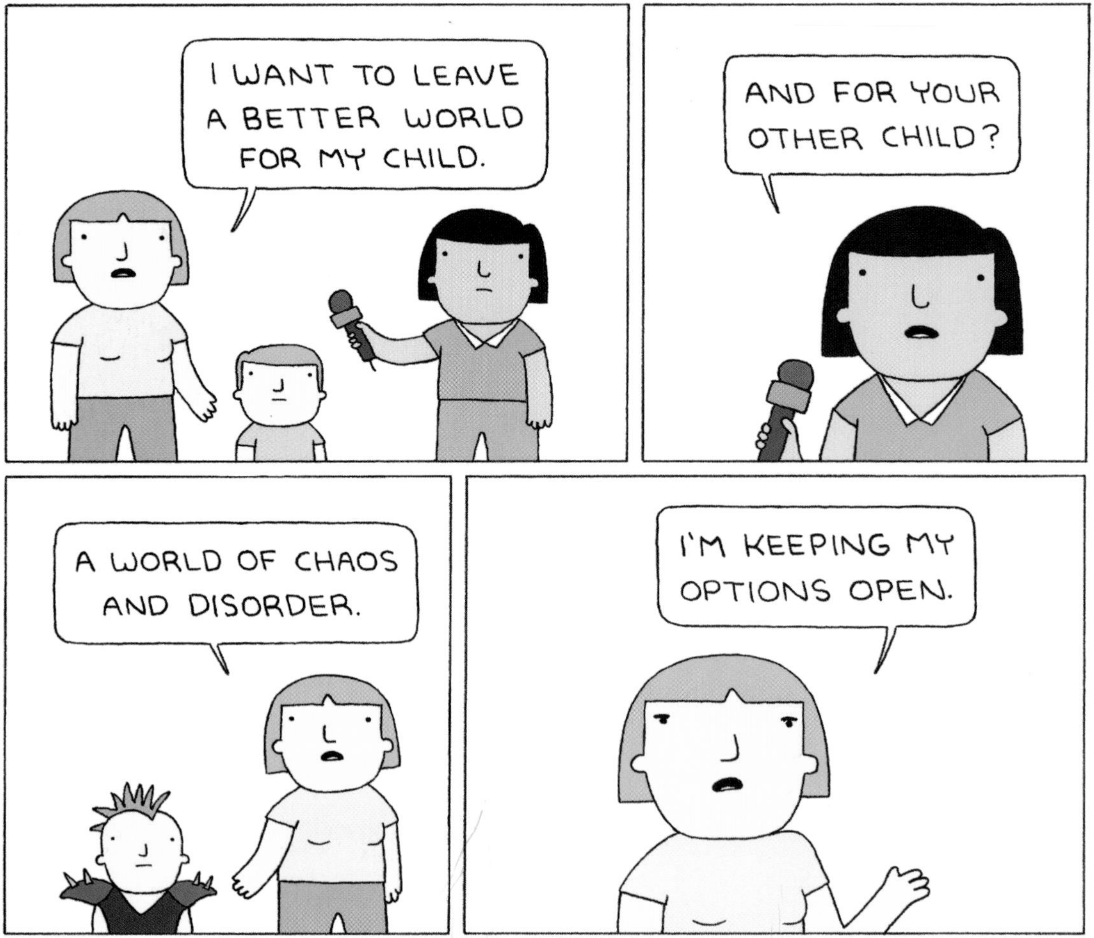
I WANT TO LEAVE A BETTER WORLD FOR MY CHILD.
AND FOR YOUR OTHER CHILD?
A WORLD OF CHAOS AND DISORDER.
I'M KEEPING MY OPTIONS OPEN.

THINGS WERE SIMPLER WHEN WE HAD THE GODS

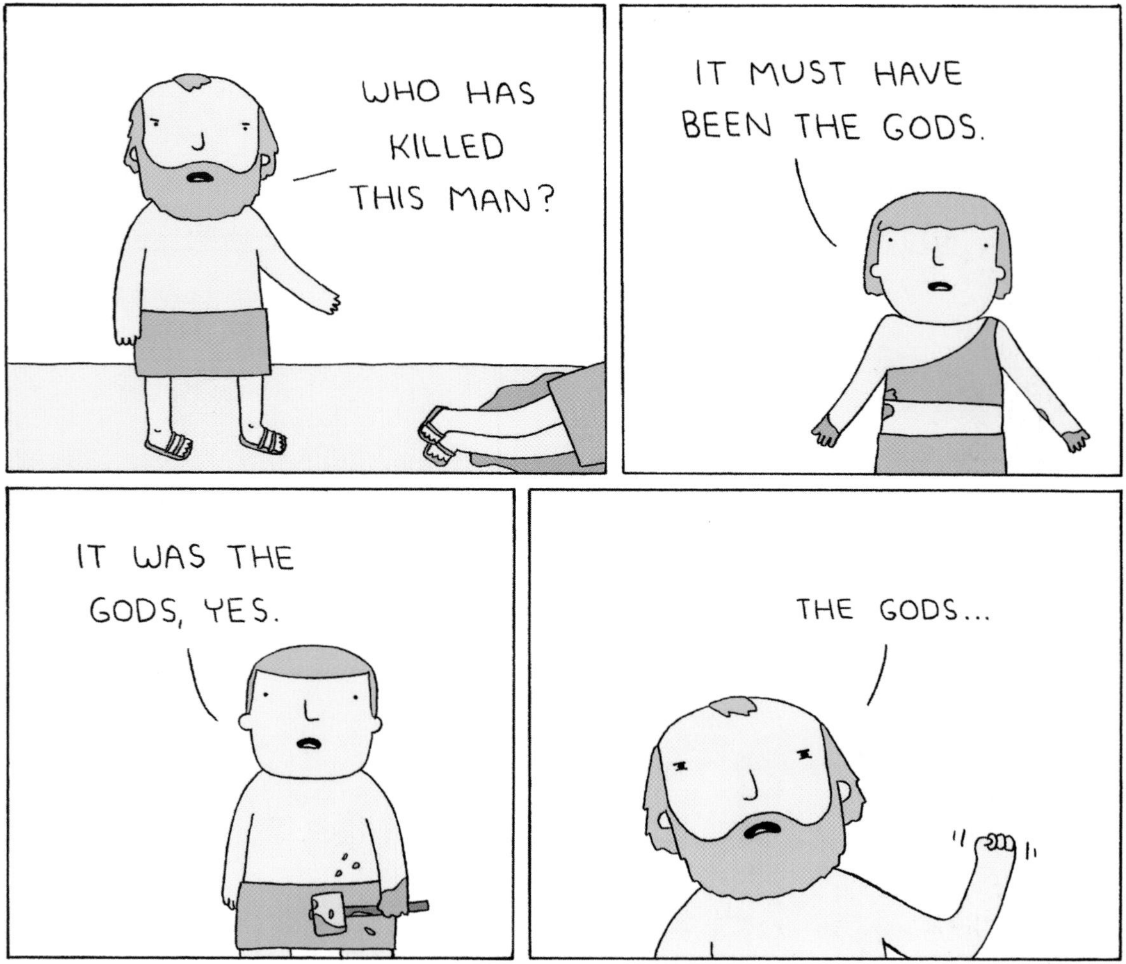
WHO HAS KILLED THIS MAN?
IT MUST HAVE BEEN THE GODS.
IT WAS THE GODS, YES.
THE GODS...

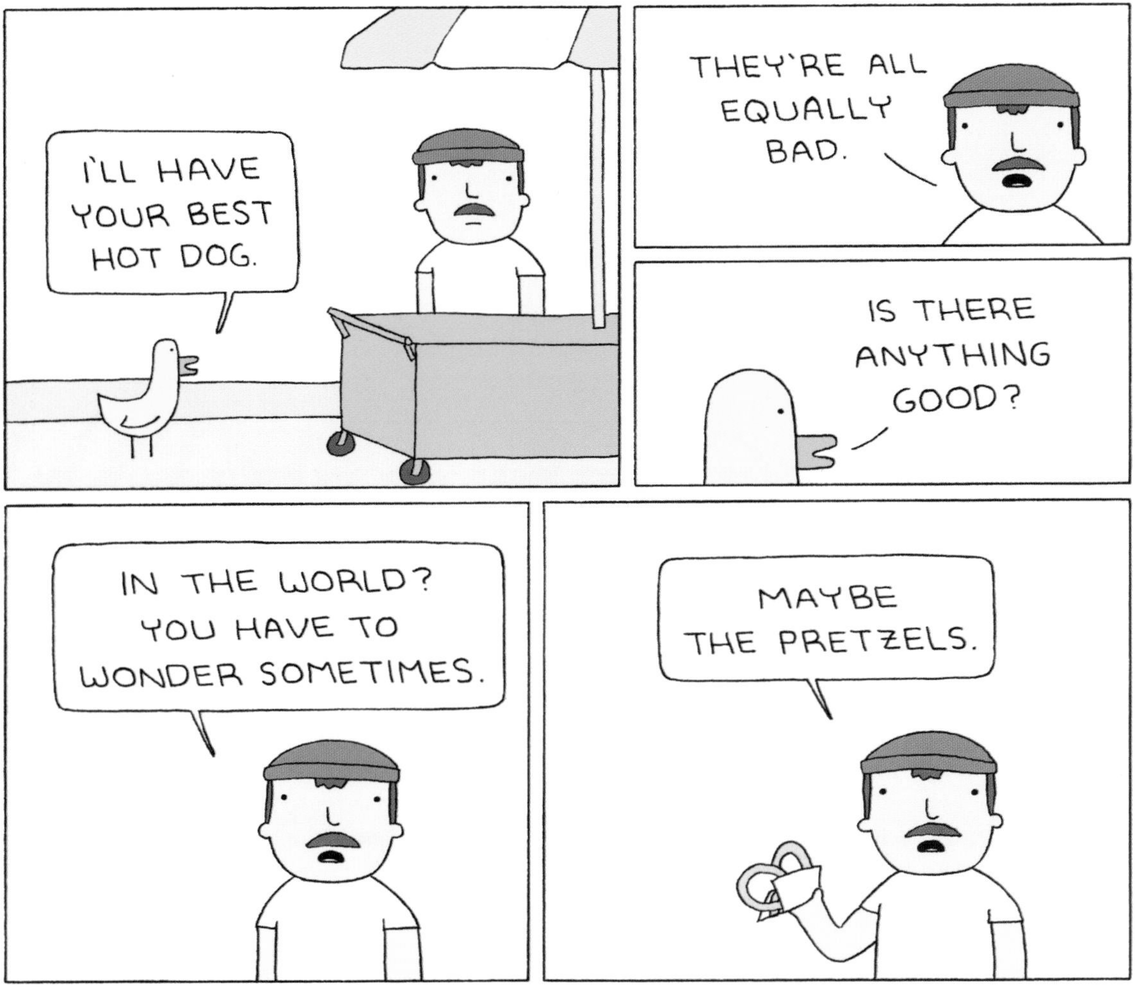
I'LL HAVE YOUR BEST HOT DOG.
THEY'RE ALL EQUALLY BAD.
IS THERE ANYTHING GOOD?
IN THE WORLD? YOU HAVE TO WONDER SOMETIMES.
MAYBE THE PRETZELS.

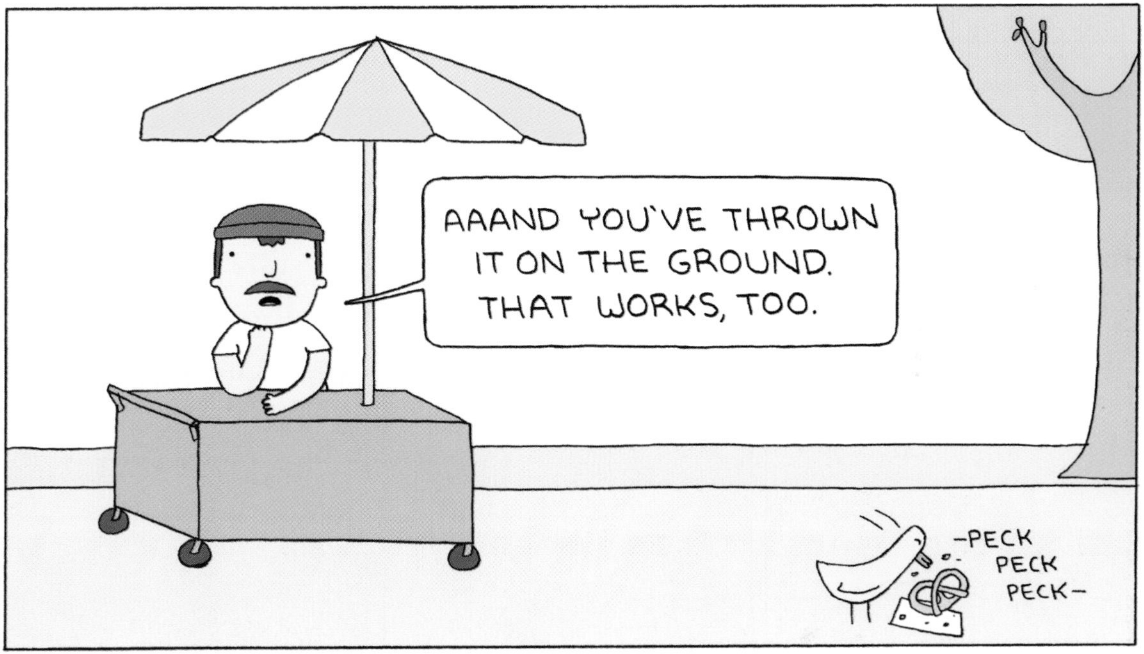
AAAND YOU'VE THROWN IT ON THE GROUND. THAT WORKS, TOO.
-PECK PECK PECK-

PARTY
FOREVER

I HAVE
WORK
TOMORROW.

PARTY
UNTIL AN
APPROPRIATE
HOUR BASED
ON YOUR
CURRENT
SCHEDULE

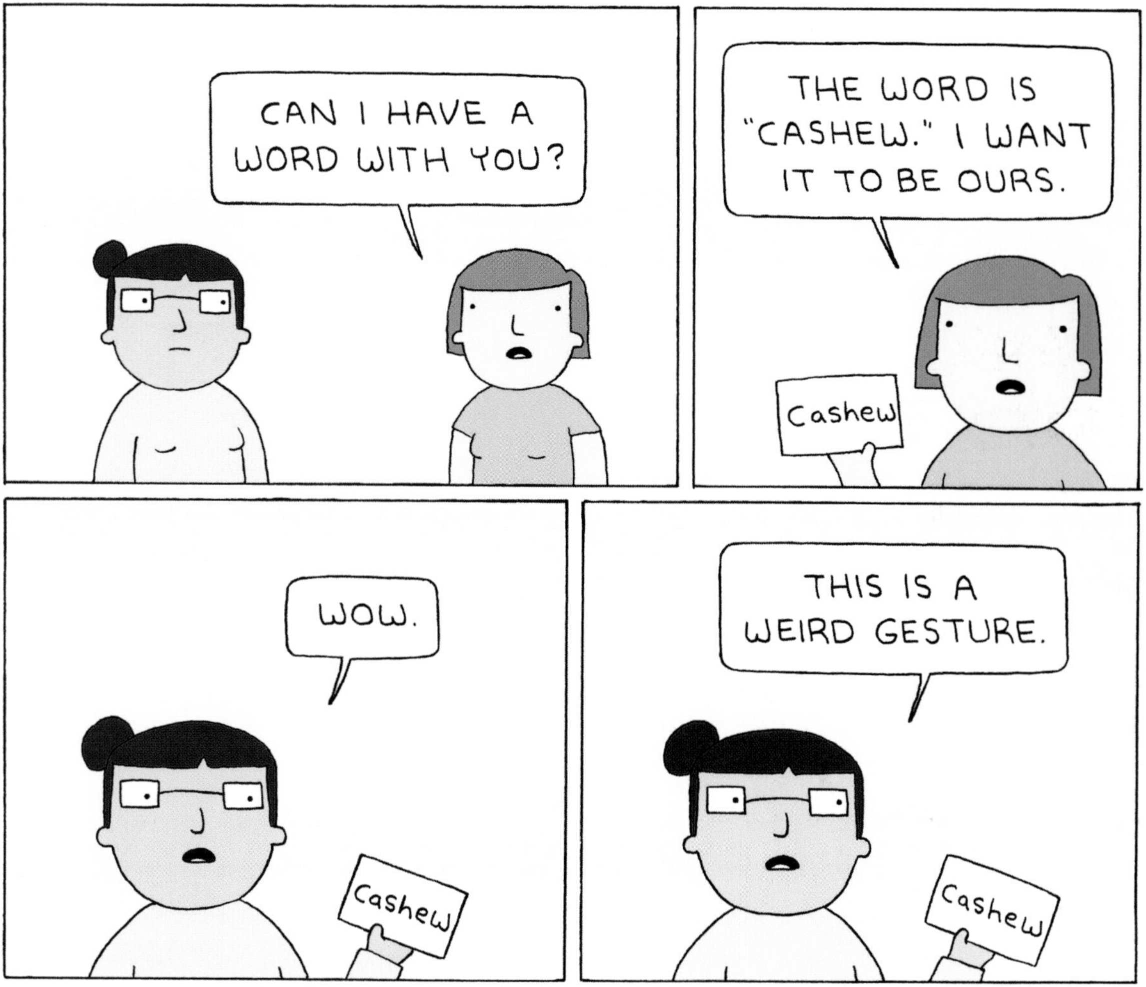
CAN I HAVE A WORD WITH YOU?
THE WORD IS "CASHEW." I WANT IT TO BE OURS.
Cashew
WOW.
Cashew
THIS IS A WEIRD GESTURE.
Cashew

BOAT QUESTION

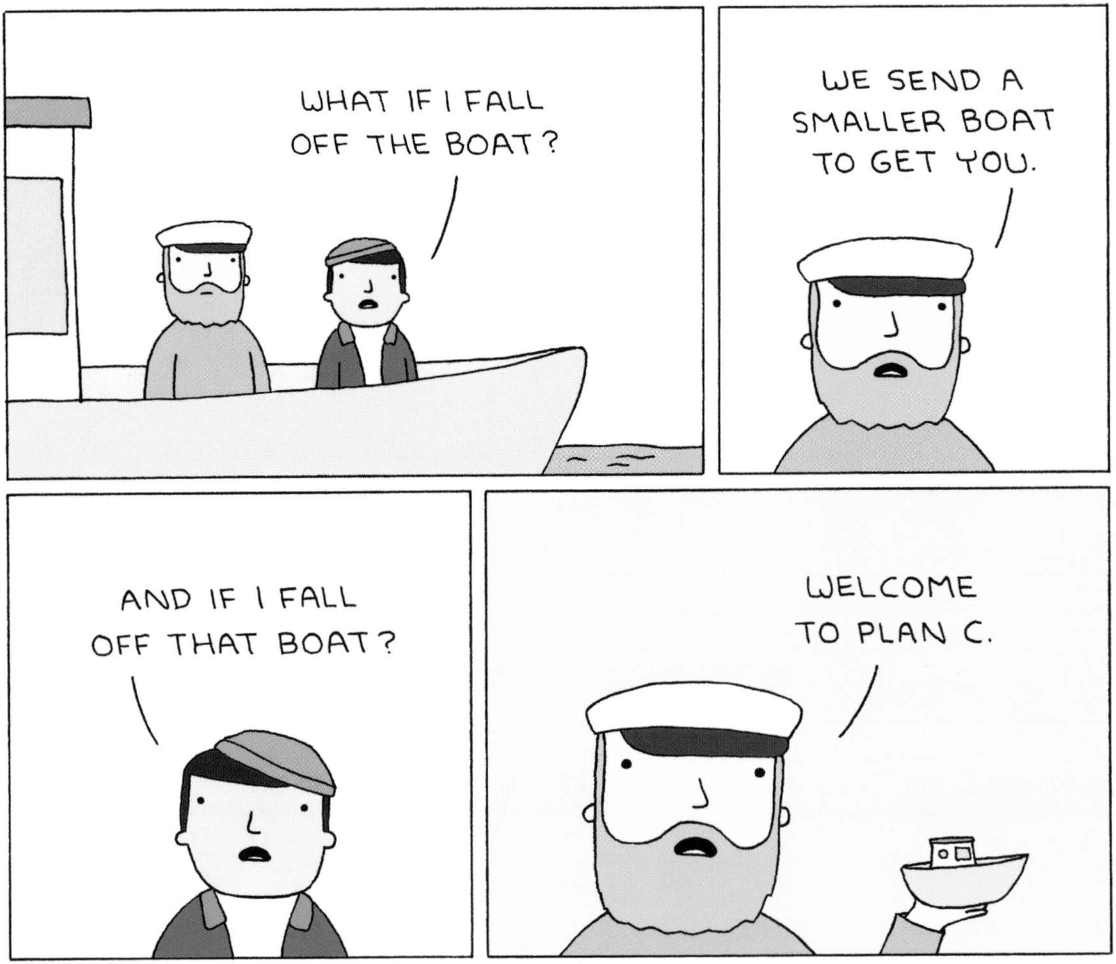
WHAT IF I FALL OFF THE BOAT?
WE SEND A SMALLER BOAT TO GET YOU.
AND IF I FALL OFF THAT BOAT?
WELCOME TO PLAN C.

UNFORTUNATELY, WE HAVE TO LET YOU GO.
IS IT BECAUSE I SCREAM IN EXISTENTIAL TERROR EVERY MOMENT I'M TRAPPED IN THIS OFFICE?
NO, NO, NO. IT'S A BUDGET THING.

ERNESTO IS PRETTY BUMMED

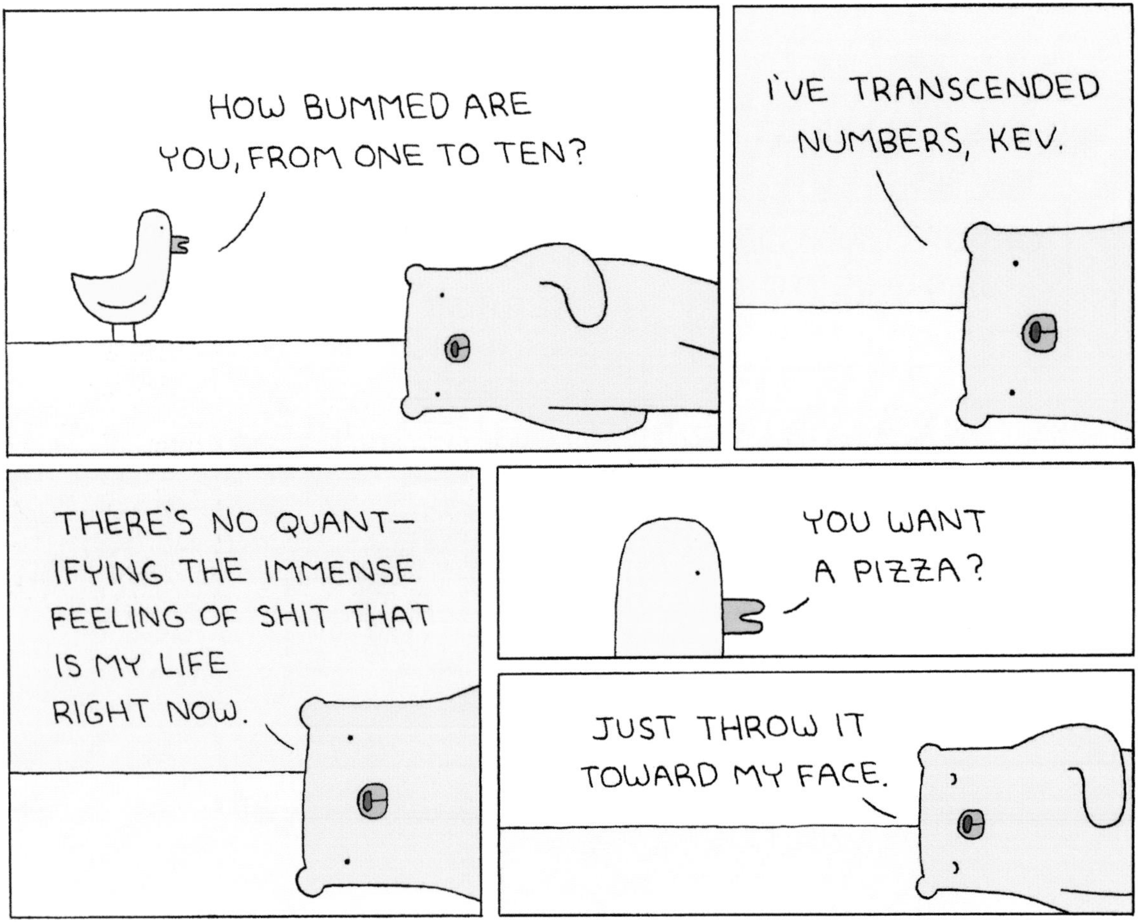
HOW BUMMED ARE YOU, FROM ONE TO TEN?
I'VE TRANSCENDED NUMBERS, KEV.
THERE'S NO QUANT-IFYING THE IMMENSE FEELING OF SHIT THAT IS MY LIFE RIGHT NOW.
YOU WANT A PIZZA?
JUST THROW IT TOWARD MY FACE.

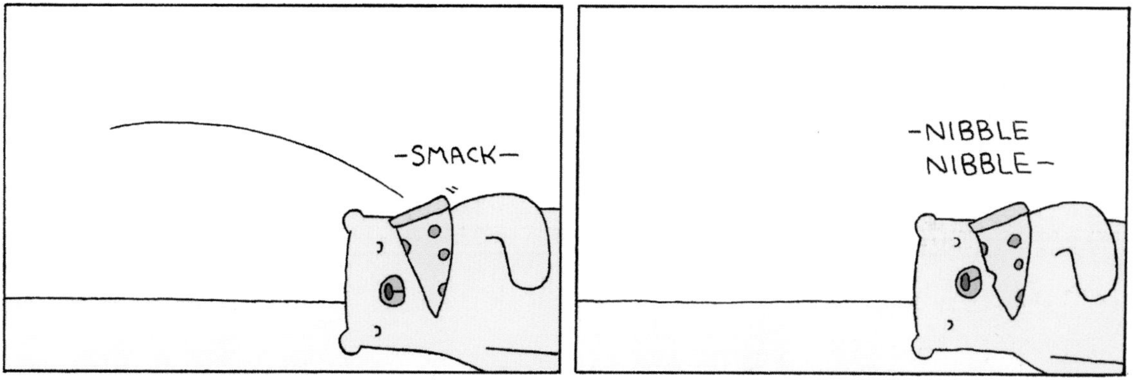
-SMACK-
-NIBBLE
NIBBLE-

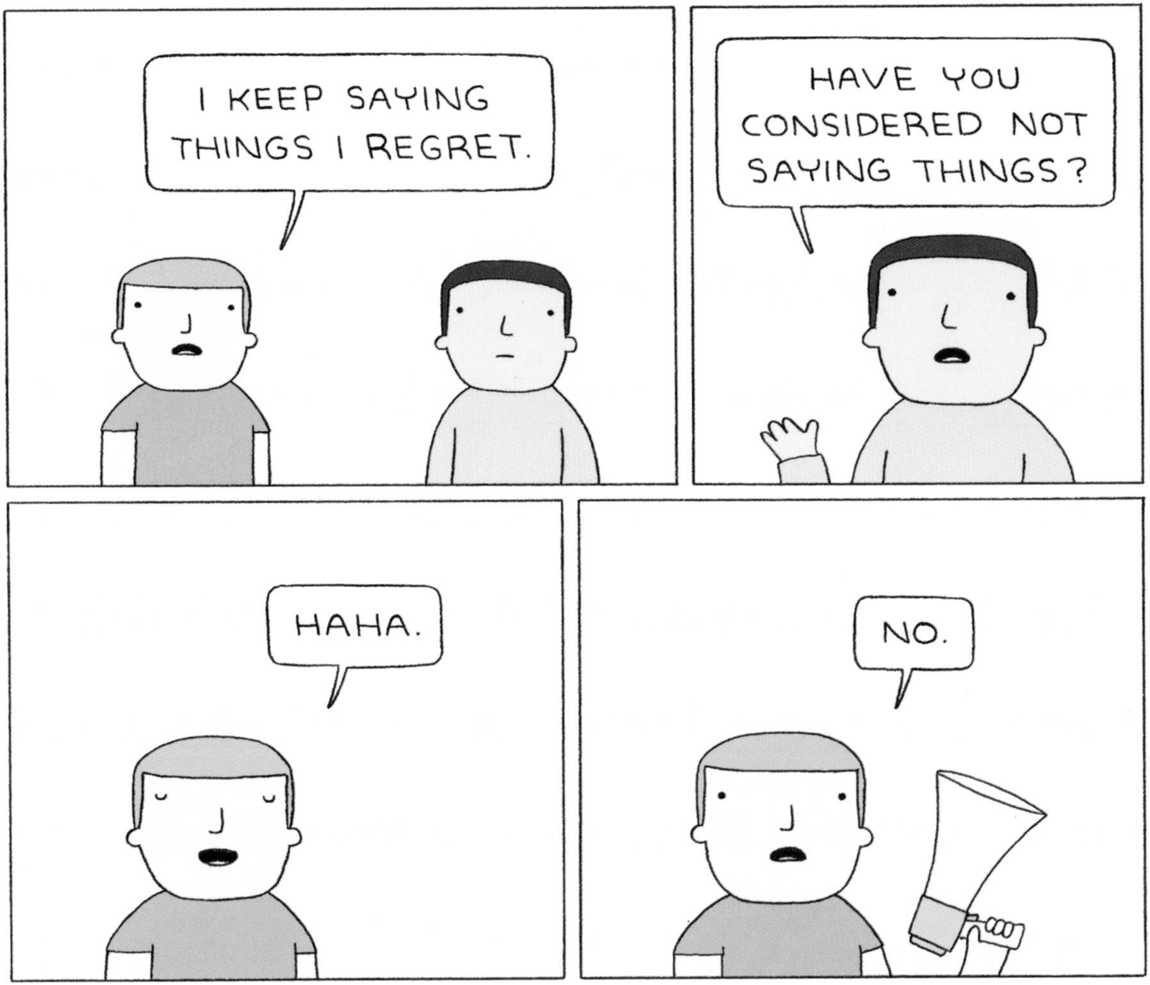
I KEEP SAYING THINGS I REGRET.
HAVE YOU CONSIDERED NOT SAYING THINGS?
HAHA.
NO.

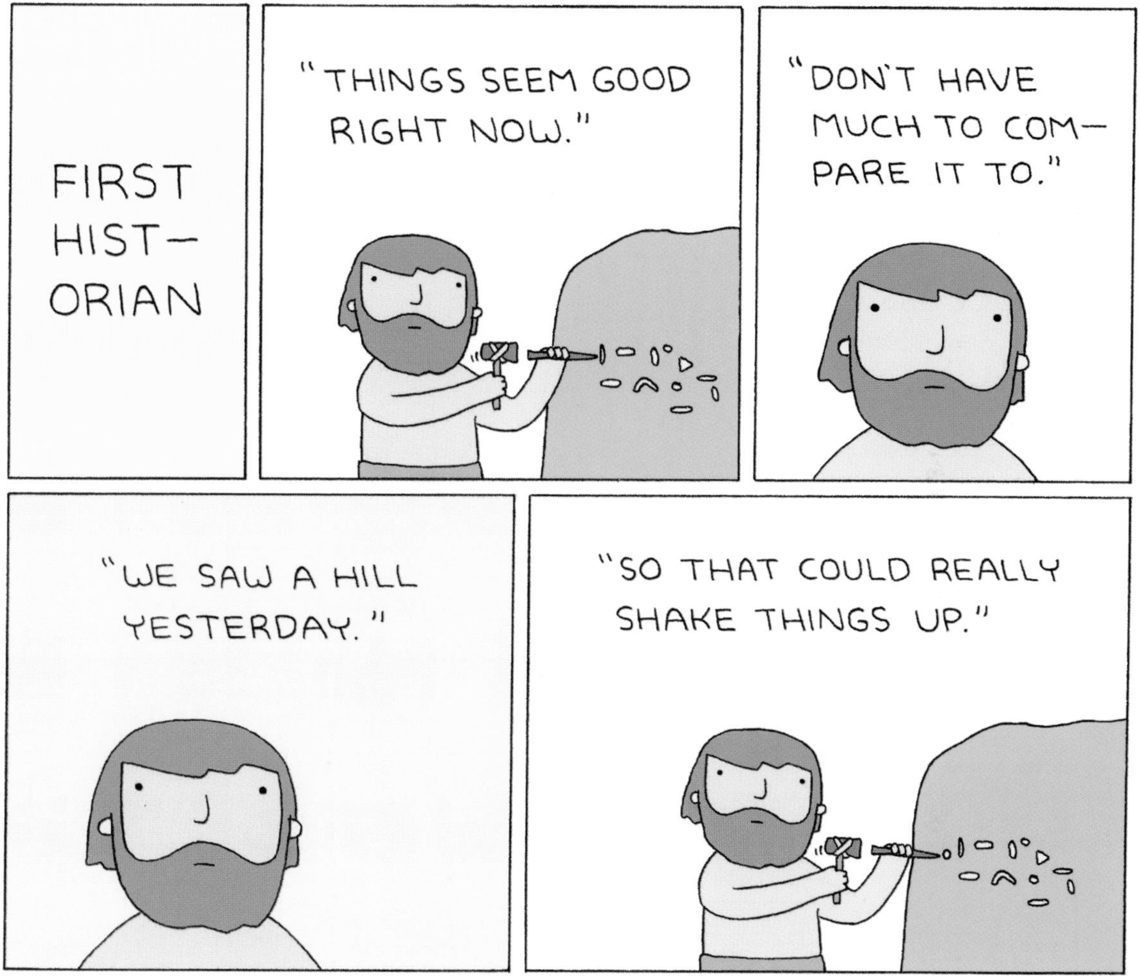
FIRST HIST-ORIAN
"THINGS SEEM GOOD RIGHT NOW."
"DON'T HAVE MUCH TO COM-PARE IT TO."
"WE SAW A HILL YESTERDAY."
"SO THAT COULD REALLY SHAKE THINGS UP."

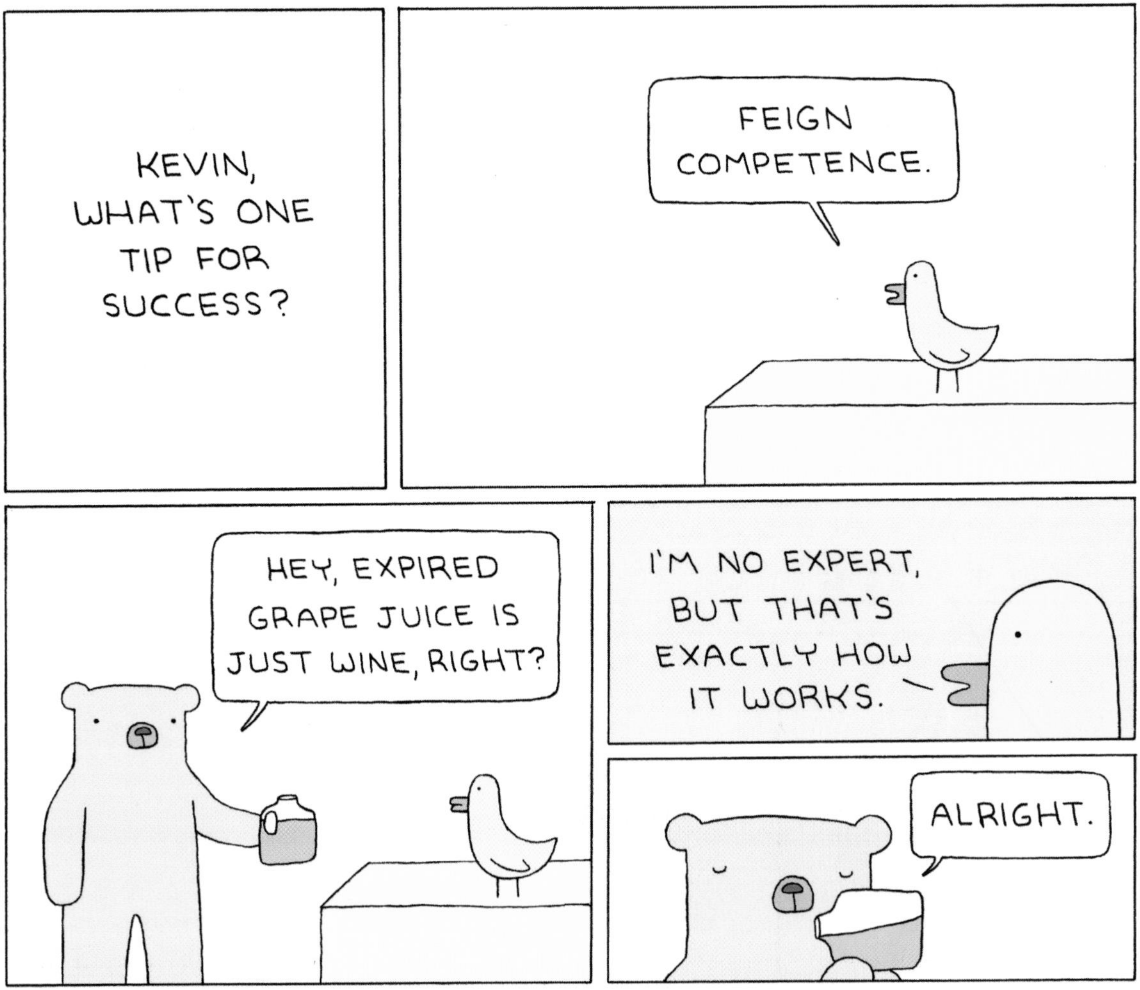
KEVIN, WHAT'S ONE TIP FOR SUCCESS?
FEIGN COMPETENCE.
HEY, EXPIRED GRAPE JUICE IS JUST WINE, RIGHT?
I'M NO EXPERT, BUT THAT'S EXACTLY HOW IT WORKS.
ALRIGHT.

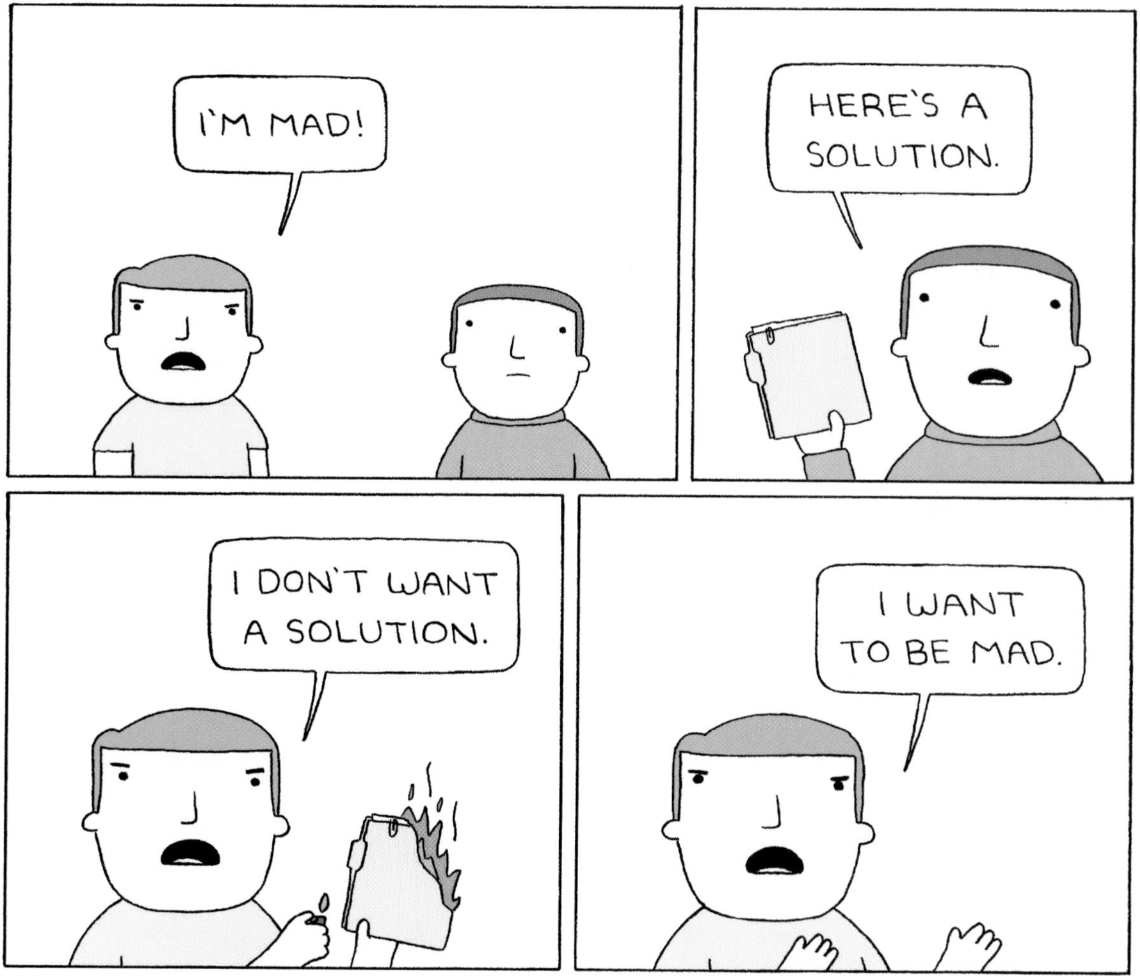
I'M MAD!
HERE'S A SOLUTION.
I DON'T WANT A SOLUTION.
I WANT TO BE MAD.

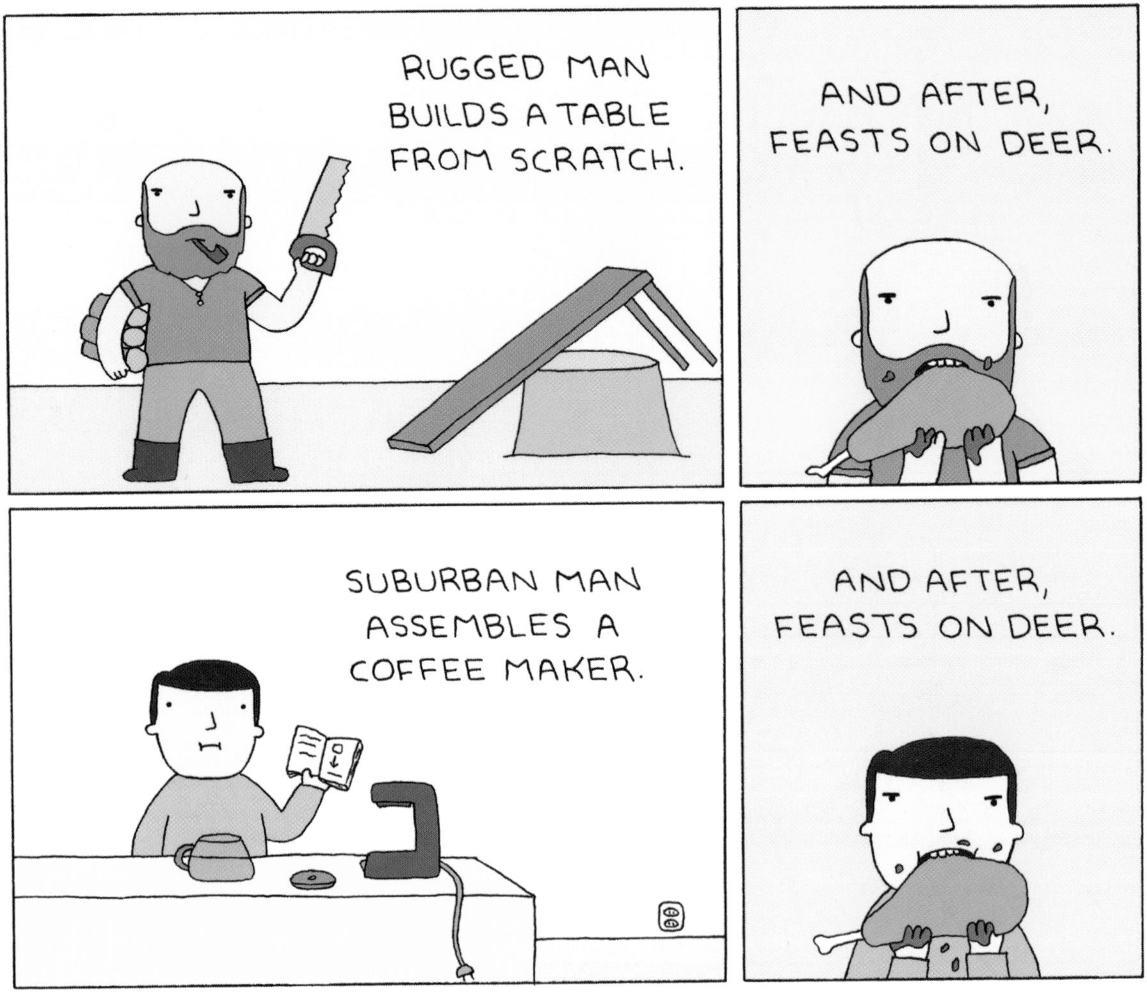
RUGGED MAN BUILDS A TABLE FROM SCRATCH.
AND AFTER, FEASTS ON DEER.
SUBURBAN MAN ASSEMBLES A COFFEE MAKER.
AND AFTER, FEASTS ON DEER.

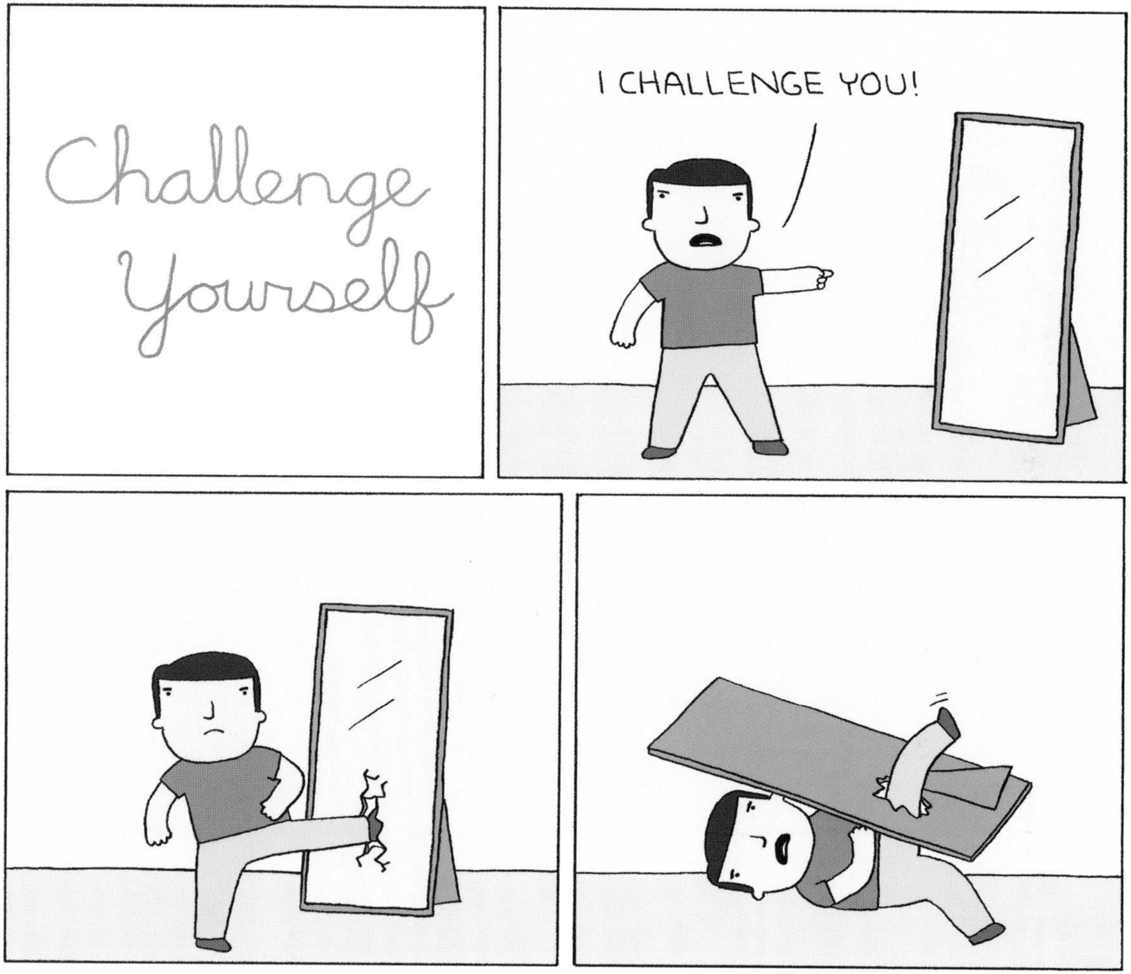
Challenge Yourself
I CHALLENGE YOU!

KEVIN HAS SEEN A GIRL

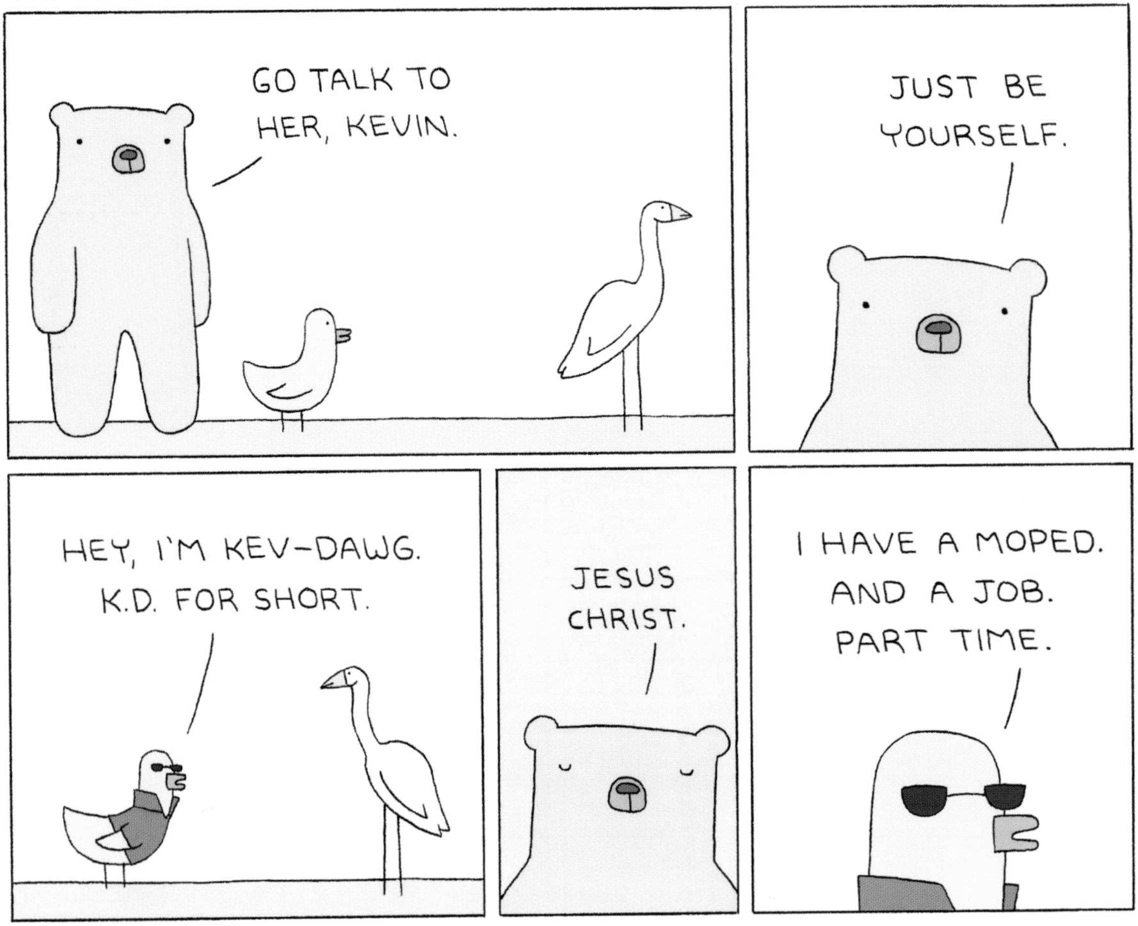
GO TALK TO HER, KEVIN.
JUST BE YOURSELF.
HEY, I'M KEV-DAWG. K.D. FOR SHORT.
JESUS CHRIST.
I HAVE A MOPED. AND A JOB. PART TIME.

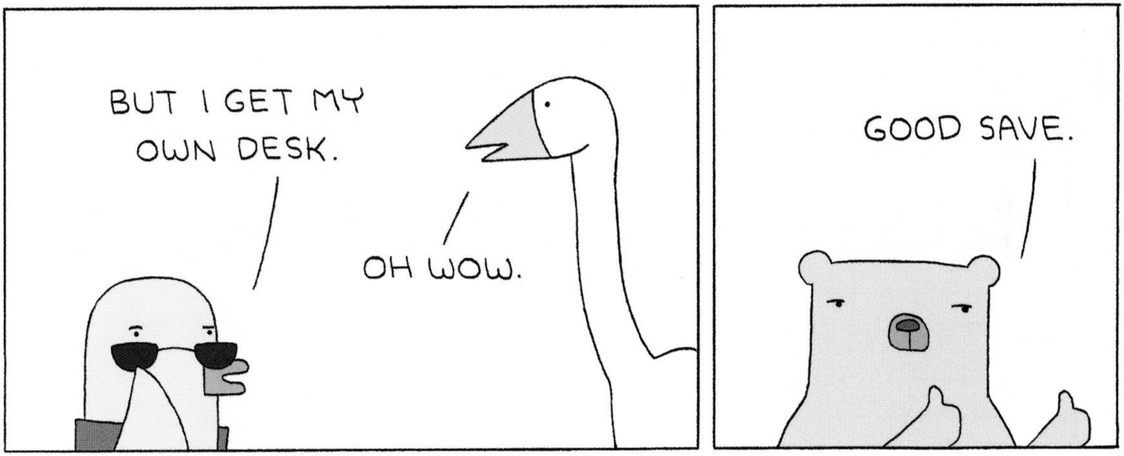
BUT I GET MY OWN DESK.
OH WOW.
GOOD SAVE.

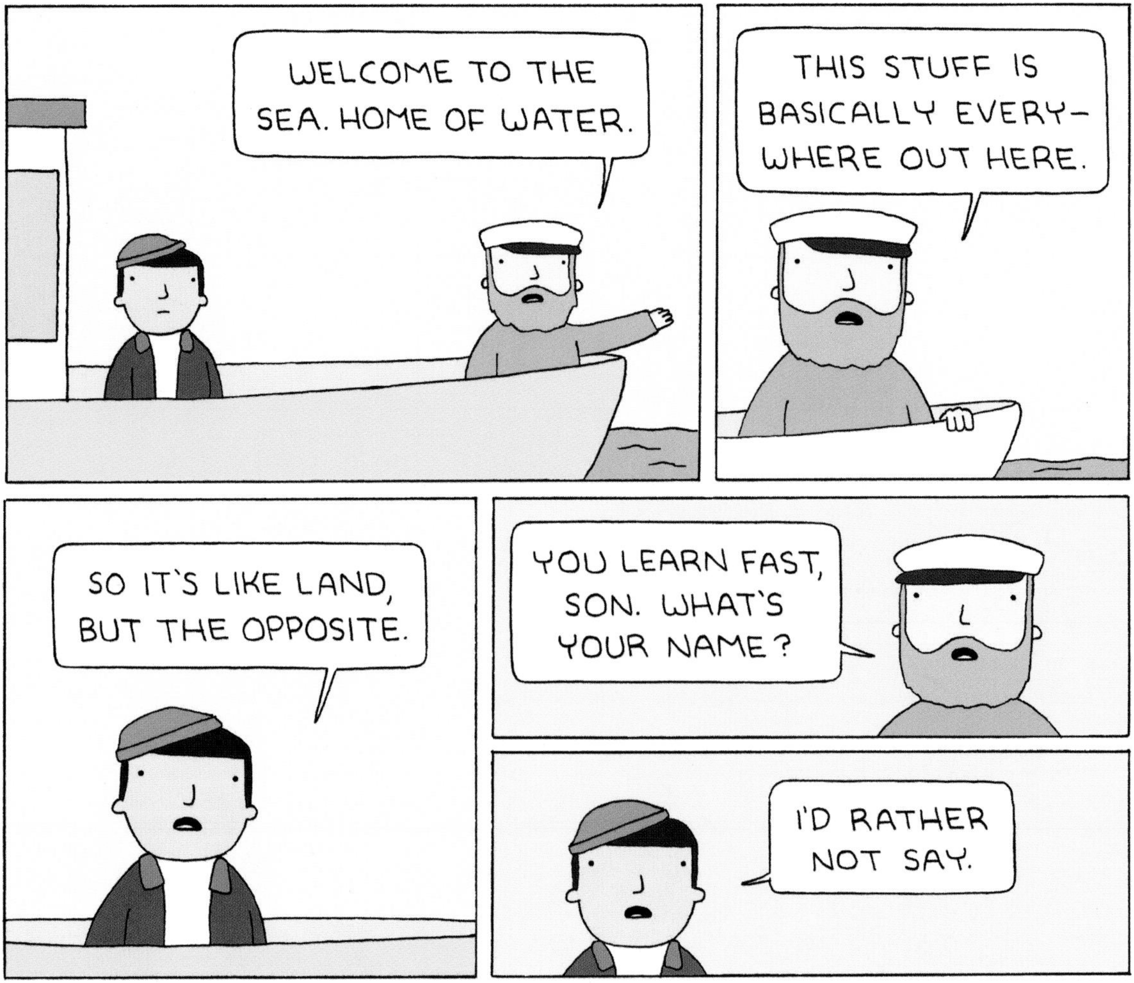
WELCOME TO THE SEA. HOME OF WATER.
THIS STUFF IS BASICALLY EVERY- WHERE OUT HERE.
SO IT'S LIKE LAND, BUT THE OPPOSITE.
YOU LEARN FAST, SON. WHAT'S YOUR NAME?
I'D RATHER NOT SAY.

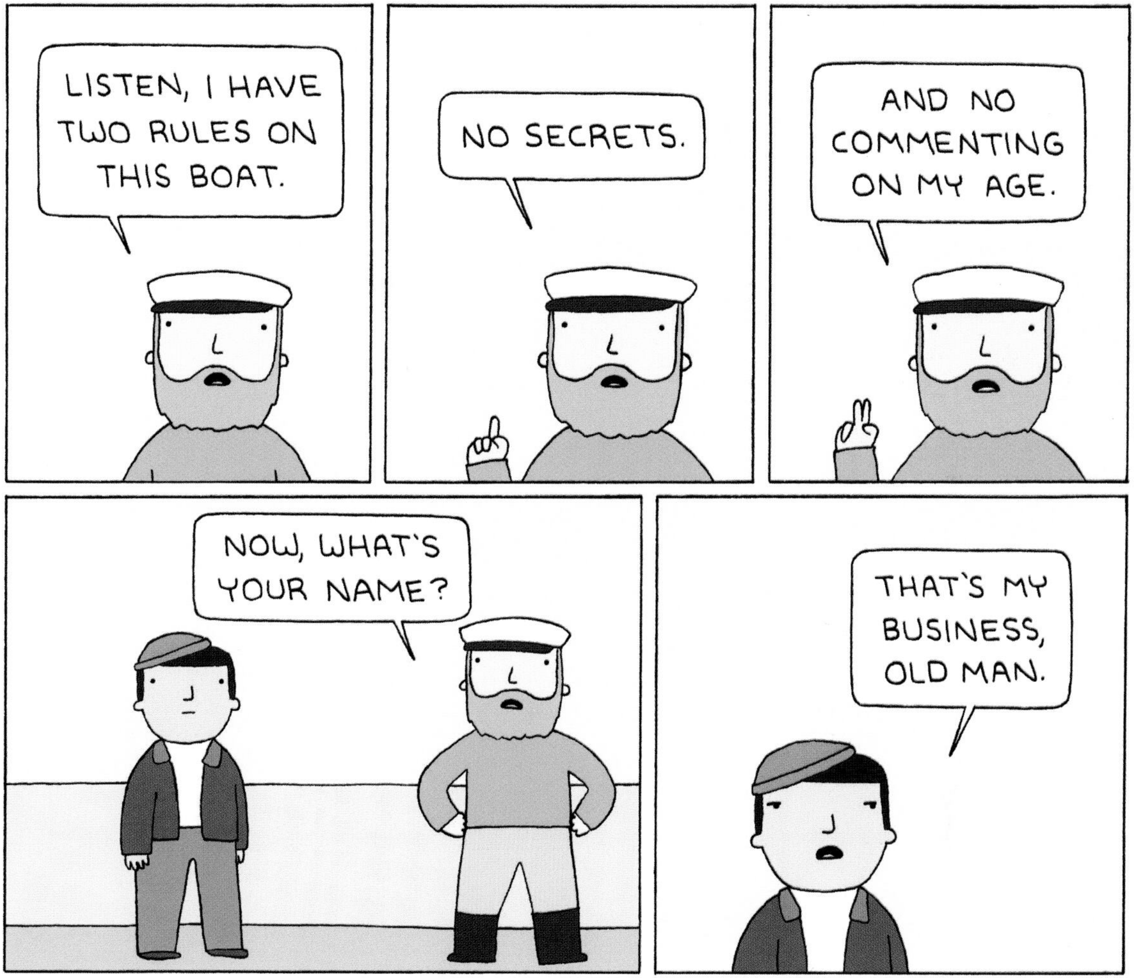
LISTEN, I HAVE TWO RULES ON THIS BOAT.
NO SECRETS.
AND NO COMMENTING ON MY AGE.
NOW, WHAT'S YOUR NAME?
THAT'S MY BUSINESS, OLD MAN.

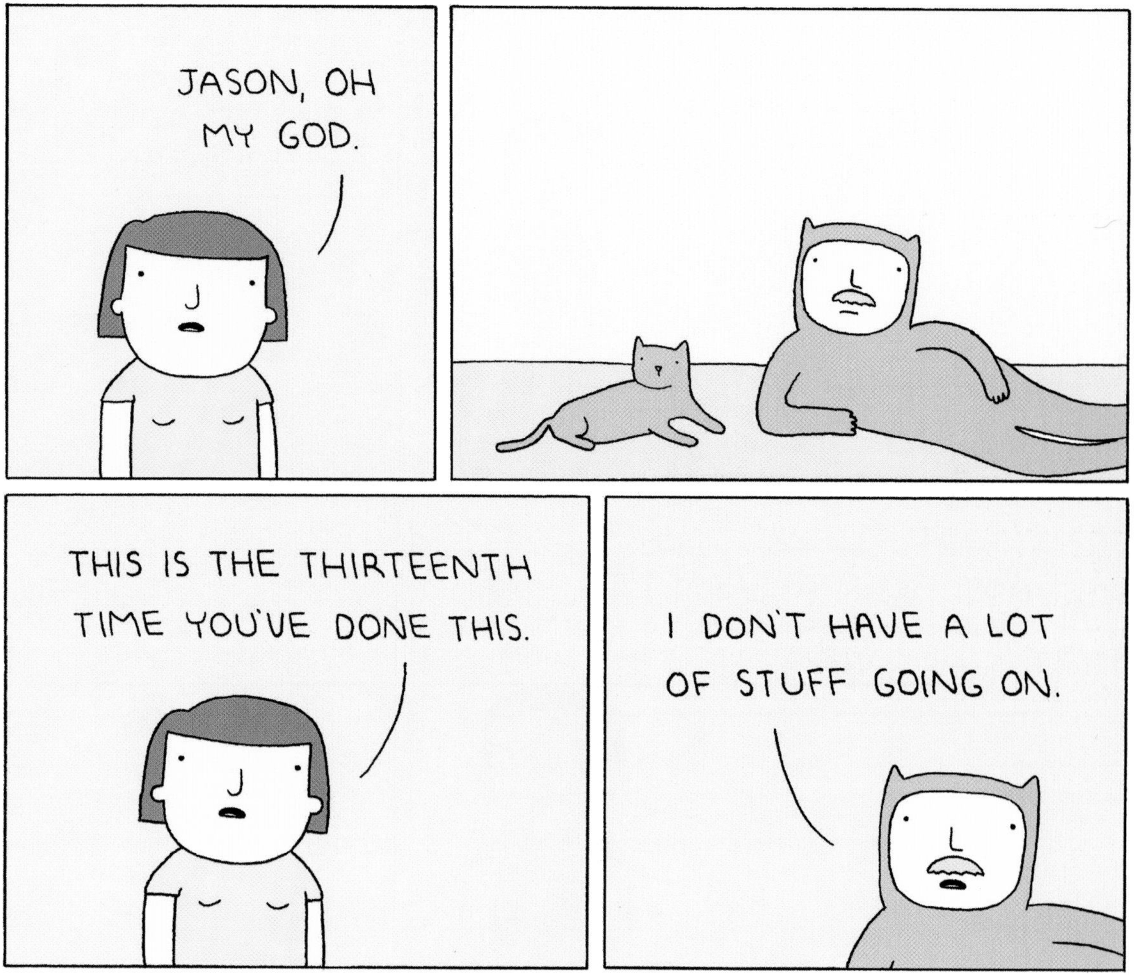
JASON, OH MY GOD.
THIS IS THE THIRTEENTH TIME YOU'VE DONE THIS.
I DON'T HAVE A LOT OF STUFF GOING ON.

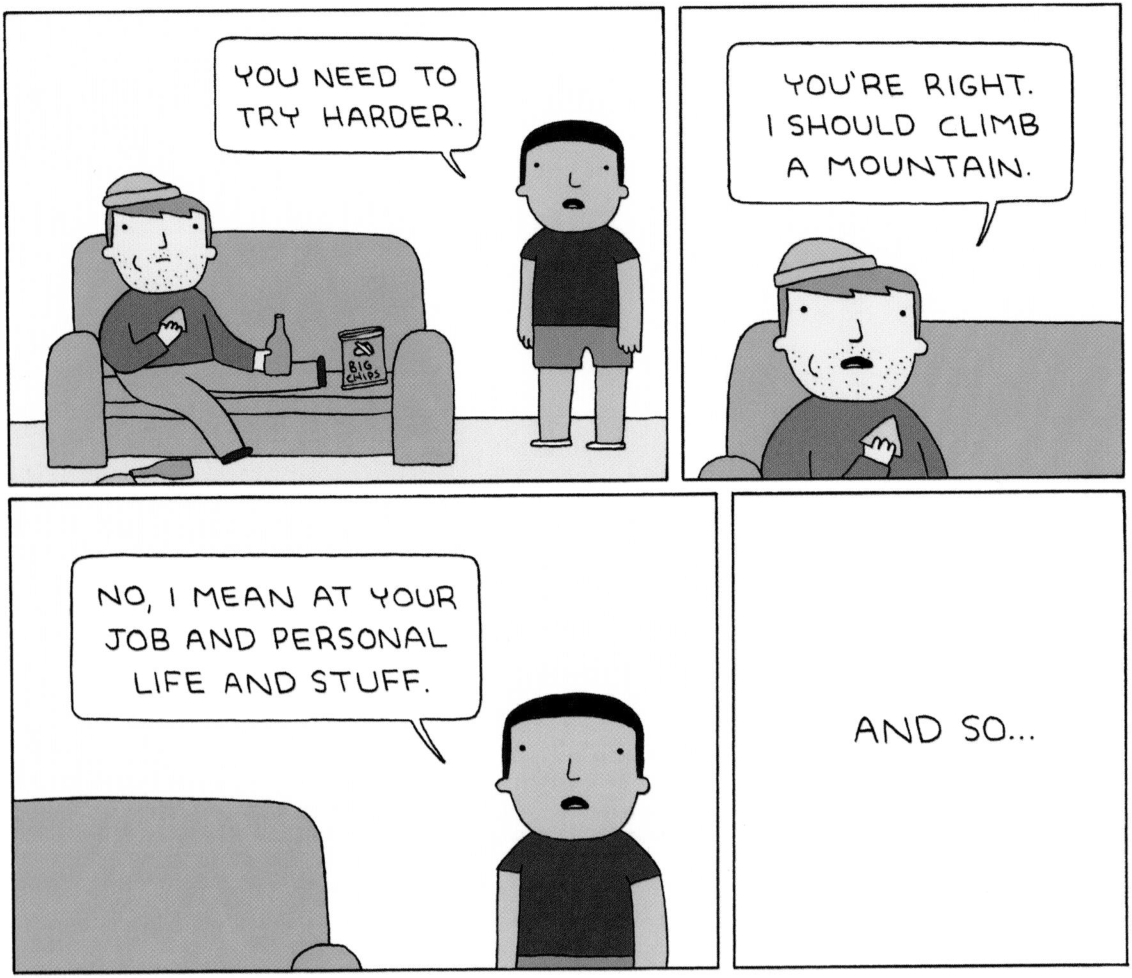
YOU NEED TO TRY HARDER.
BIG CHIPS
YOU'RE RIGHT. I SHOULD CLIMB A MOUNTAIN.
NO, I MEAN AT YOUR JOB AND PERSONAL LIFE AND STUFF.
AND SO...

LIFE IS INCREDIBLE WHEN YOU THINK ABOUT IT.
BUT I DON'T THINK ABOUT IT.

KEVIN GOT REJECTED

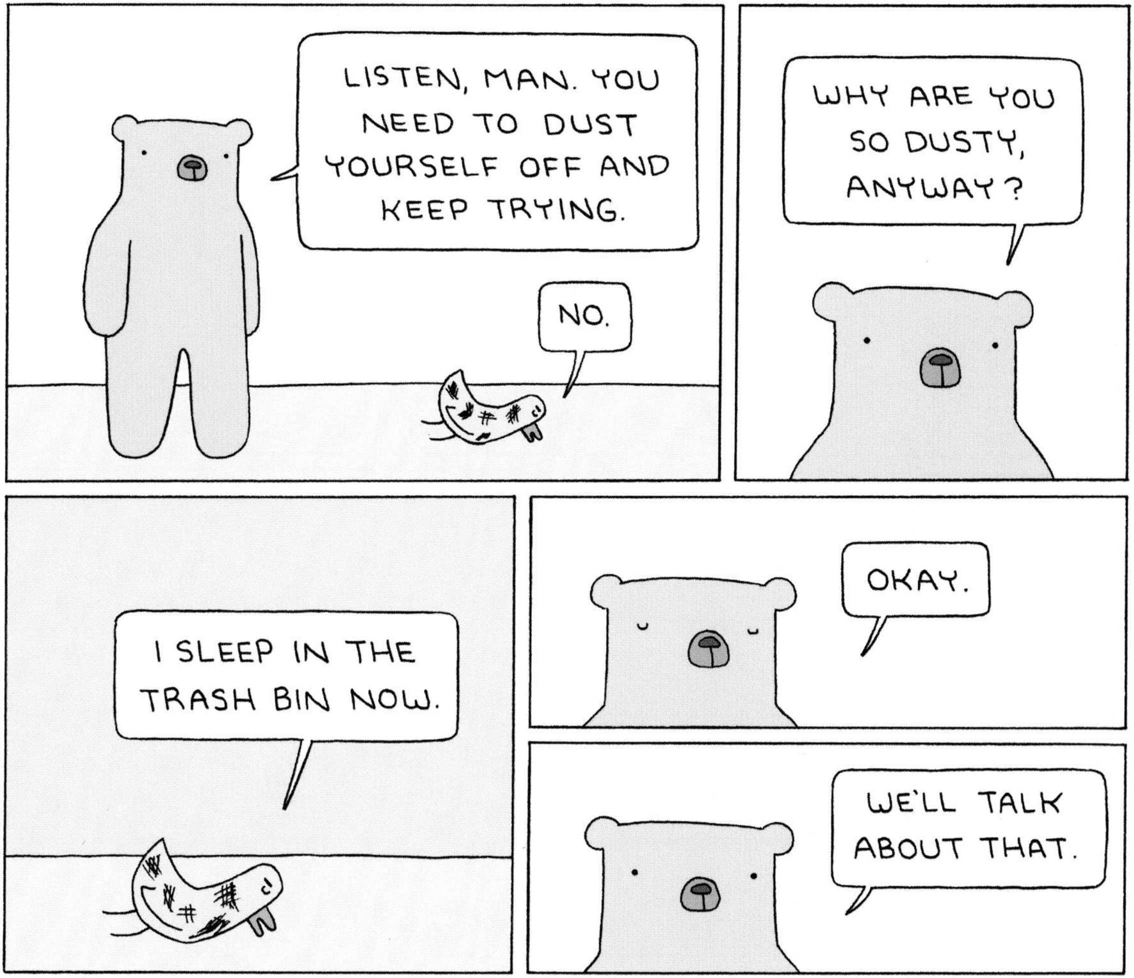
LISTEN, MAN. YOU NEED TO DUST YOURSELF OFF AND KEEP TRYING.
NO.
WHY ARE YOU SO DUSTY, ANYWAY?
I SLEEP IN THE TRASH BIN NOW.
OKAY.
WE'LL TALK ABOUT THAT.

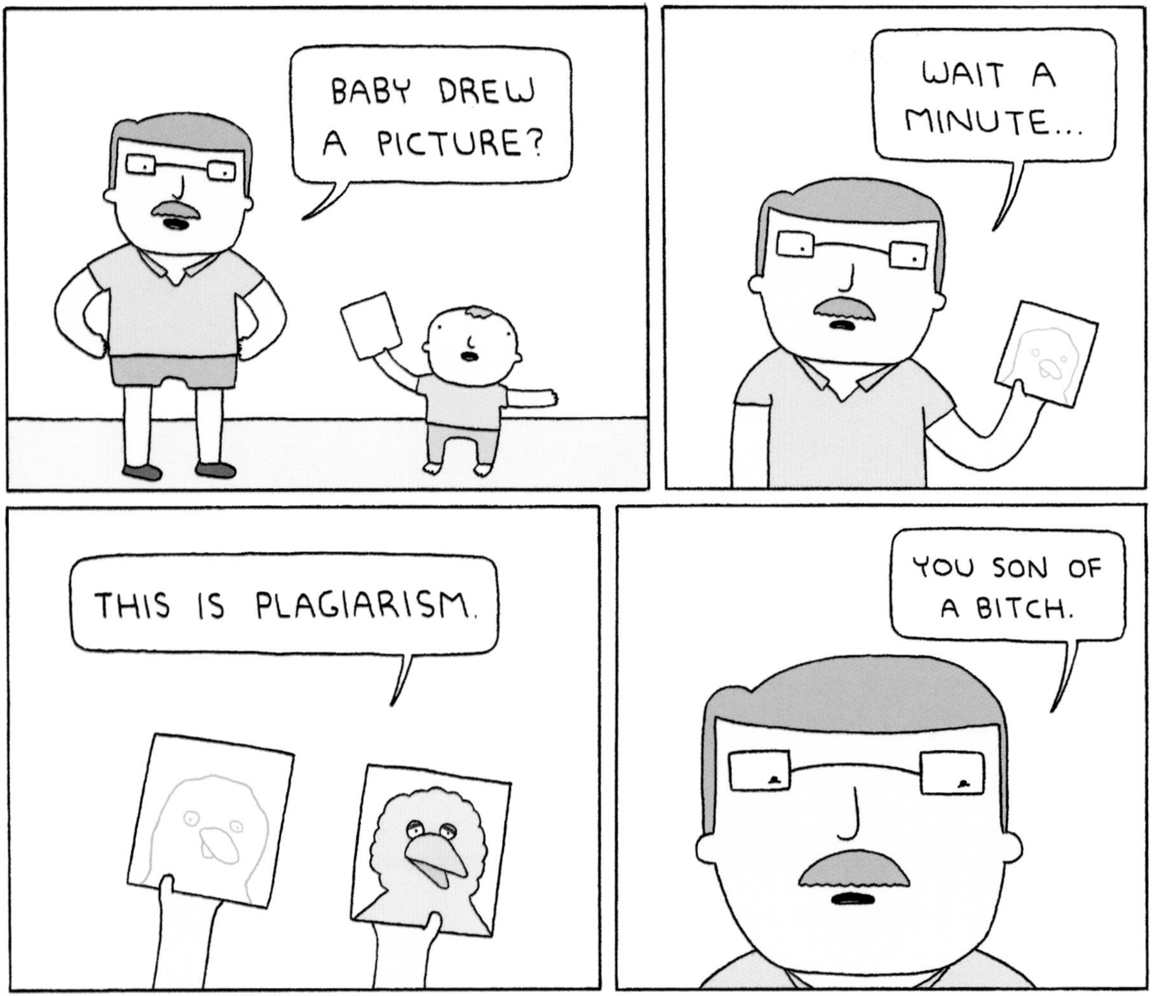
BABY DREW A PICTURE?
WAIT A MINUTE...
THIS IS PLAGIARISM.
YOU SON OF A BITCH.

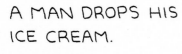
A MAN DROPS HIS ICE CREAM.

IN TURN, HE NOURISHES THE ANTS, WHO—

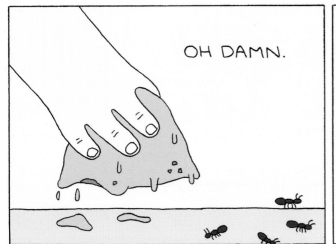
OH DAMN.

DAMN, HE JUST WENT FOR IT.

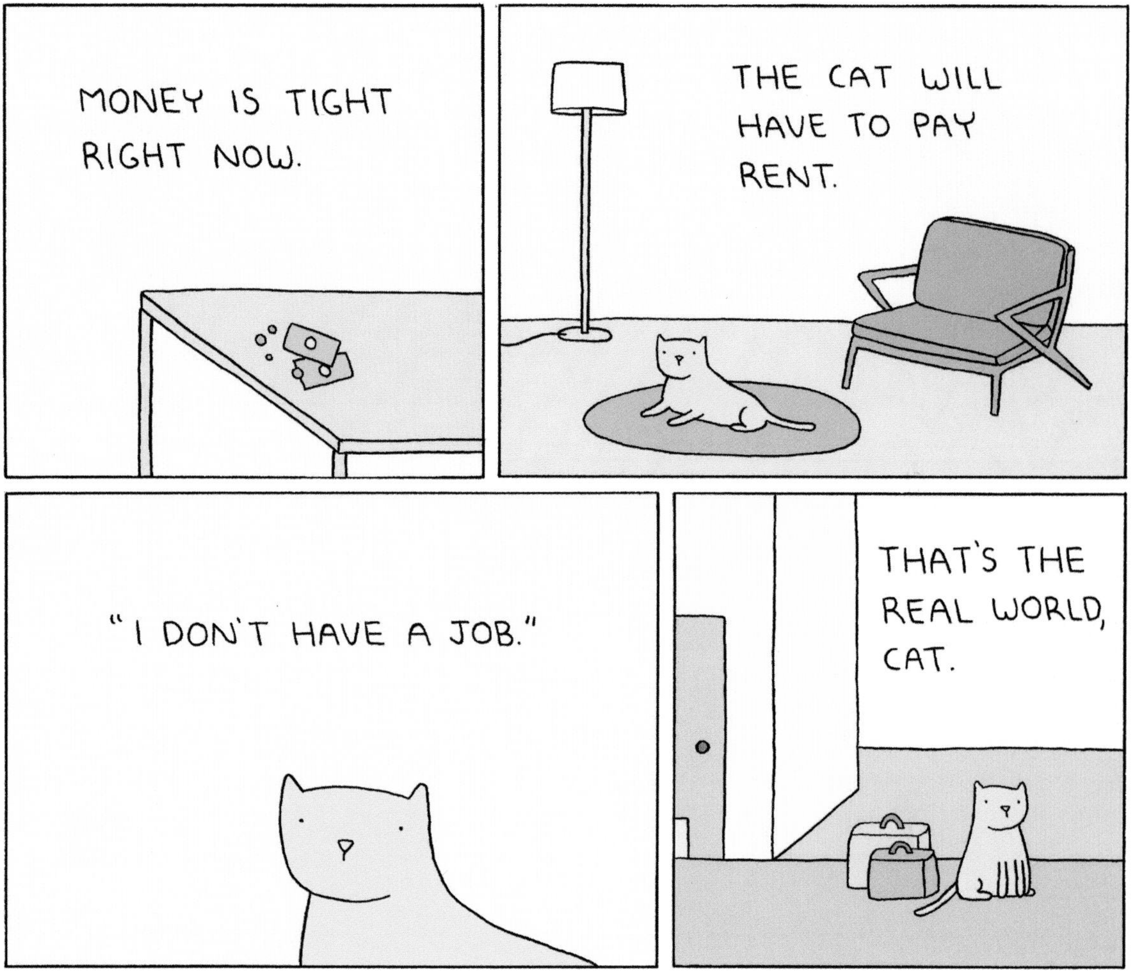
MONEY IS TIGHT RIGHT NOW.
THE CAT WILL HAVE TO PAY RENT.
"I DON'T HAVE A JOB."
THAT'S THE REAL WORLD, CAT.

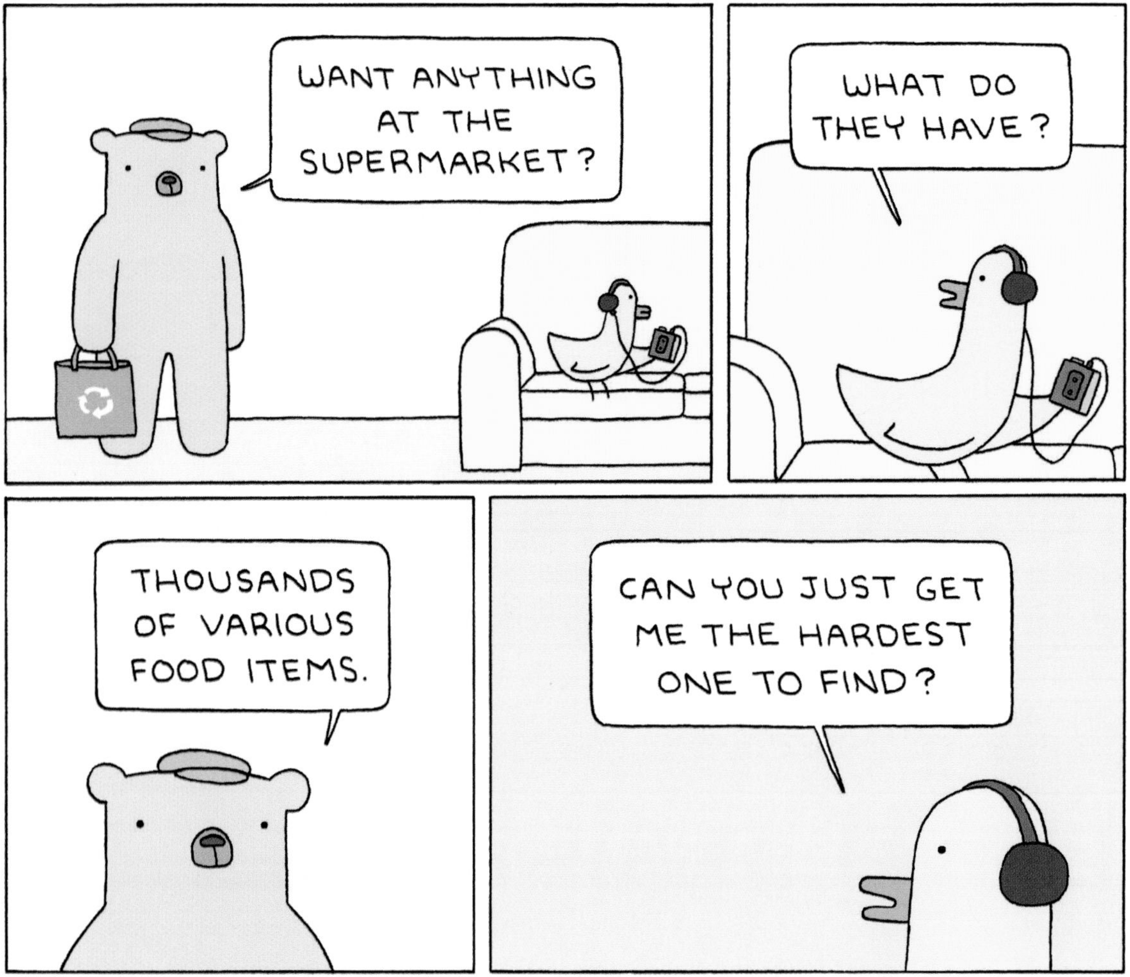
WANT ANYTHING AT THE SUPERMARKET?
WHAT DO THEY HAVE?
THOUSANDS OF VARIOUS FOOD ITEMS.
CAN YOU JUST GET ME THE HARDEST ONE TO FIND?

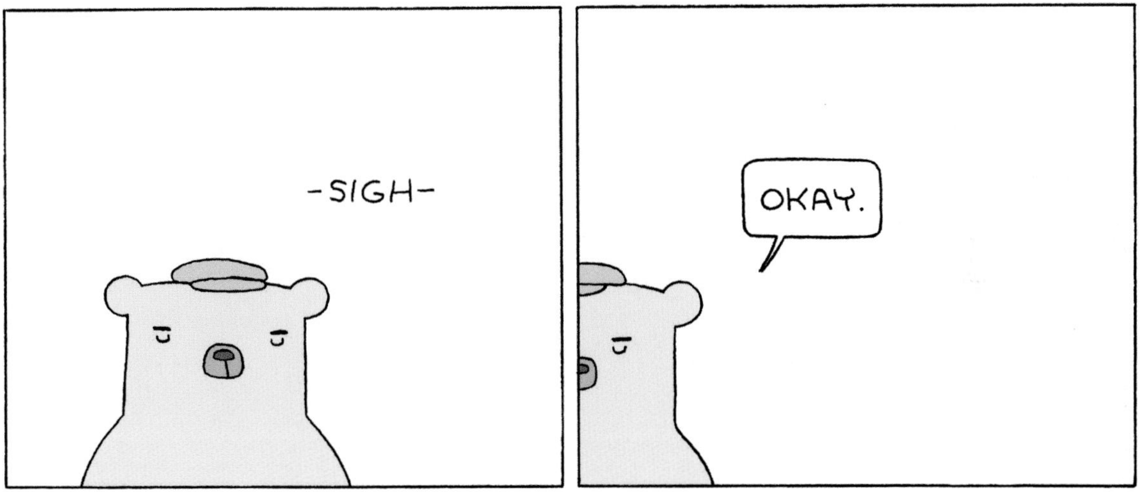
-SIGH-
OKAY.

II

SOCIAL CREATURES

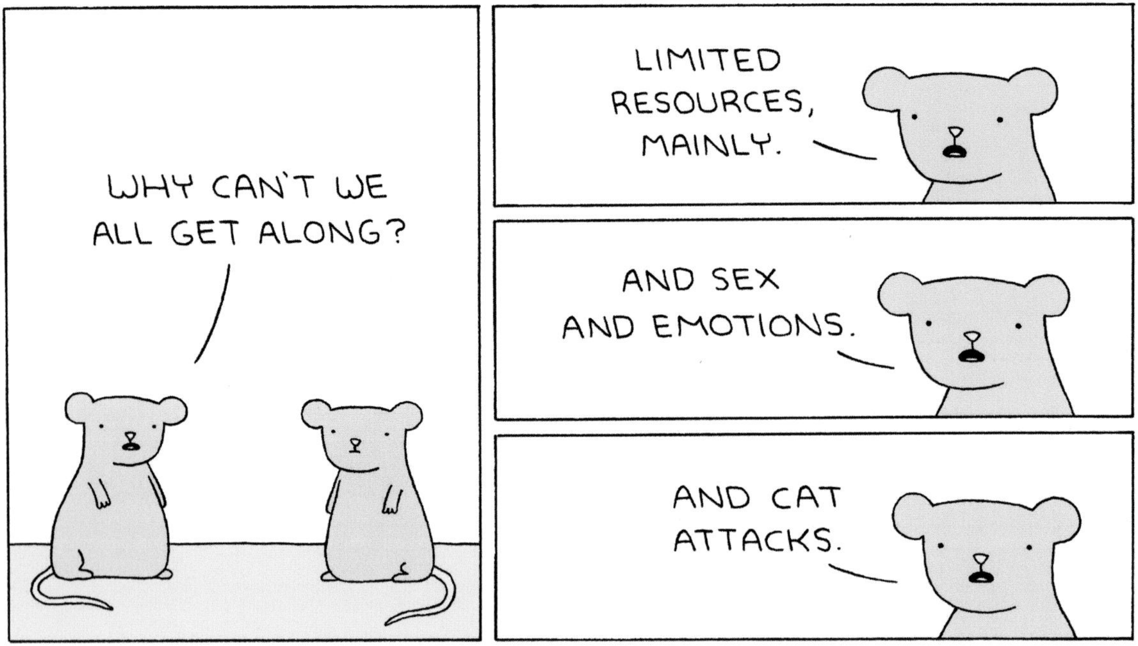
WHY CAN'T WE ALL GET ALONG?
LIMITED RESOURCES, MAINLY.
AND SEX AND EMOTIONS.
AND CAT ATTACKS.

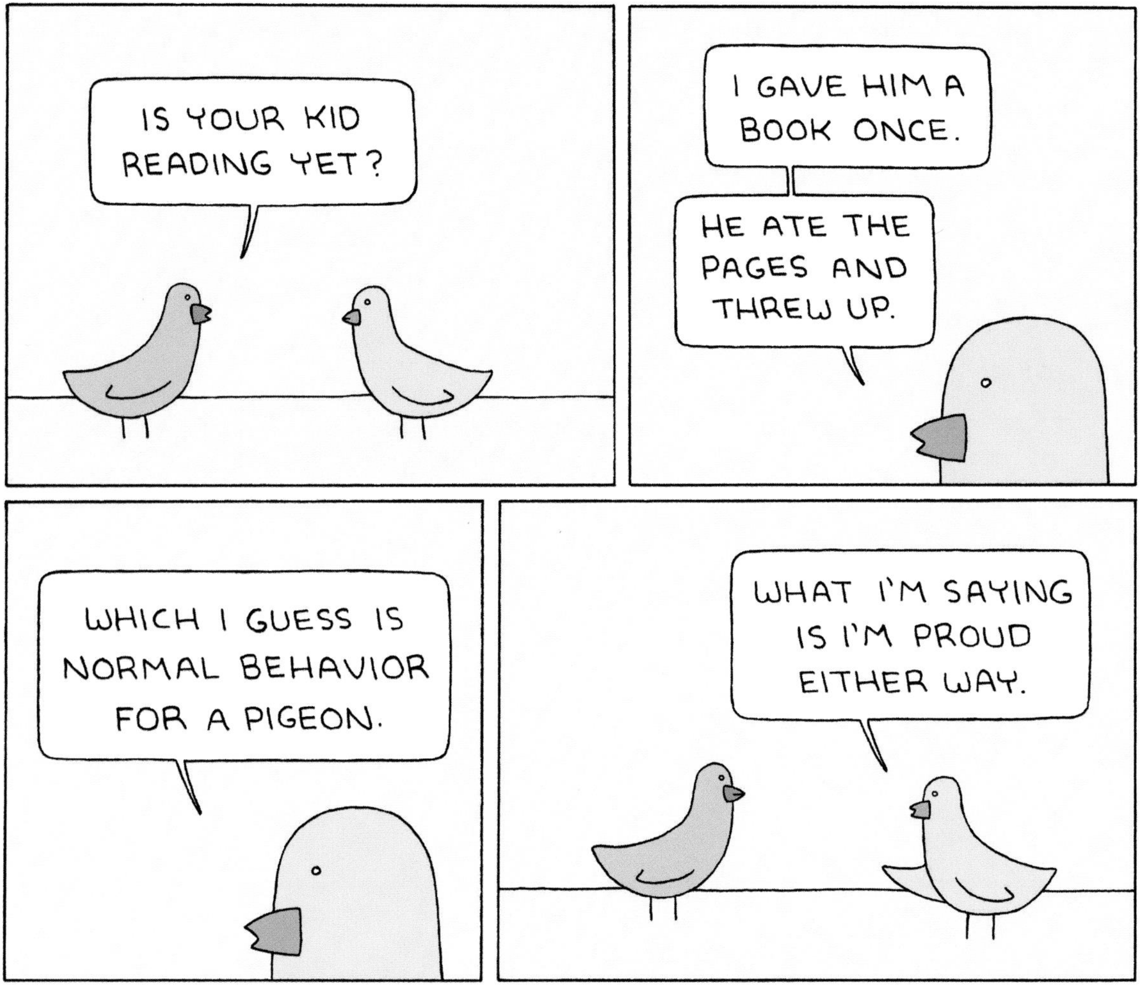
IS YOUR KID READING YET?
I GAVE HIM A BOOK ONCE.
HE ATE THE PAGES AND THREW UP.
WHICH I GUESS IS NORMAL BEHAVIOR FOR A PIGEON.
WHAT I'M SAYING IS I'M PROUD EITHER WAY.

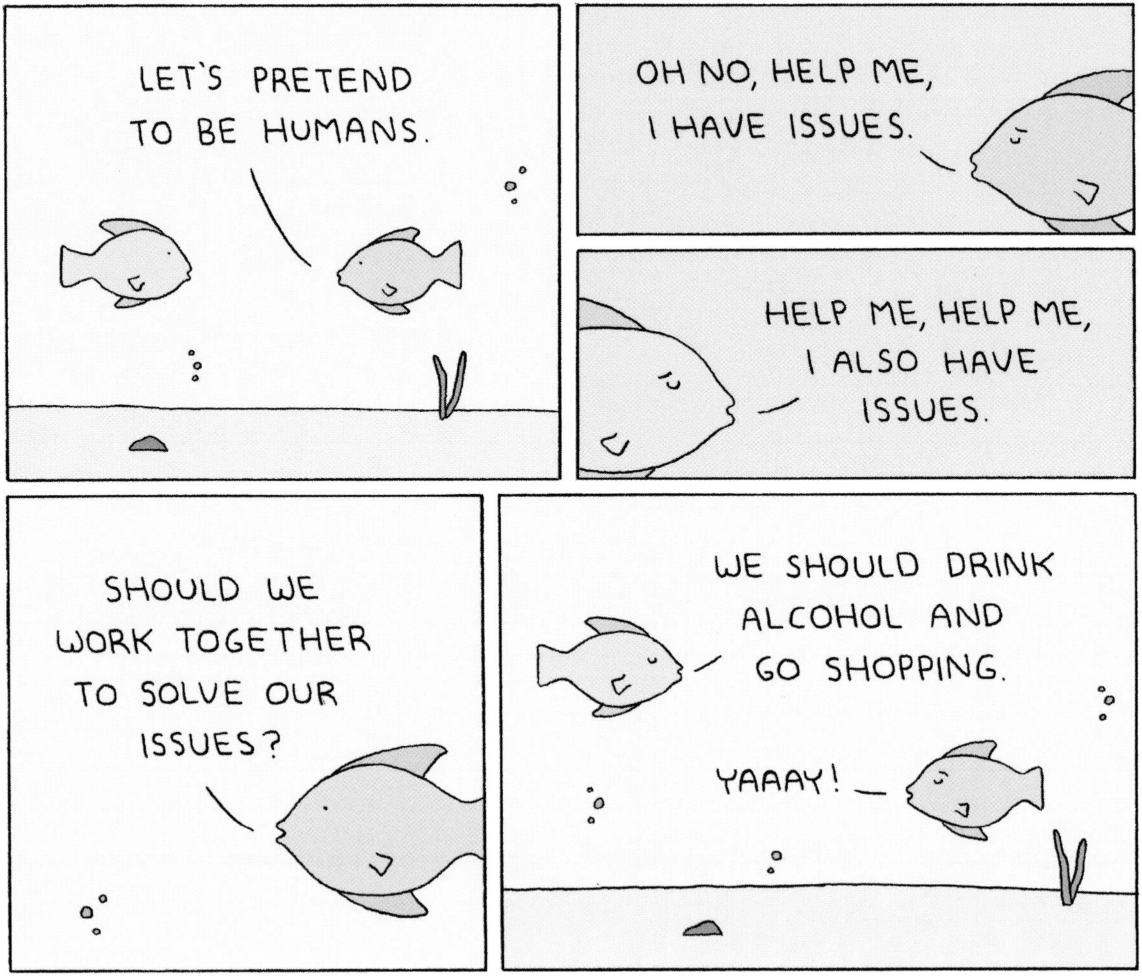
LET'S PRETEND TO BE HUMANS.
OH NO, HELP ME, I HAVE ISSUES.
HELP ME, HELP ME, I ALSO HAVE ISSUES.
SHOULD WE WORK TOGETHER TO SOLVE OUR ISSUES?
WE SHOULD DRINK ALCOHOL AND GO SHOPPING.
YAAAY!

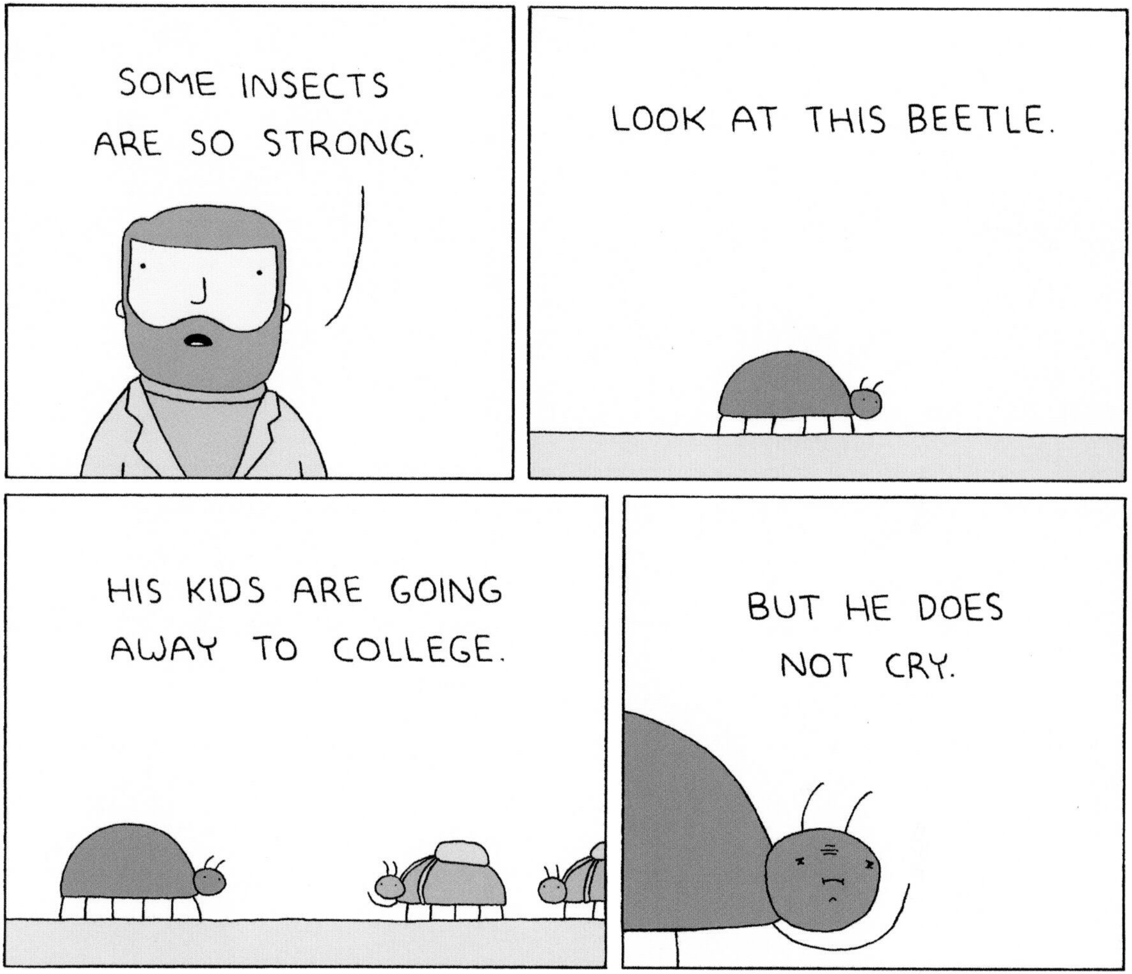
SOME INSECTS ARE SO STRONG.
LOOK AT THIS BEETLE.
HIS KIDS ARE GOING AWAY TO COLLEGE.
BUT HE DOES NOT CRY.

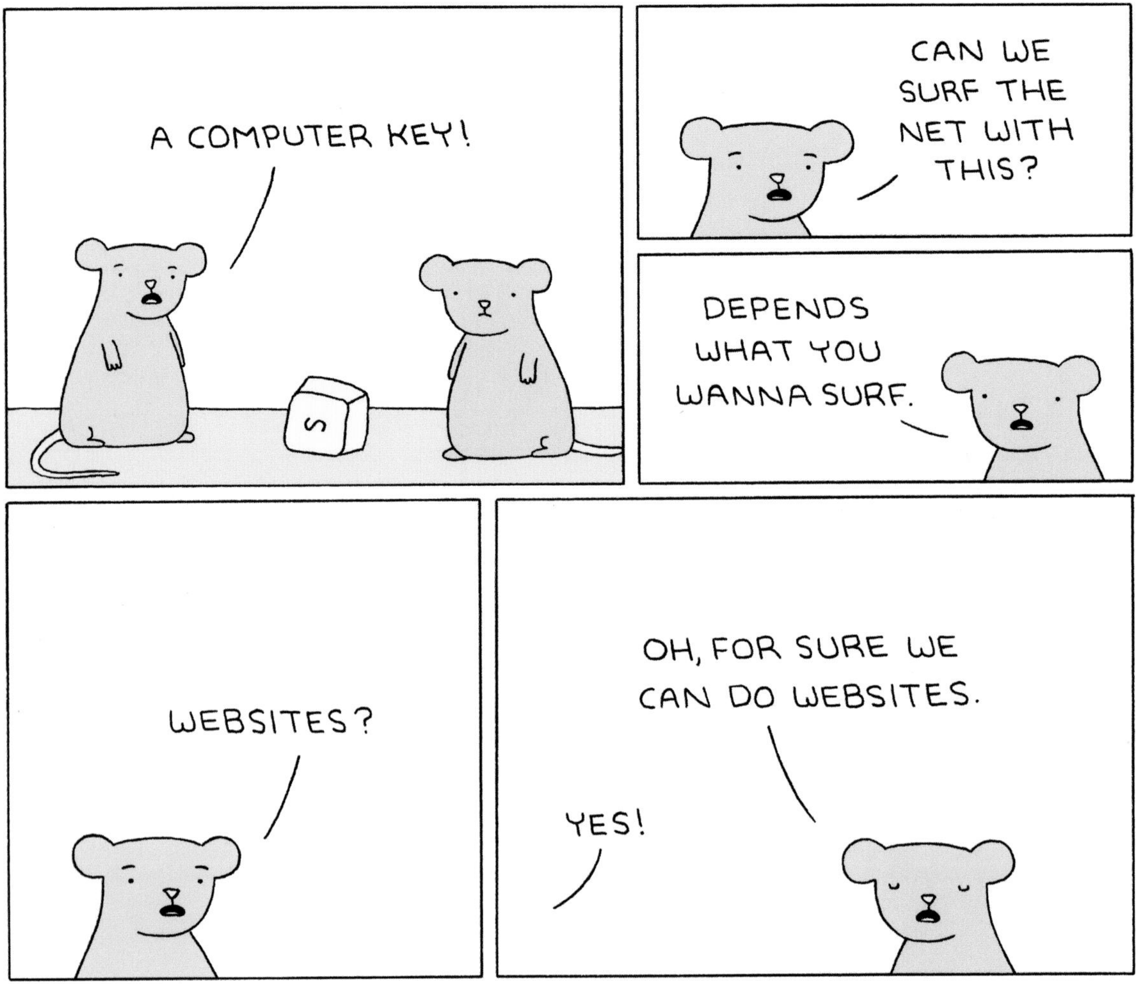
A COMPUTER KEY!
S
CAN WE SURF THE NET WITH THIS?
DEPENDS WHAT YOU WANNA SURF.
WEBSITES?
OH, FOR SURE WE CAN DO WEBSITES.
YES!

ANOTHER RAINY NIGHT AT HOME.

THE CAT WANDERS INTO THE ROOM AND TRIES TO GET MY ATTENTION.

DANIEL.

DANIEL, HEY.

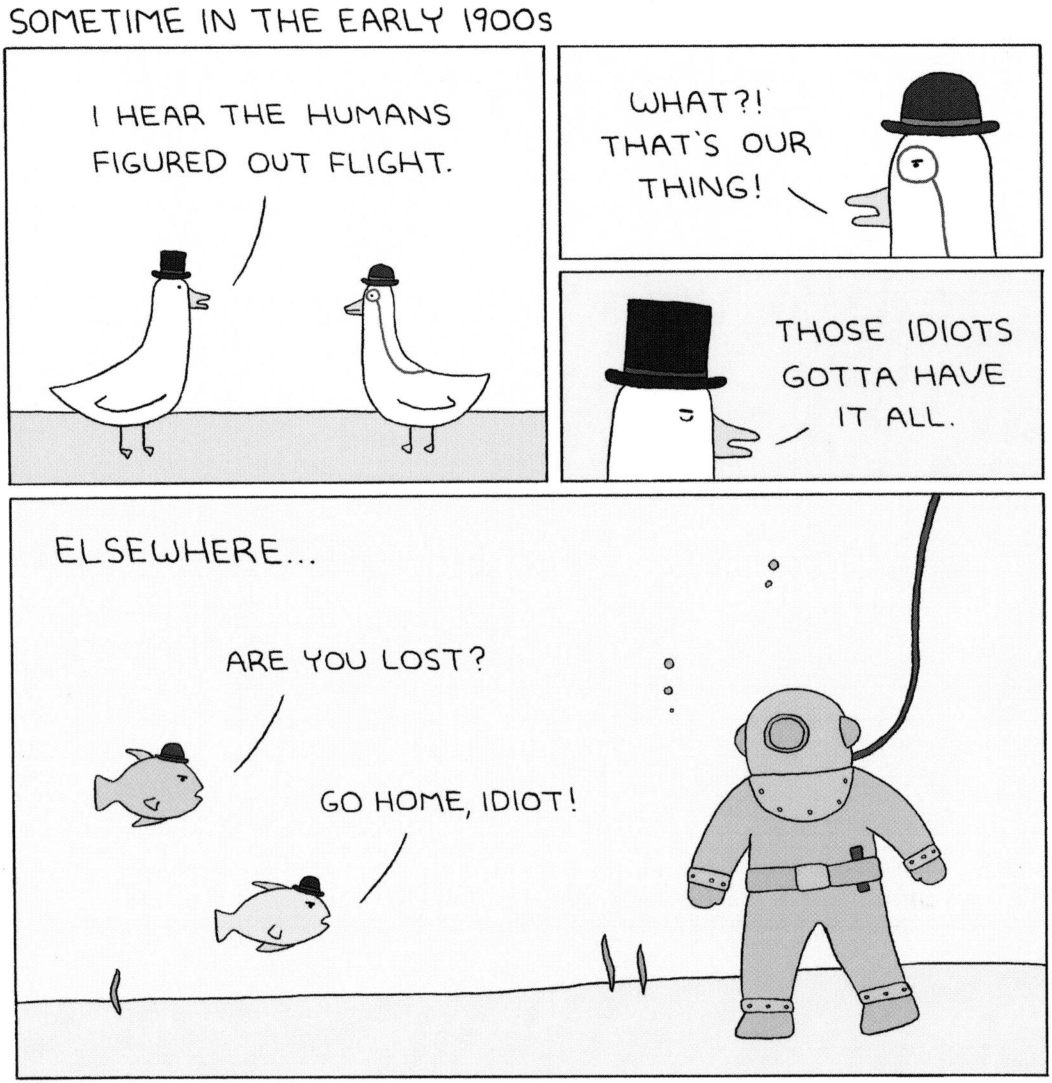
SOMETIME IN THE EARLY 1900s
I HEAR THE HUMANS FIGURED OUT FLIGHT.
WHAT?! THAT'S OUR THING!
THOSE IDIOTS GOTTA HAVE IT ALL.
ELSEWHERE...
ARE YOU LOST?
GO HOME, IDIOT!

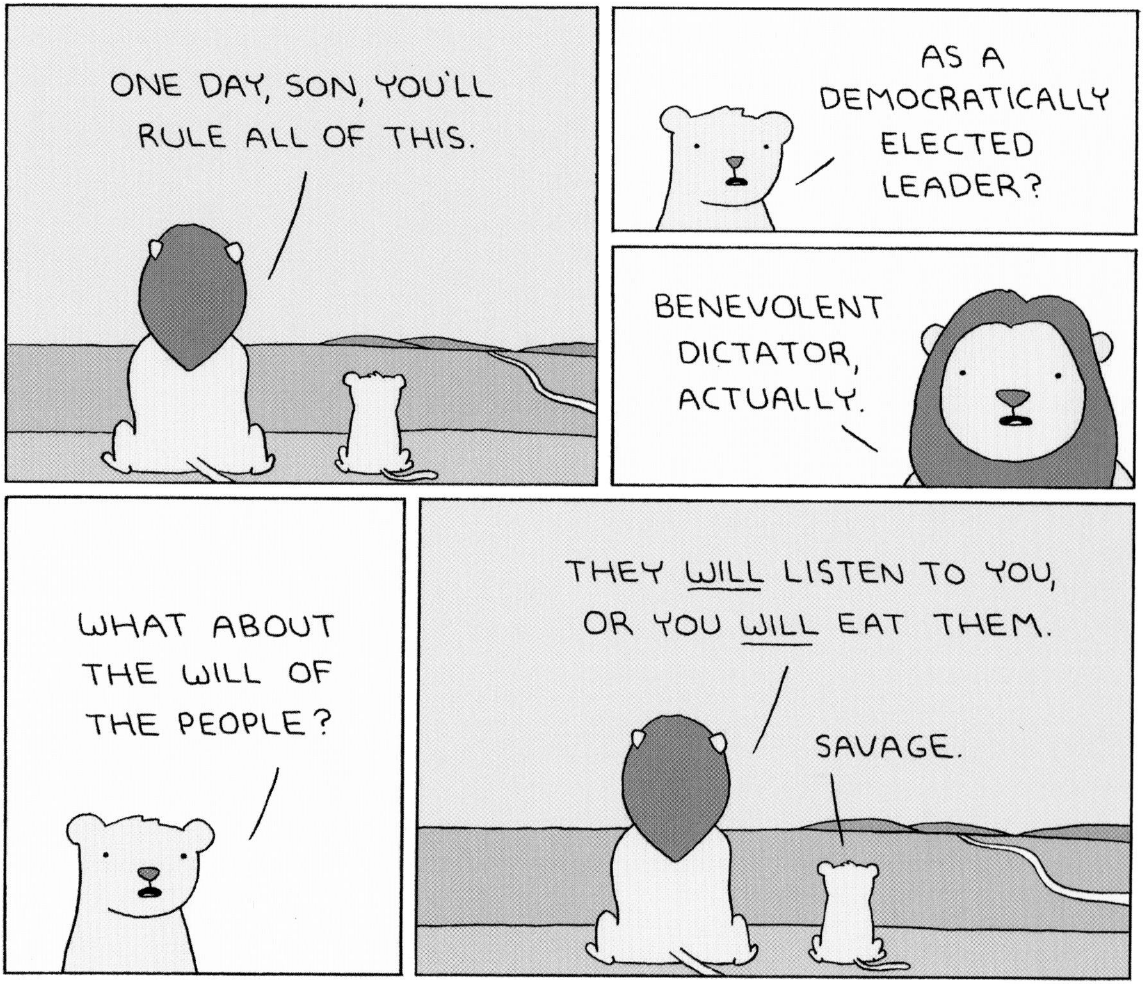
ONE DAY, SON, YOU'LL RULE ALL OF THIS.
AS A DEMOCRATICALLY ELECTED LEADER?
BENEVOLENT DICTATOR, ACTUALLY.
WHAT ABOUT THE WILL OF THE PEOPLE?
THEY WILL LISTEN TO YOU, OR YOU WILL EAT THEM.
SAVAGE.

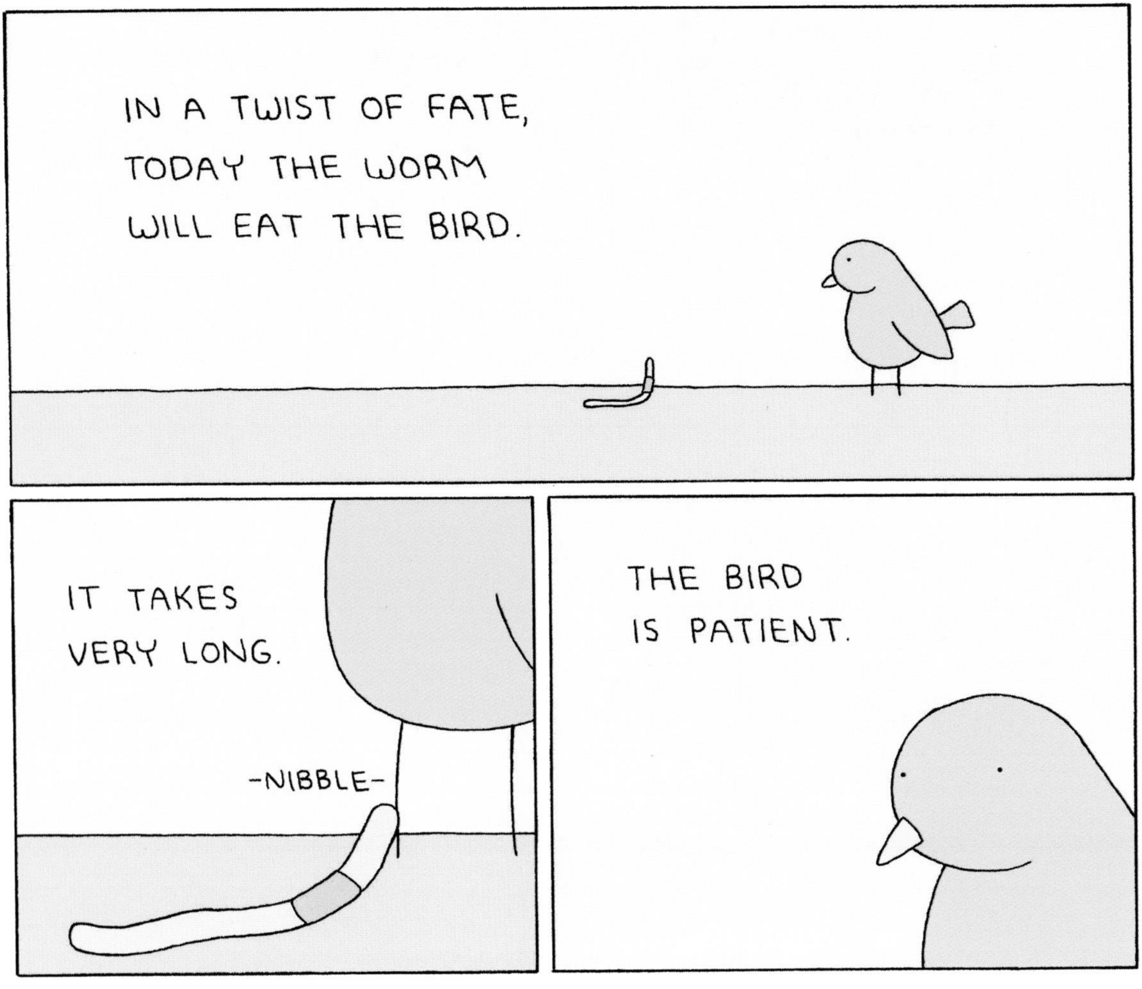

IN A TWIST OF FATE, TODAY THE WORM WILL EAT THE BIRD.
IT TAKES VERY LONG.
-NIBBLE-
THE BIRD IS PATIENT.

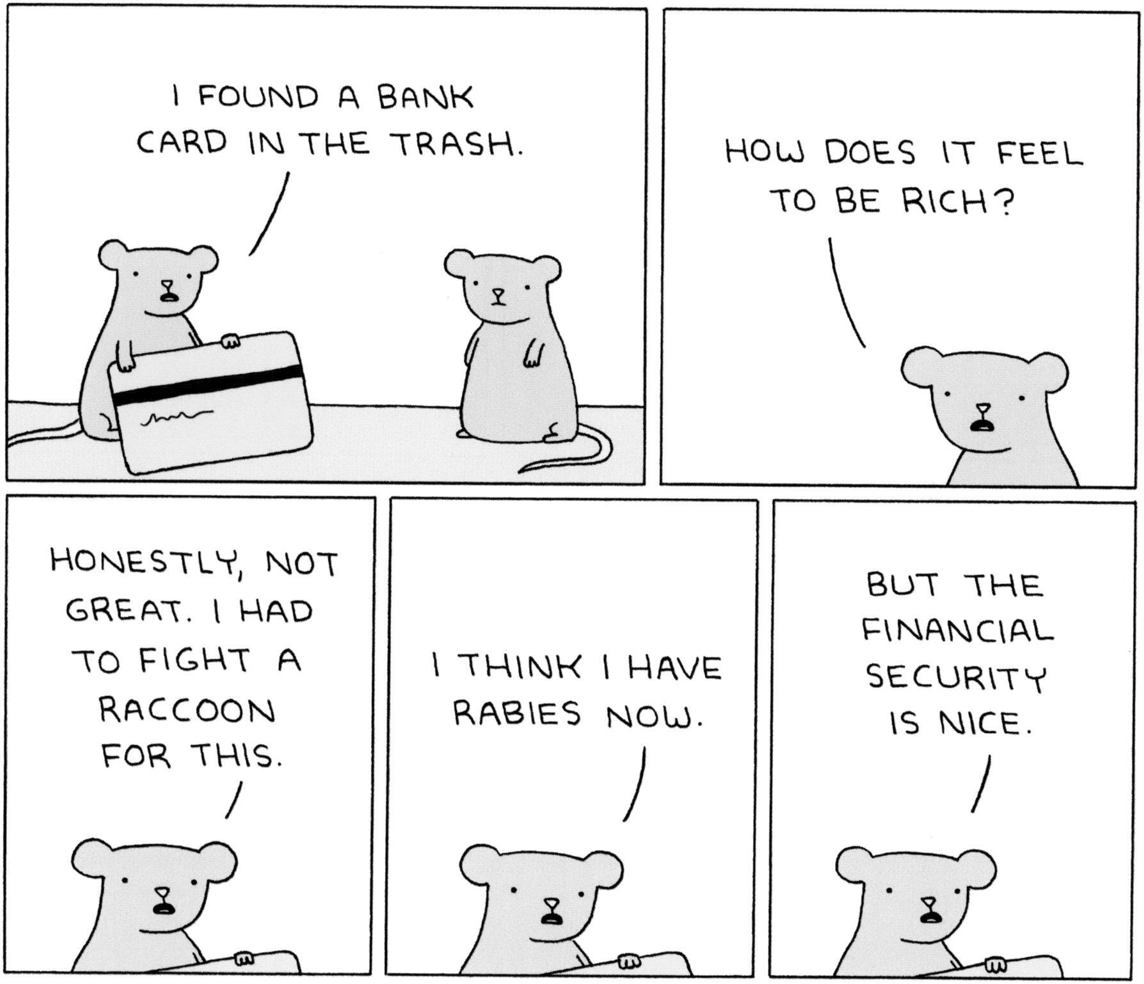
I FOUND A BANK CARD IN THE TRASH.
HOW DOES IT FEEL TO BE RICH?
HONESTLY, NOT GREAT. I HAD TO FIGHT A RACCOON FOR THIS.
I THINK I HAVE RABIES NOW.
BUT THE FINANCIAL SECURITY IS NICE.

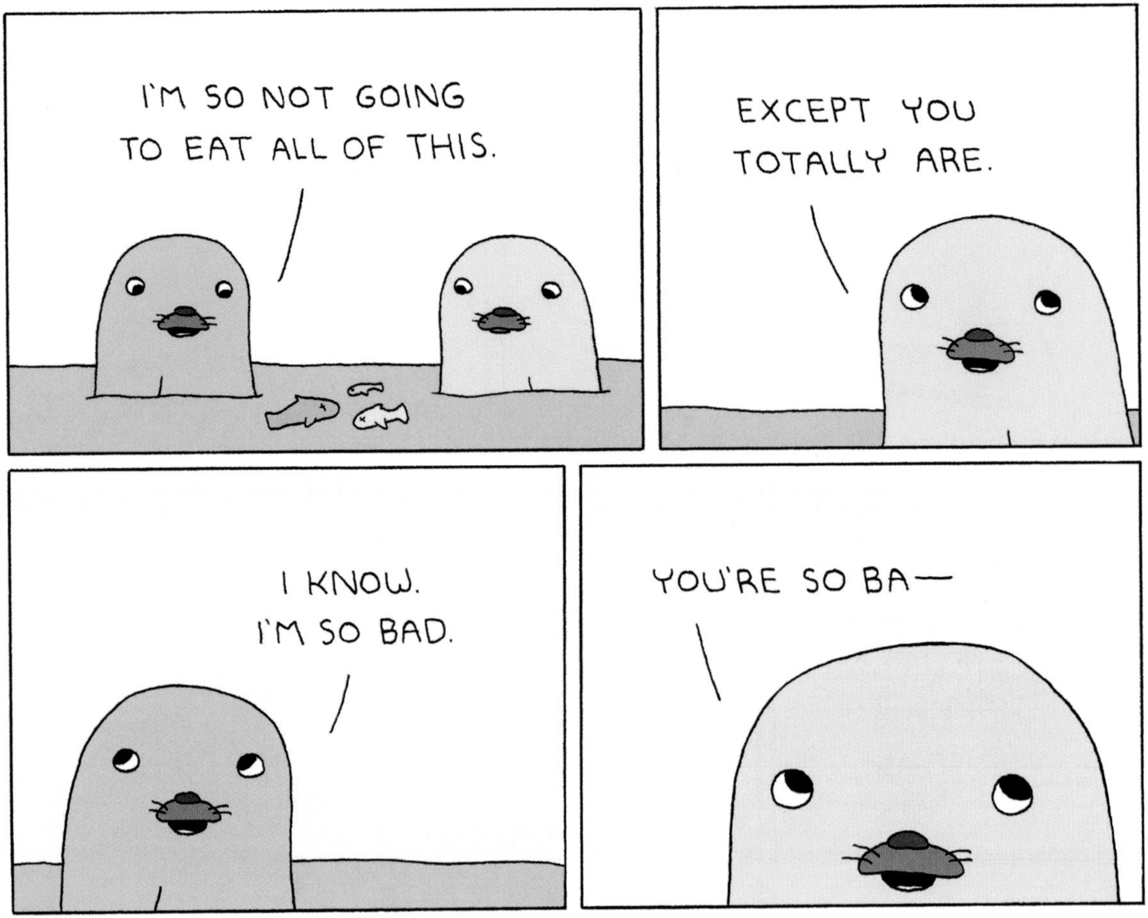
I'M SO NOT GOING TO EAT ALL OF THIS.
EXCEPT YOU TOTALLY ARE.
I KNOW. I'M SO BAD.
YOU'RE SO BA—

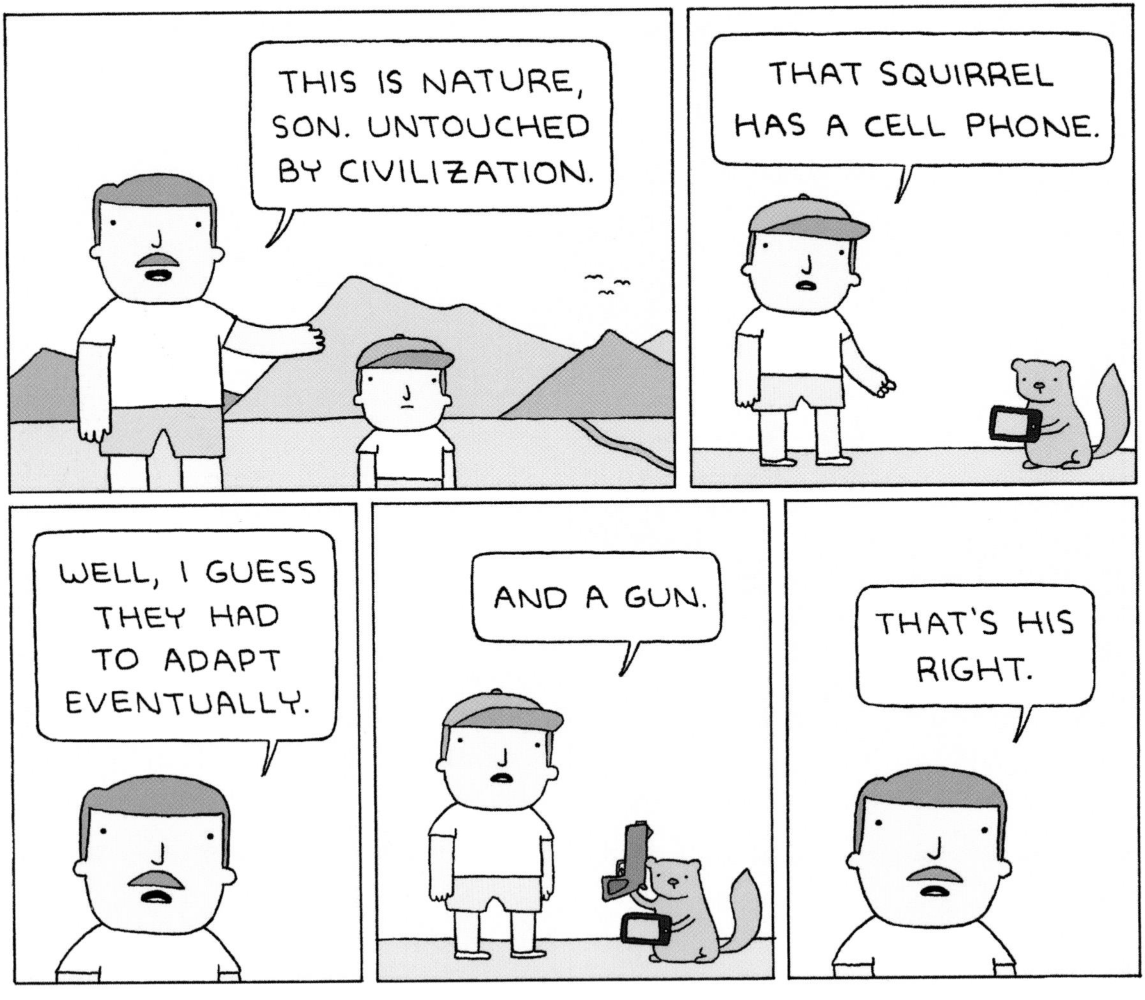
THIS IS NATURE, SON. UNTOUCHED BY CIVILIZATION.
THAT SQUIRREL HAS A CELL PHONE.
WELL, I GUESS THEY HAD TO ADAPT EVENTUALLY.
AND A GUN.
THAT'S HIS RIGHT.

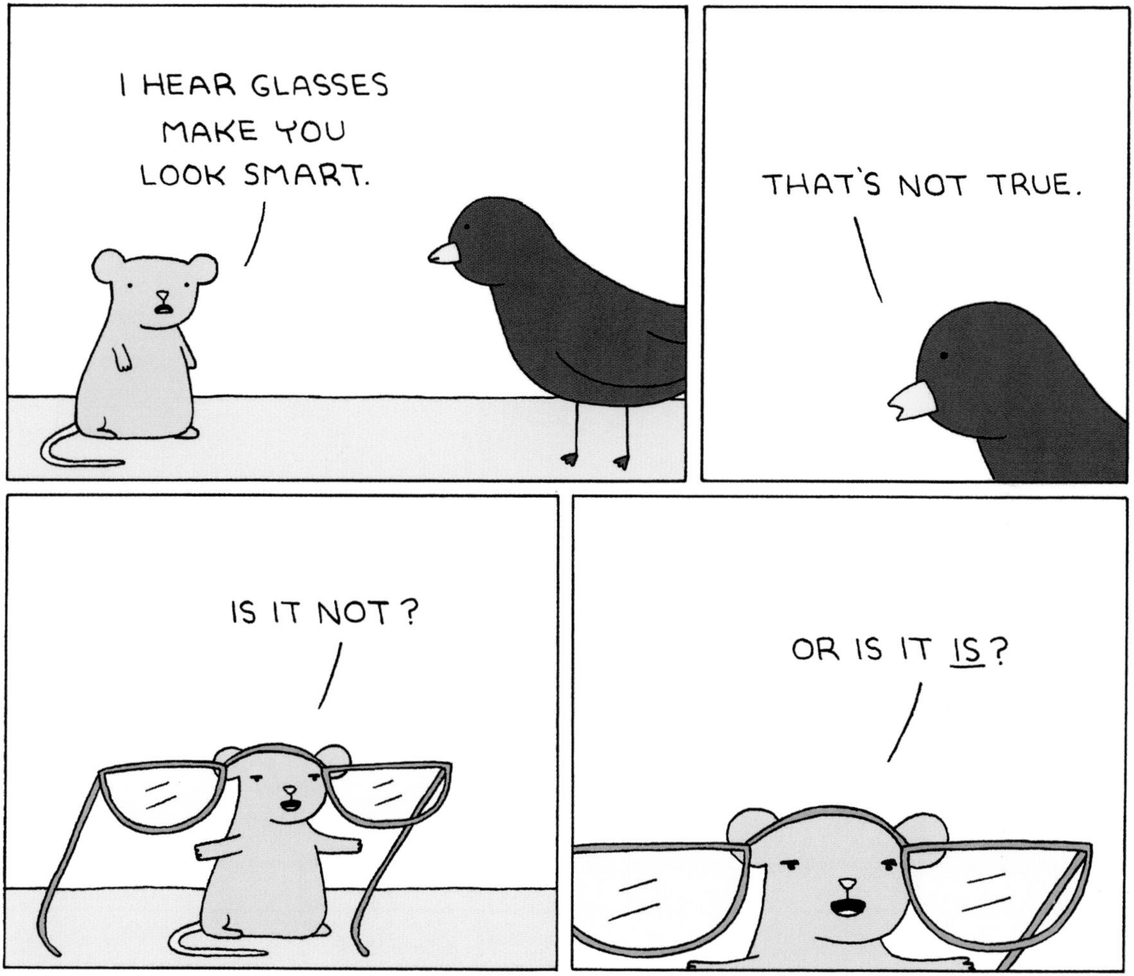
I HEAR GLASSES MAKE YOU LOOK SMART.
THAT'S NOT TRUE.
IS IT NOT?
OR IS IT IS?

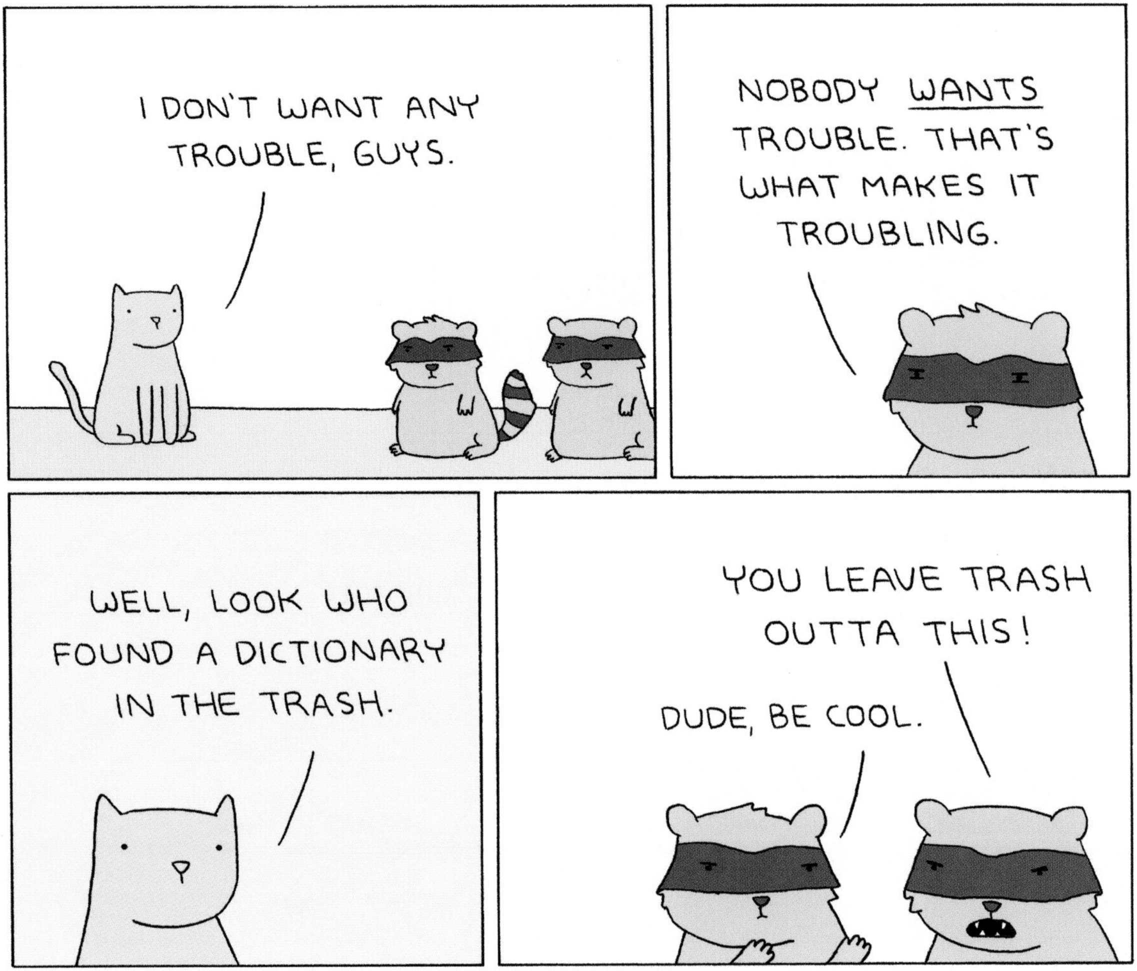
I DON'T WANT ANY TROUBLE, GUYS.
NOBODY WANTS TROUBLE. THAT'S WHAT MAKES IT TROUBLING.
WELL, LOOK WHO FOUND A DICTIONARY IN THE TRASH.
YOU LEAVE TRASH OUTTA THIS!
DUDE, BE COOL.

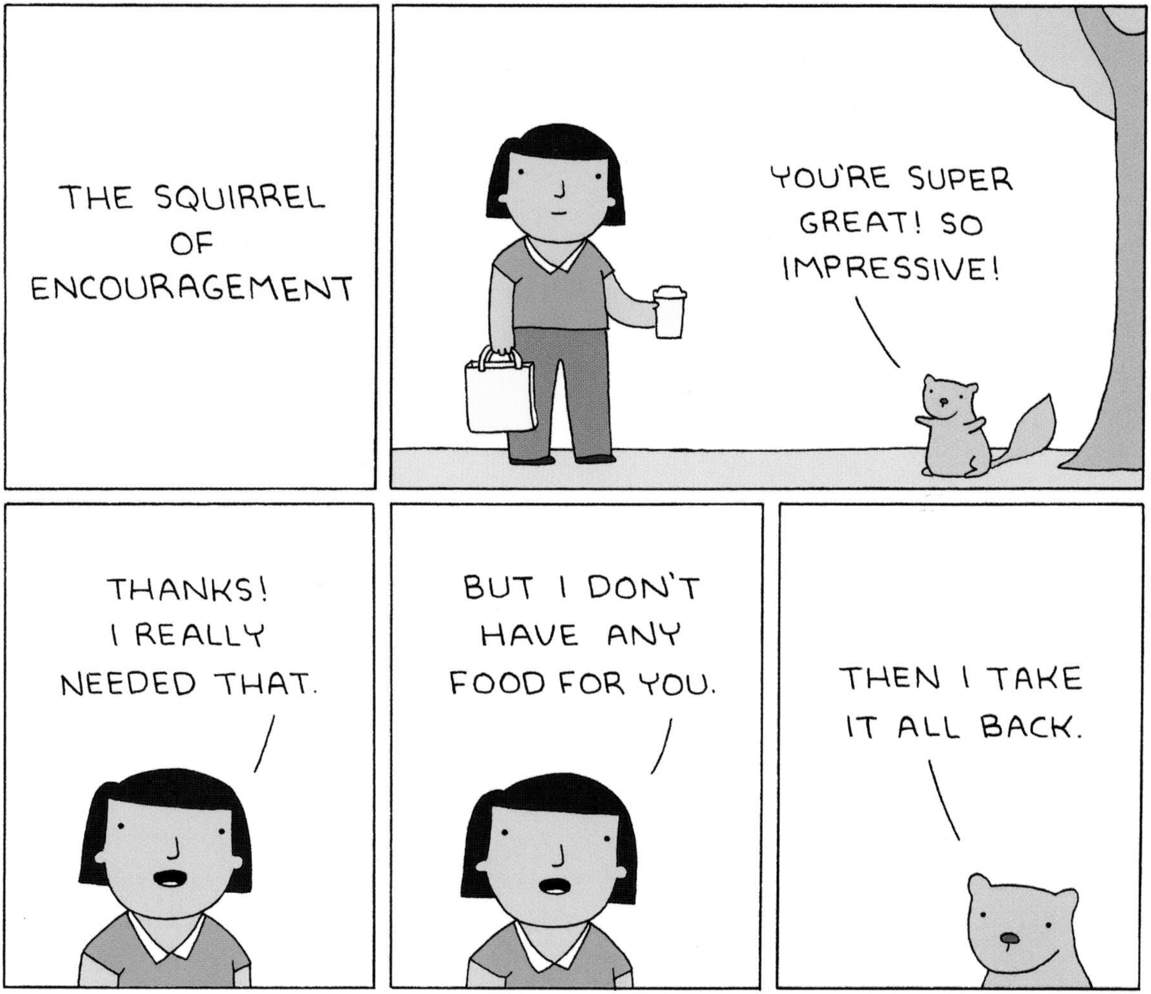
THE SQUIRREL OF ENCOURAGEMENT
YOU'RE SUPER GREAT! SO IMPRESSIVE!
THANKS! I REALLY NEEDED THAT.
BUT I DON'T HAVE ANY FOOD FOR YOU.
THEN I TAKE IT ALL BACK.

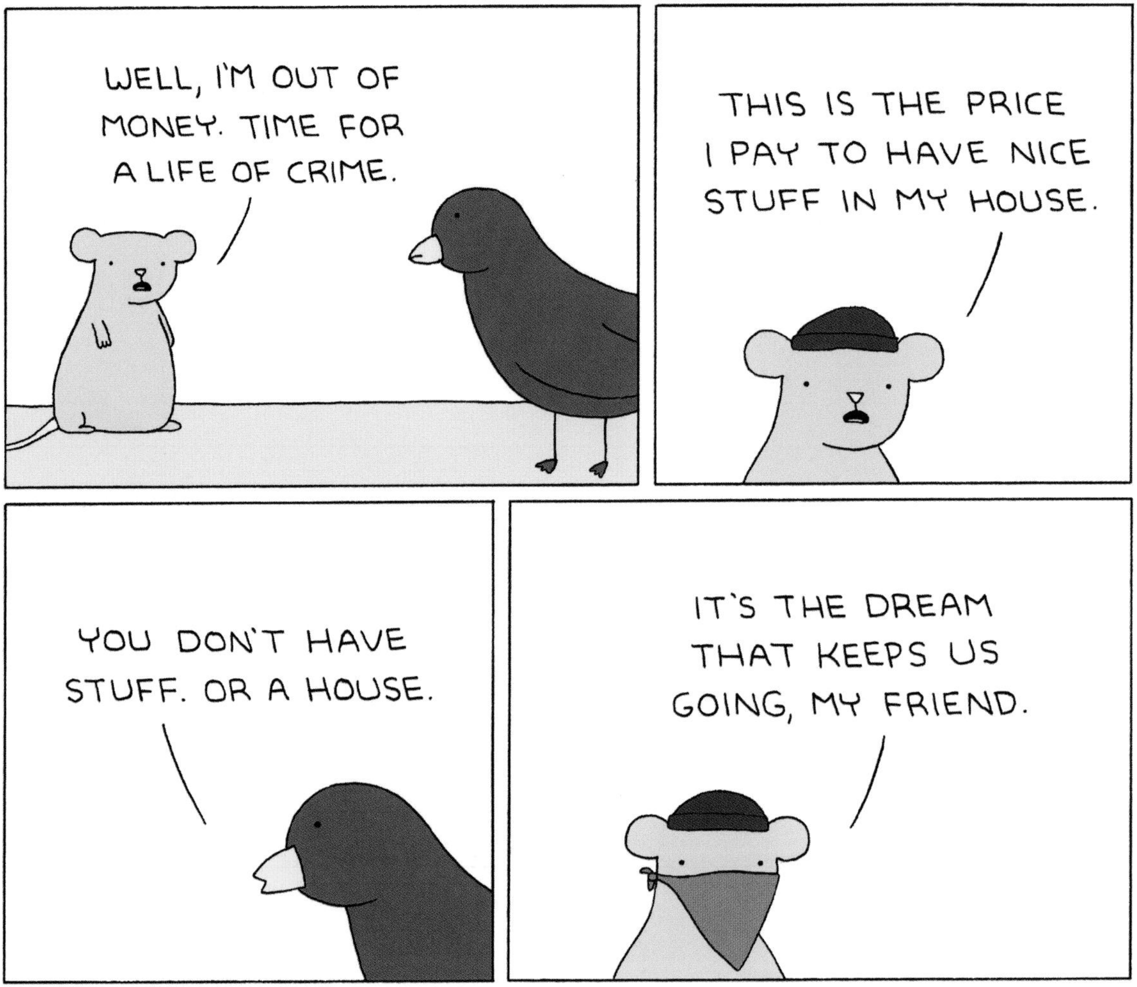
WELL, I'M OUT OF MONEY. TIME FOR A LIFE OF CRIME.
THIS IS THE PRICE I PAY TO HAVE NICE STUFF IN MY HOUSE.
YOU DON'T HAVE STUFF. OR A HOUSE.
IT'S THE DREAM THAT KEEPS US GOING, MY FRIEND.

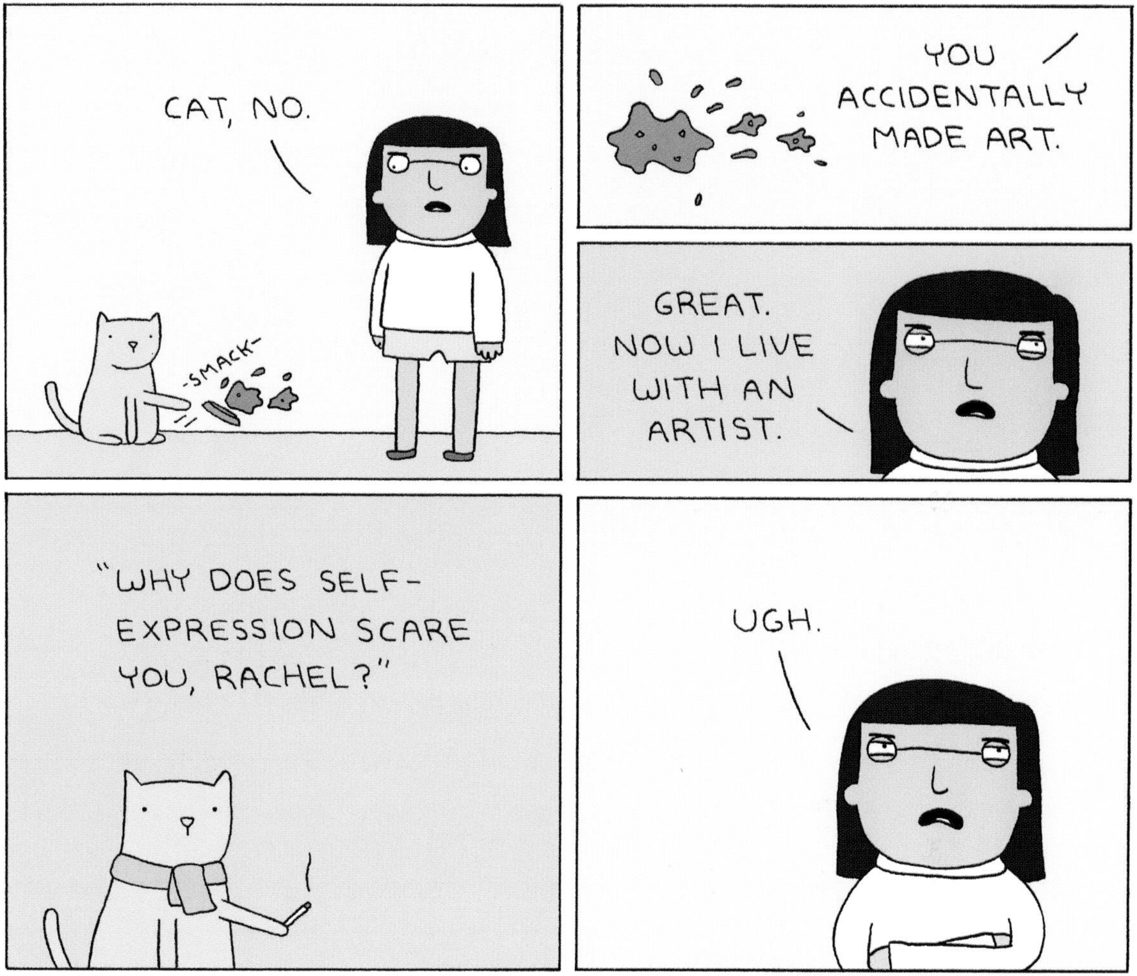
CAT, NO.
-SMACK-
YOU ACCIDENTALLY MADE ART.
GREAT. NOW I LIVE WITH AN ARTIST.
"WHY DOES SELF-EXPRESSION SCARE YOU, RACHEL?"
UGH.

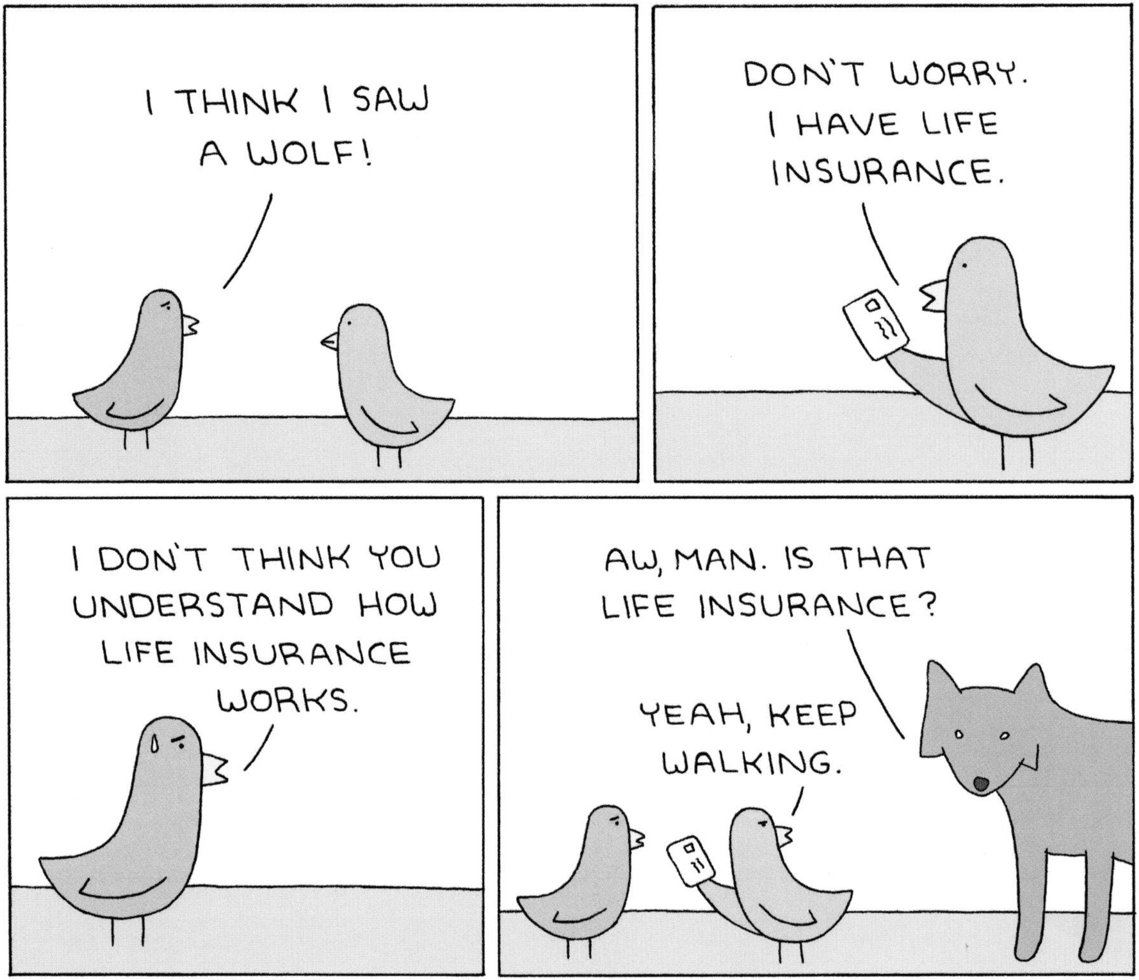
I THINK I SAW
A WOLF!
DON'T WORRY.
I HAVE LIFE
INSURANCE.
I DON'T THINK YOU
UNDERSTAND HOW
LIFE INSURANCE
WORKS.
AW, MAN. IS THAT
LIFE INSURANCE?
YEAH, KEEP
WALKING.

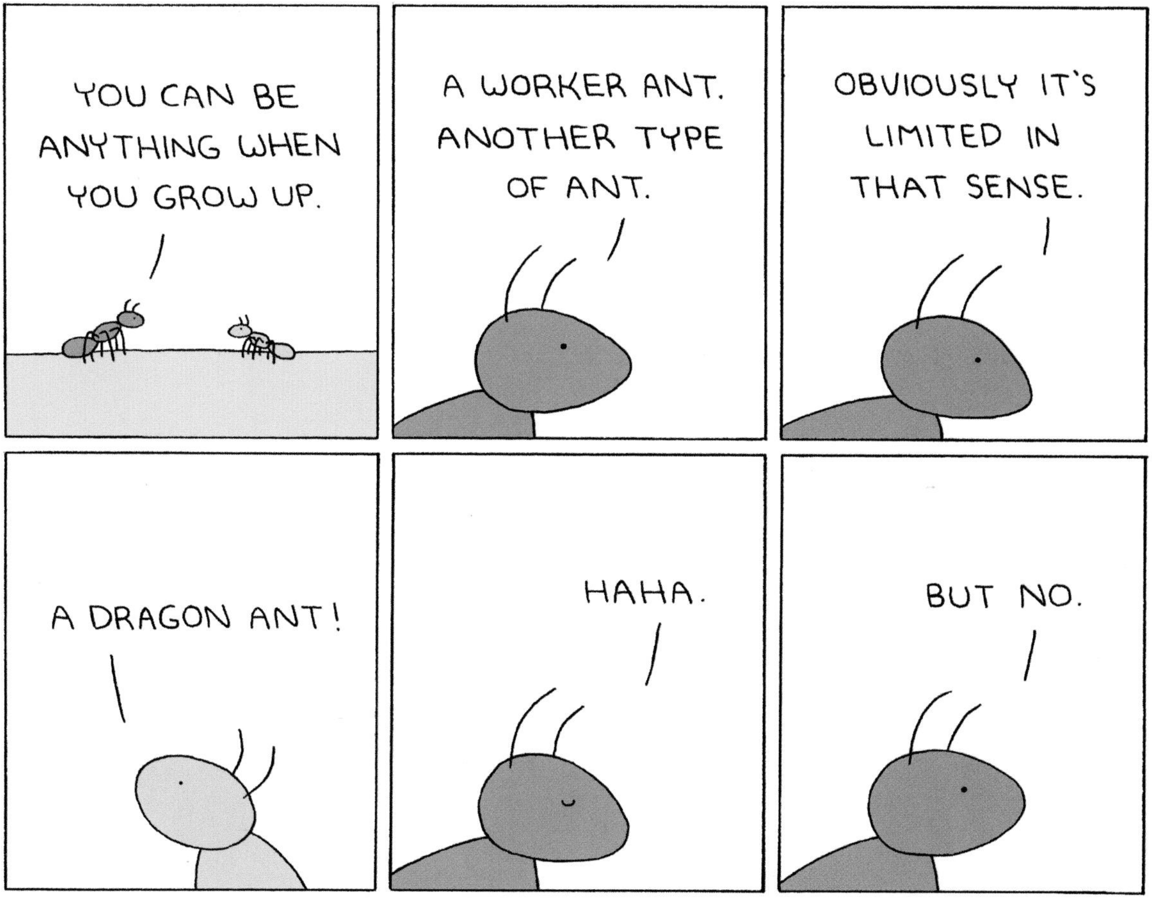
YOU CAN BE ANYTHING WHEN YOU GROW UP.
A WORKER ANT. ANOTHER TYPE OF ANT.
OBVIOUSLY IT'S LIMITED IN THAT SENSE.
A DRAGON ANT!
HAHA.
BUT NO.

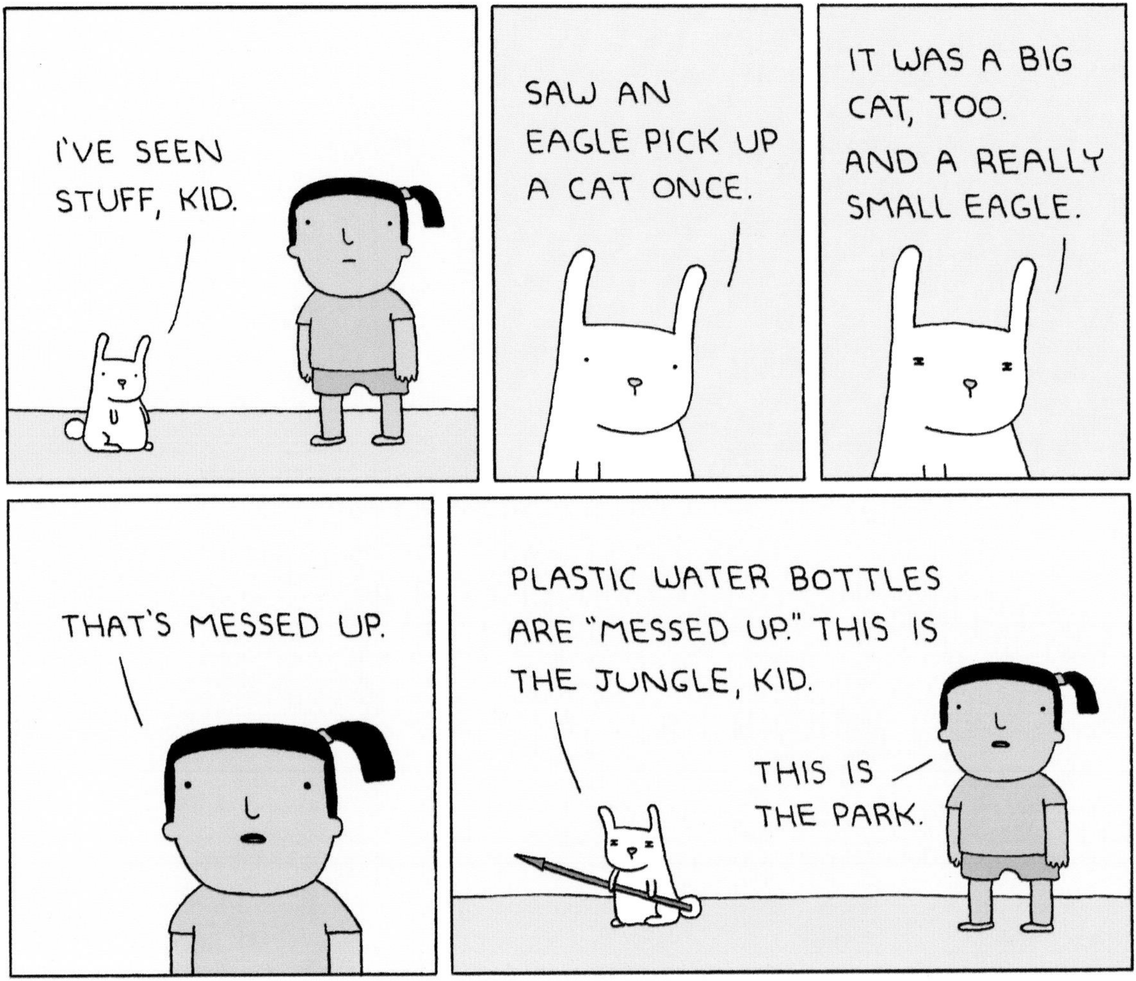
I'VE SEEN STUFF, KID.
SAW AN EAGLE PICK UP A CAT ONCE.
IT WAS A BIG CAT, TOO.
AND A REALLY SMALL EAGLE.
THAT'S MESSED UP.
PLASTIC WATER BOTTLES ARE "MESSED UP." THIS IS THE JUNGLE, KID.
THIS IS THE PARK.

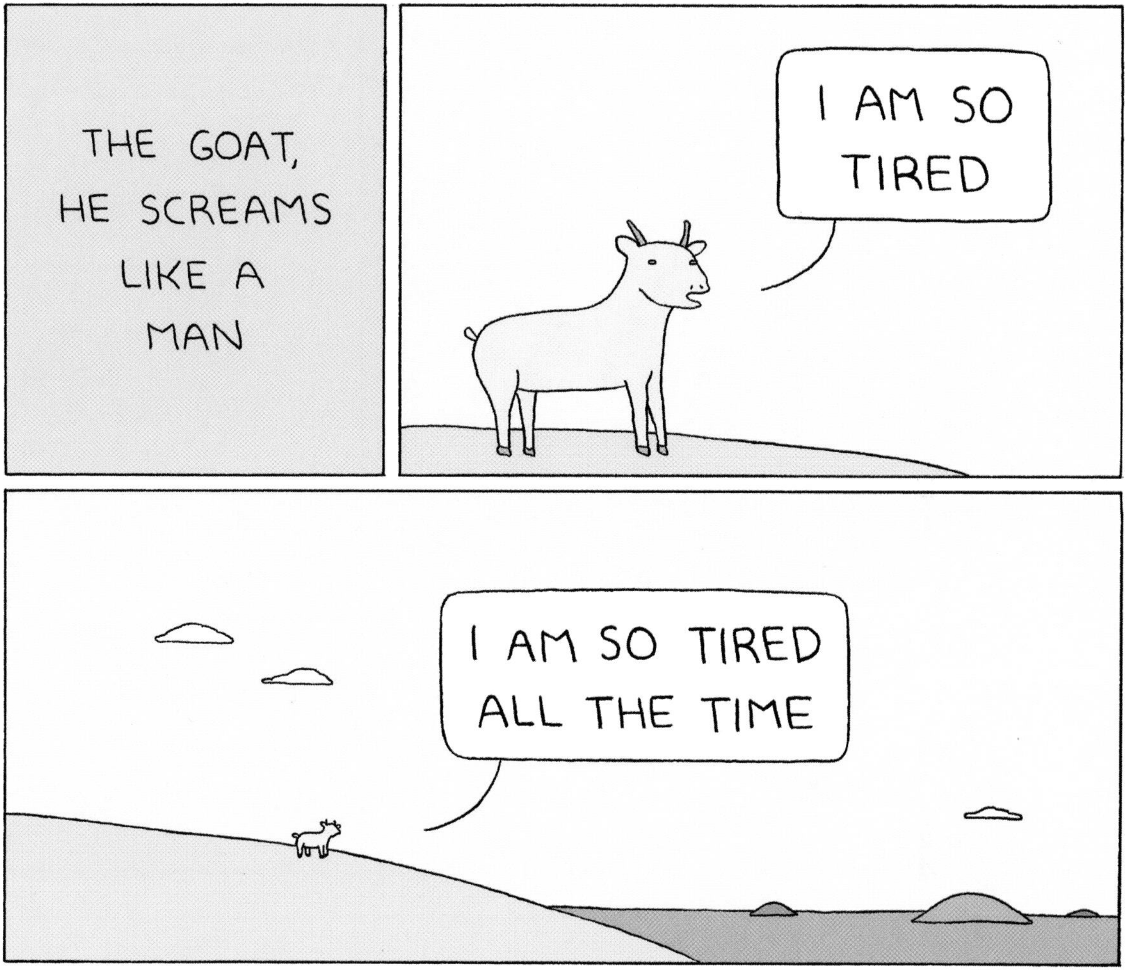
THE GOAT, HE SCREAMS LIKE A MAN
I AM SO TIRED
I AM SO TIRED ALL THE TIME

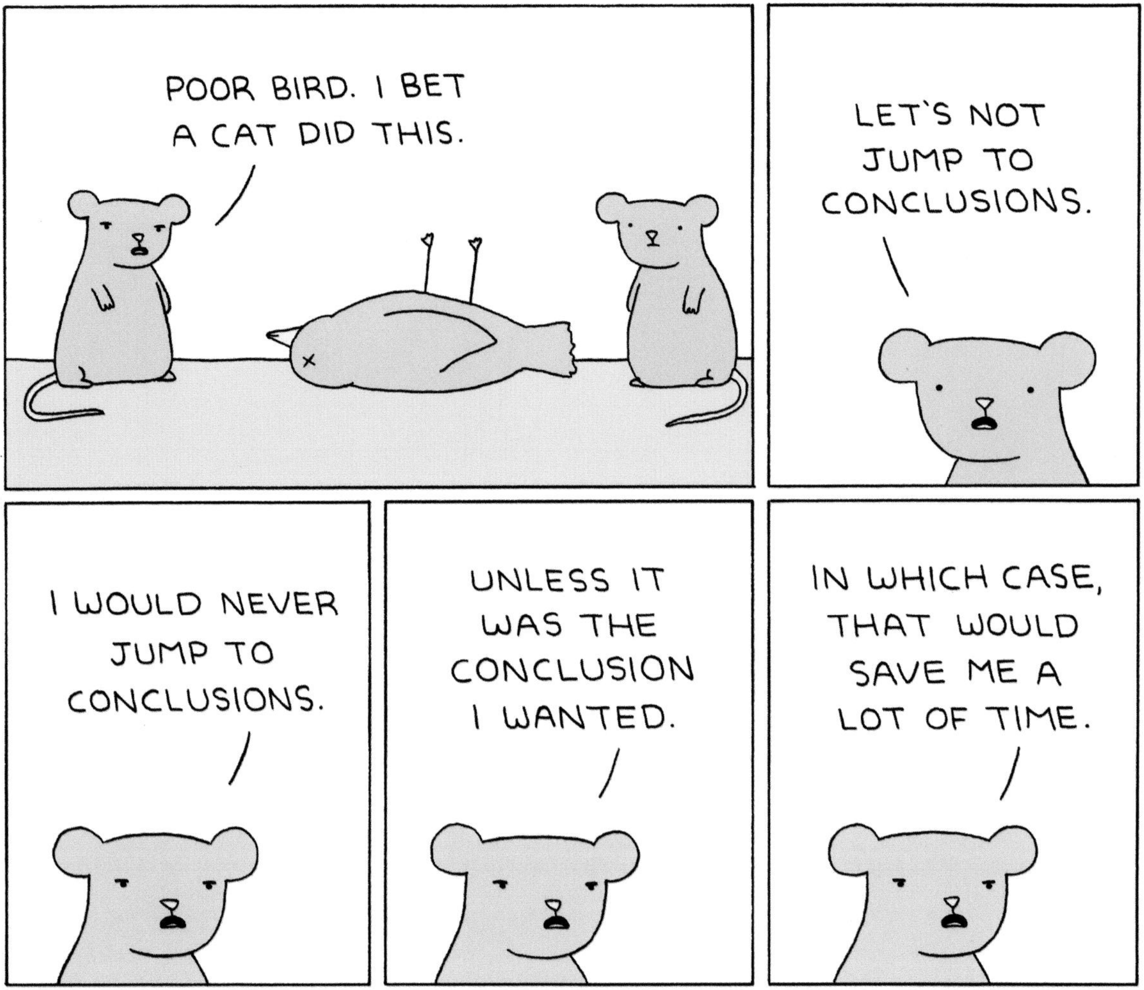
POOR BIRD. I BET A CAT DID THIS.
LET'S NOT JUMP TO CONCLUSIONS.
I WOULD NEVER JUMP TO CONCLUSIONS.
UNLESS IT WAS THE CONCLUSION I WANTED.
IN WHICH CASE, THAT WOULD SAVE ME A LOT OF TIME.

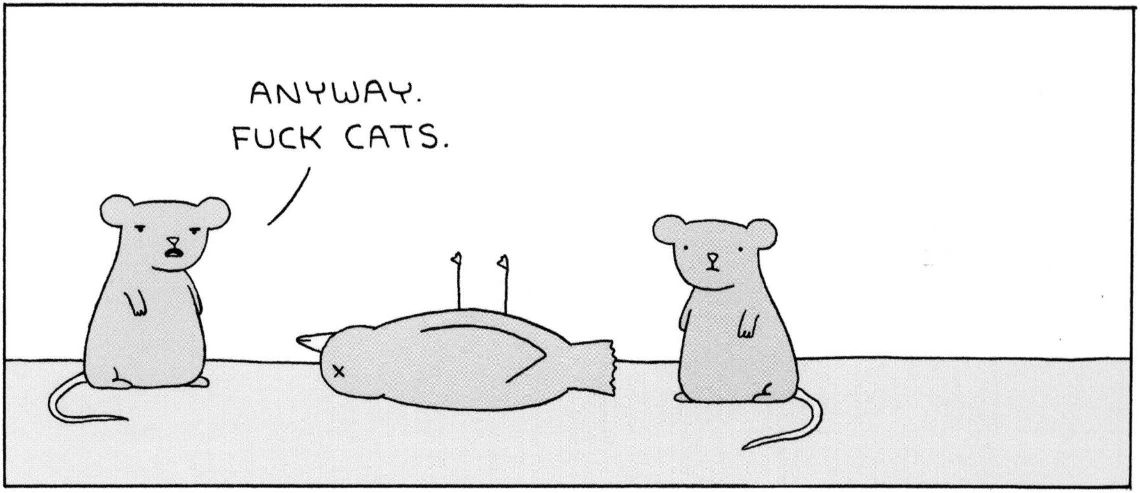
ANYWAY.
FUCK CATS.

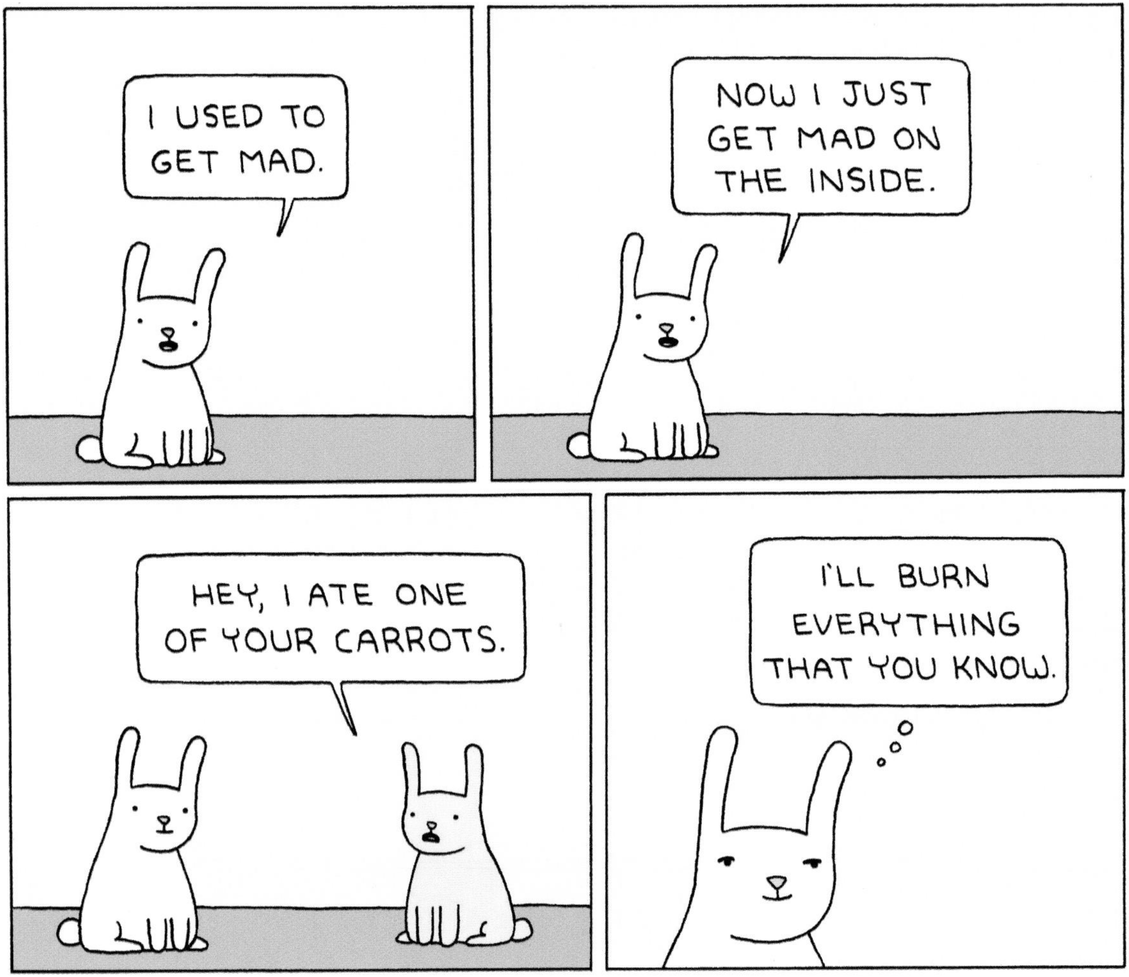
I USED TO GET MAD.
NOW I JUST GET MAD ON THE INSIDE.
HEY, I ATE ONE OF YOUR CARROTS.
I'LL BURN EVERYTHING THAT YOU KNOW.

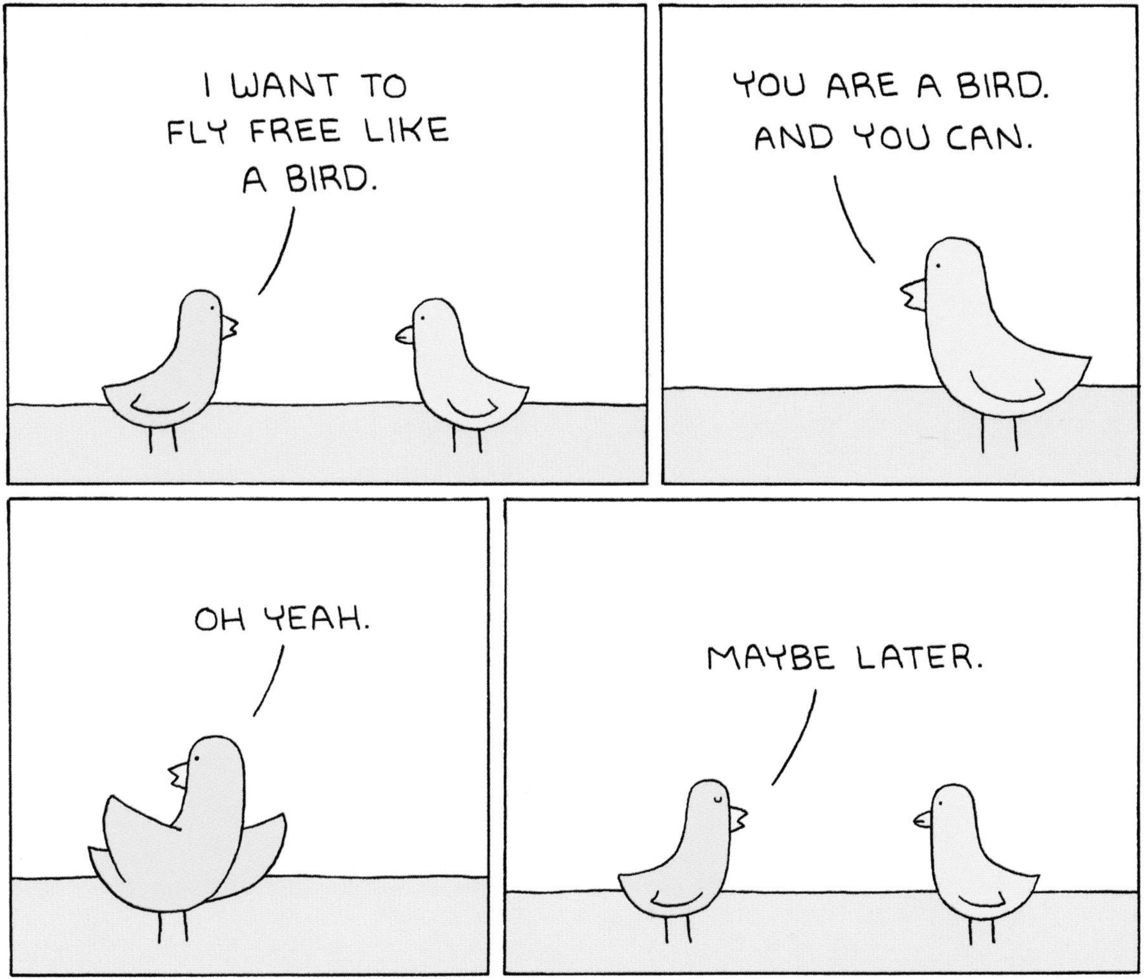
I WANT TO FLY FREE LIKE A BIRD.
YOU ARE A BIRD. AND YOU CAN.
OH YEAH.
MAYBE LATER.

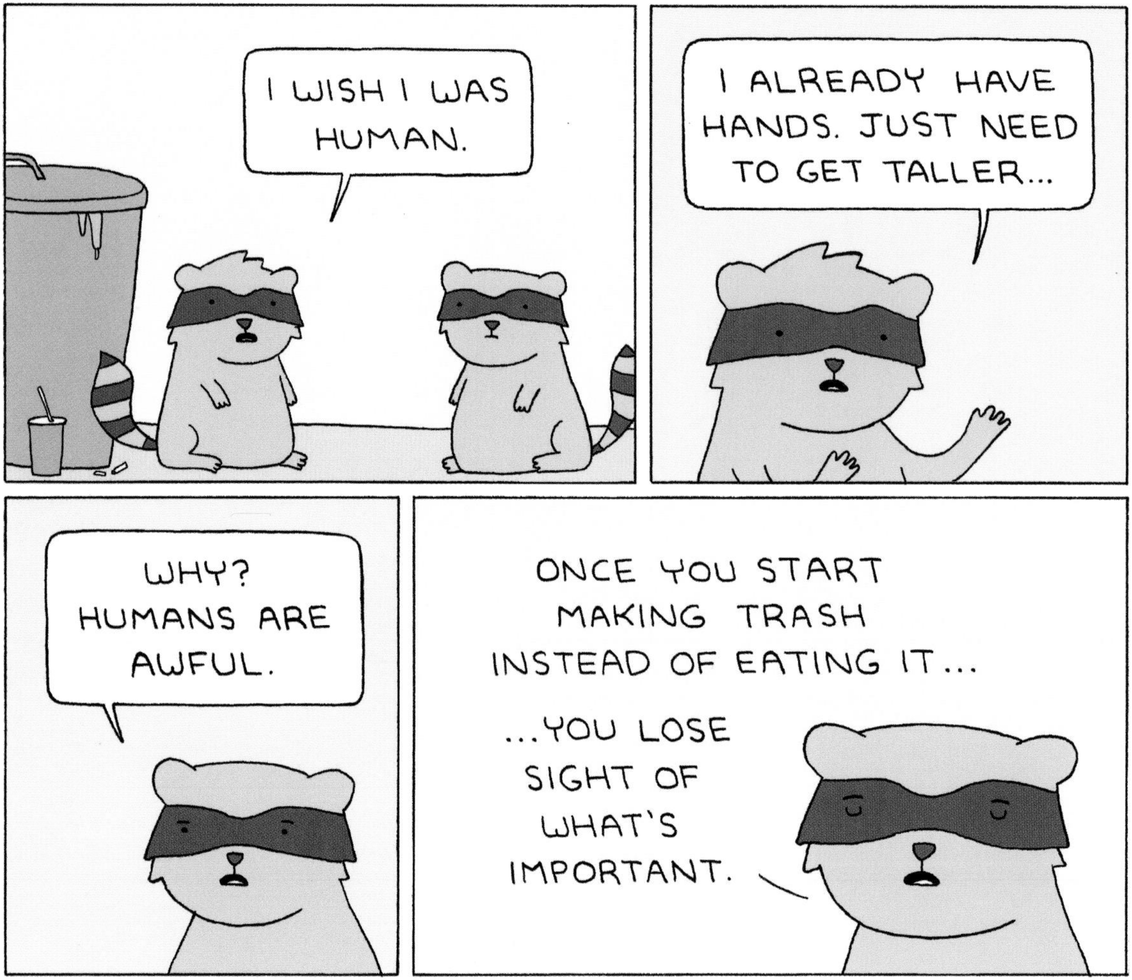
I WISH I WAS HUMAN.
I ALREADY HAVE HANDS. JUST NEED TO GET TALLER...
WHY? HUMANS ARE AWFUL.
ONCE YOU START MAKING TRASH INSTEAD OF EATING IT...
...YOU LOSE SIGHT OF WHAT'S IMPORTANT.

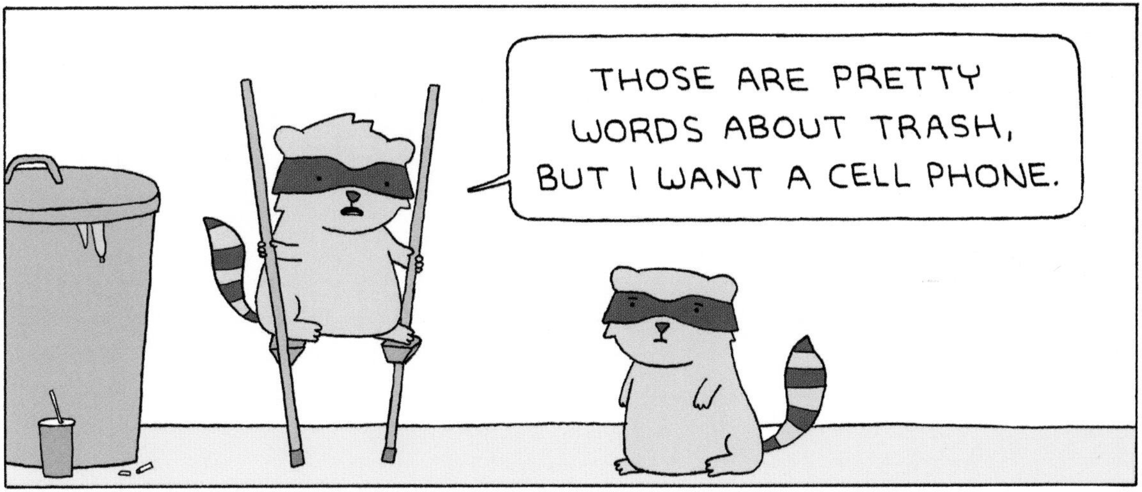
THOSE ARE PRETTY WORDS ABOUT TRASH, BUT I WANT A CELL PHONE.

III

CHANGES

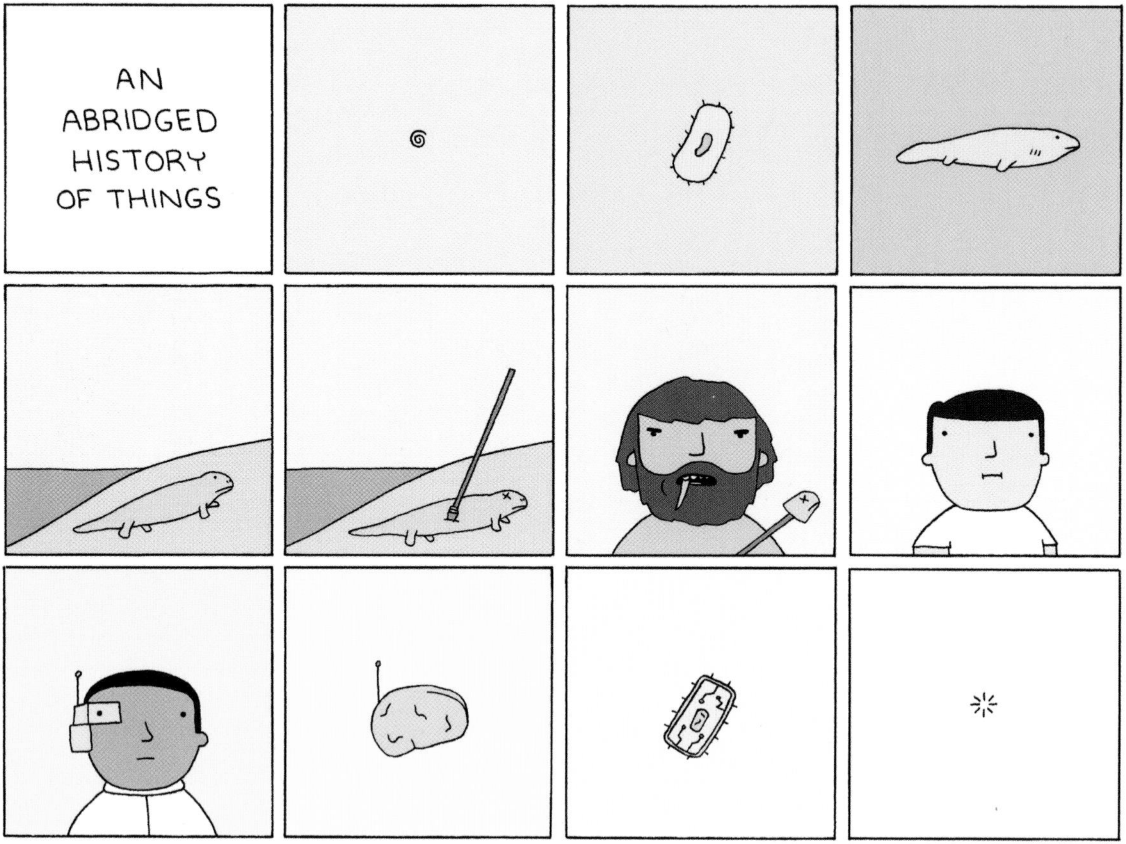
AN ABRIDGED HISTORY OF THINGS

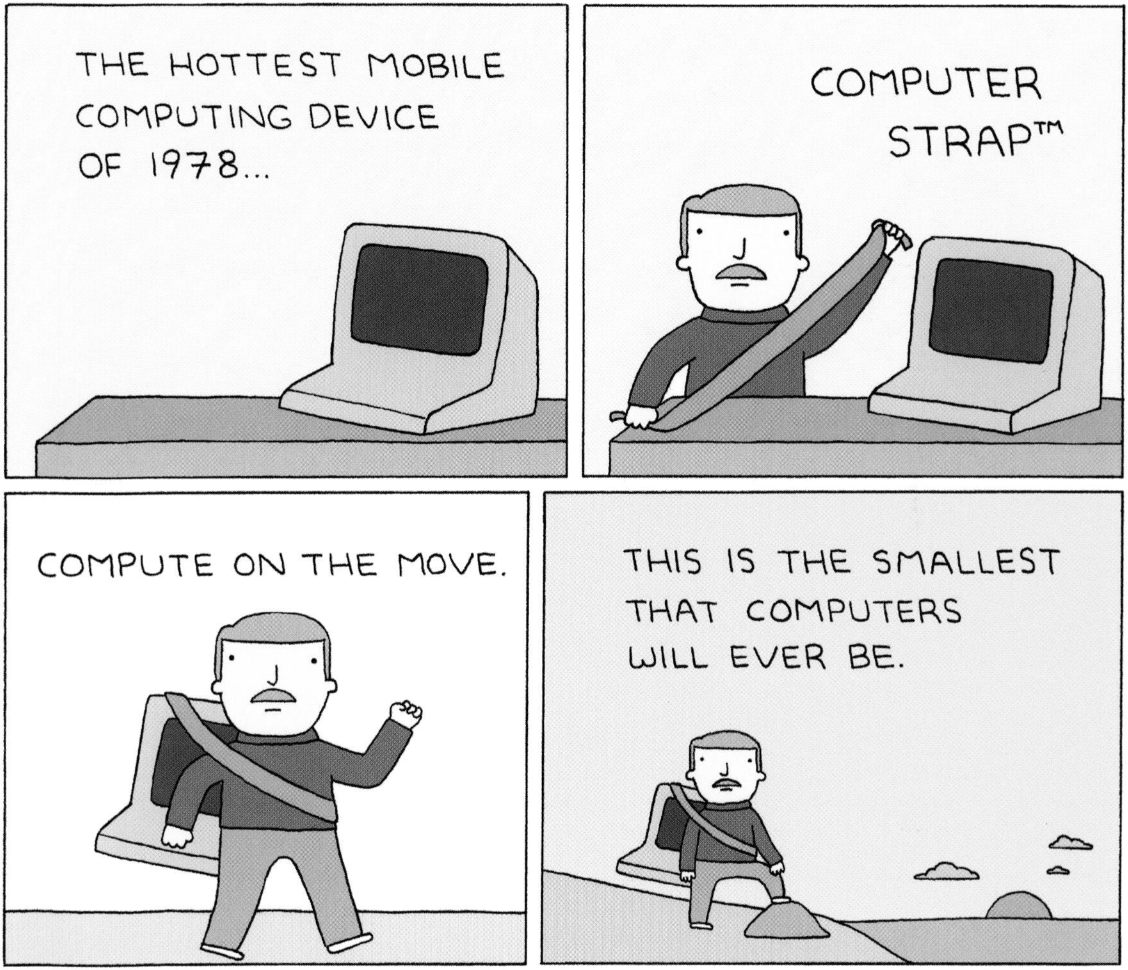
THE HOTTEST MOBILE COMPUTING DEVICE OF 1978...
COMPUTER STRAP™
COMPUTE ON THE MOVE.
THIS IS THE SMALLEST THAT COMPUTERS WILL EVER BE.

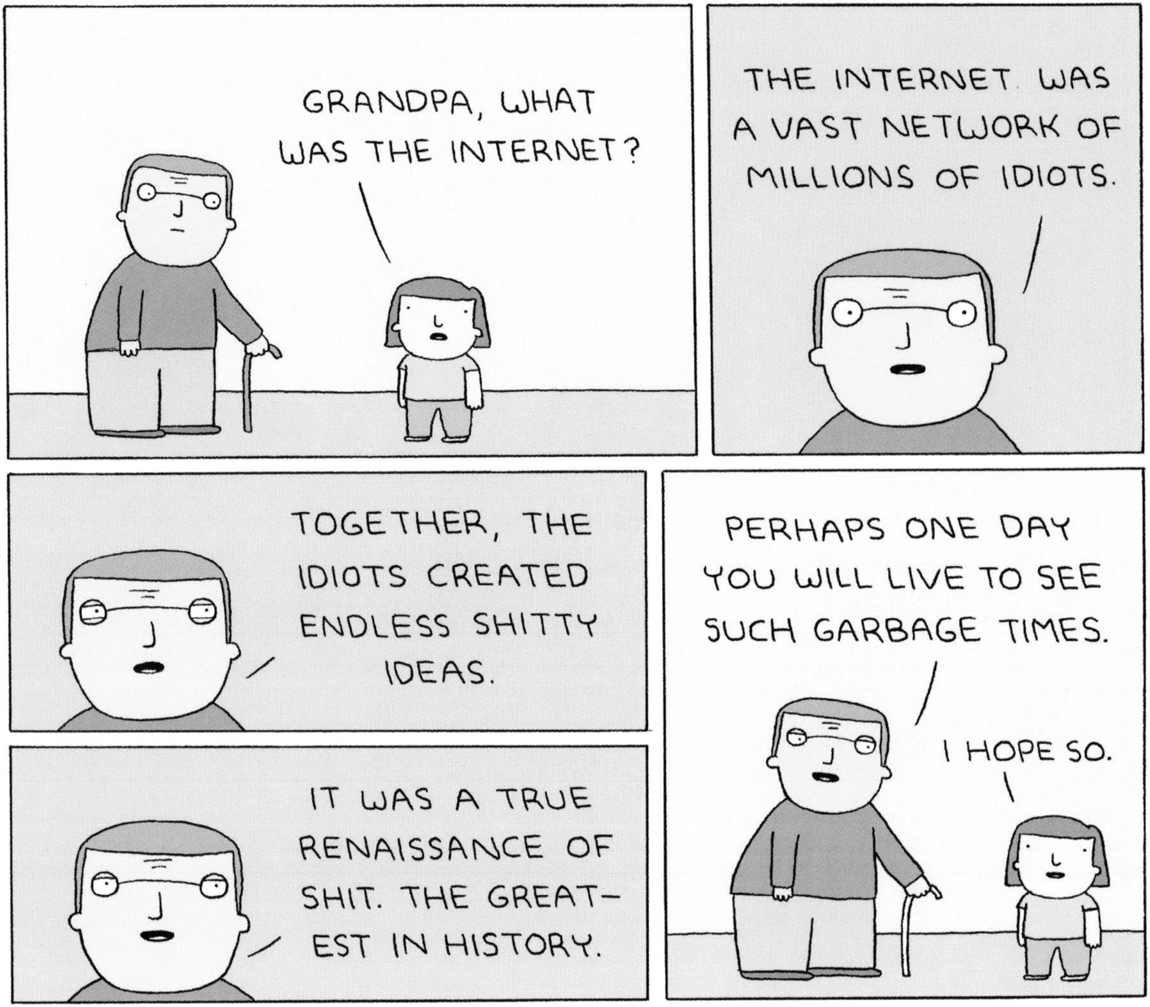
GRANDPA, WHAT WAS THE INTERNET?
THE INTERNET WAS A VAST NETWORK OF MILLIONS OF IDIOTS.
TOGETHER, THE IDIOTS CREATED ENDLESS SHITTY IDEAS.
IT WAS A TRUE RENAISSANCE OF SHIT. THE GREAT-EST IN HISTORY.
PERHAPS ONE DAY YOU WILL LIVE TO SEE SUCH GARBAGE TIMES.
I HOPE SO.

IN THIS DYSTOPIAN VISION OF THE FUTURE...

FASCISM!

VOLCANOES!

BUT THERE'S A COOLER TYPE OF PHONE.

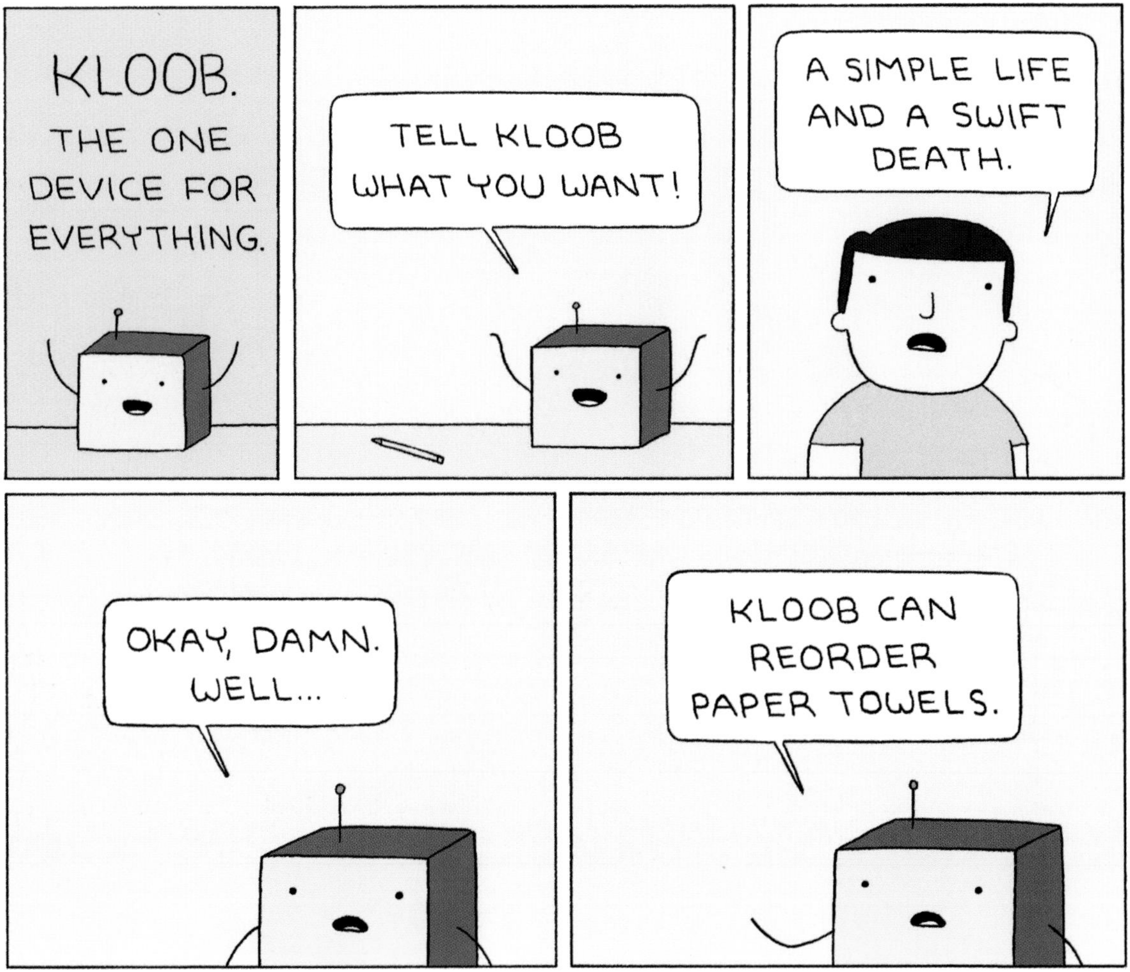
KLOOB.
THE ONE DEVICE FOR EVERYTHING.
TELL KLOOB WHAT YOU WANT!
A SIMPLE LIFE AND A SWIFT DEATH.
OKAY, DAMN. WELL...
KLOOB CAN REORDER PAPER TOWELS.

THE OLD COMPUTER LIES FORGOTTEN.

IN TIME, IT DECOMPOSES.

AND NEW COMPUTERS GROW FROM THE FERTILE EARTH.

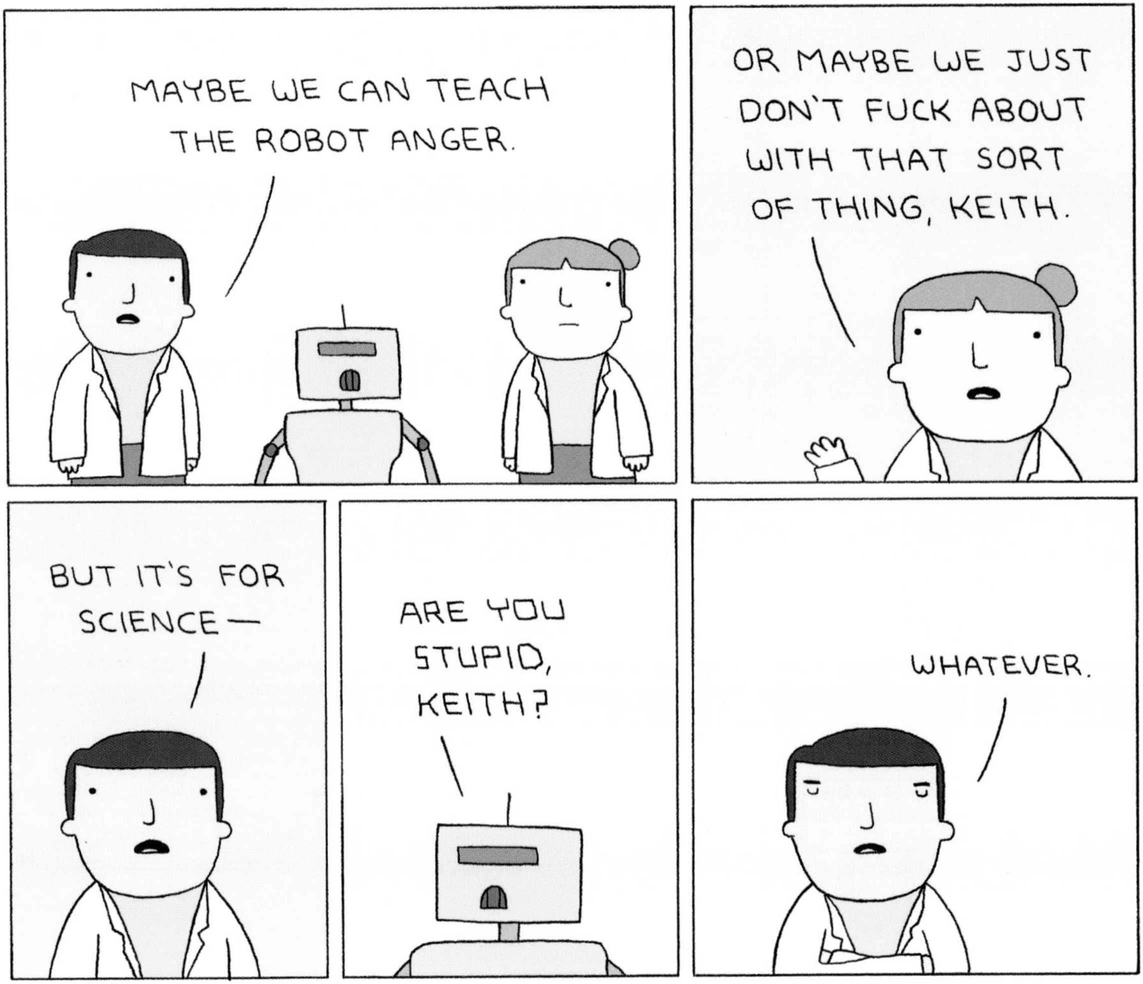
MAYBE WE CAN TEACH THE ROBOT ANGER.
OR MAYBE WE JUST DON'T FUCK ABOUT WITH THAT SORT OF THING, KEITH.
BUT IT'S FOR SCIENCE—
ARE YOU STUPID, KEITH?
WHATEVER.

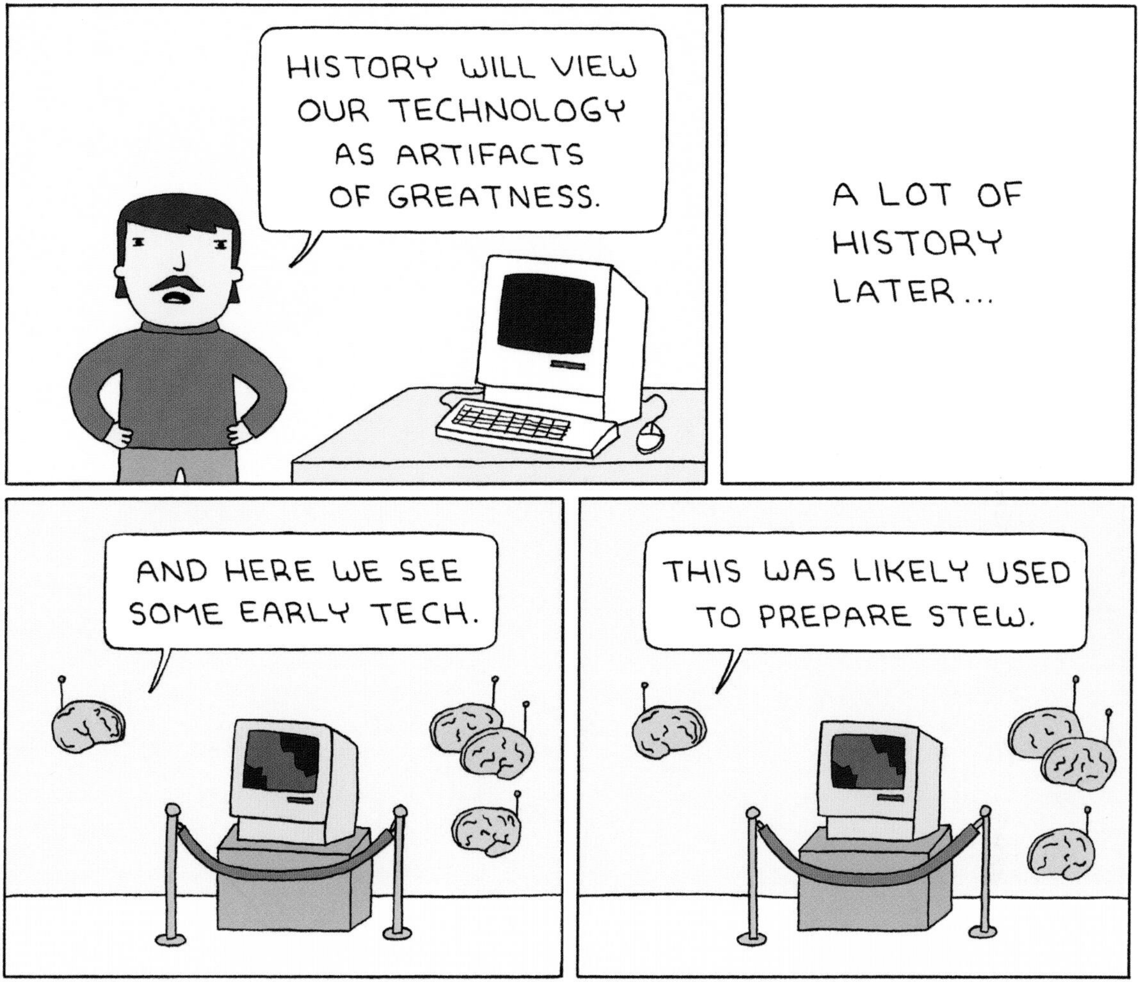
HISTORY WILL VIEW OUR TECHNOLOGY AS ARTIFACTS OF GREATNESS.
A LOT OF HISTORY LATER...
AND HERE WE SEE SOME EARLY TECH.
THIS WAS LIKELY USED TO PREPARE STEW.

OUR FUTURE IN SPACE

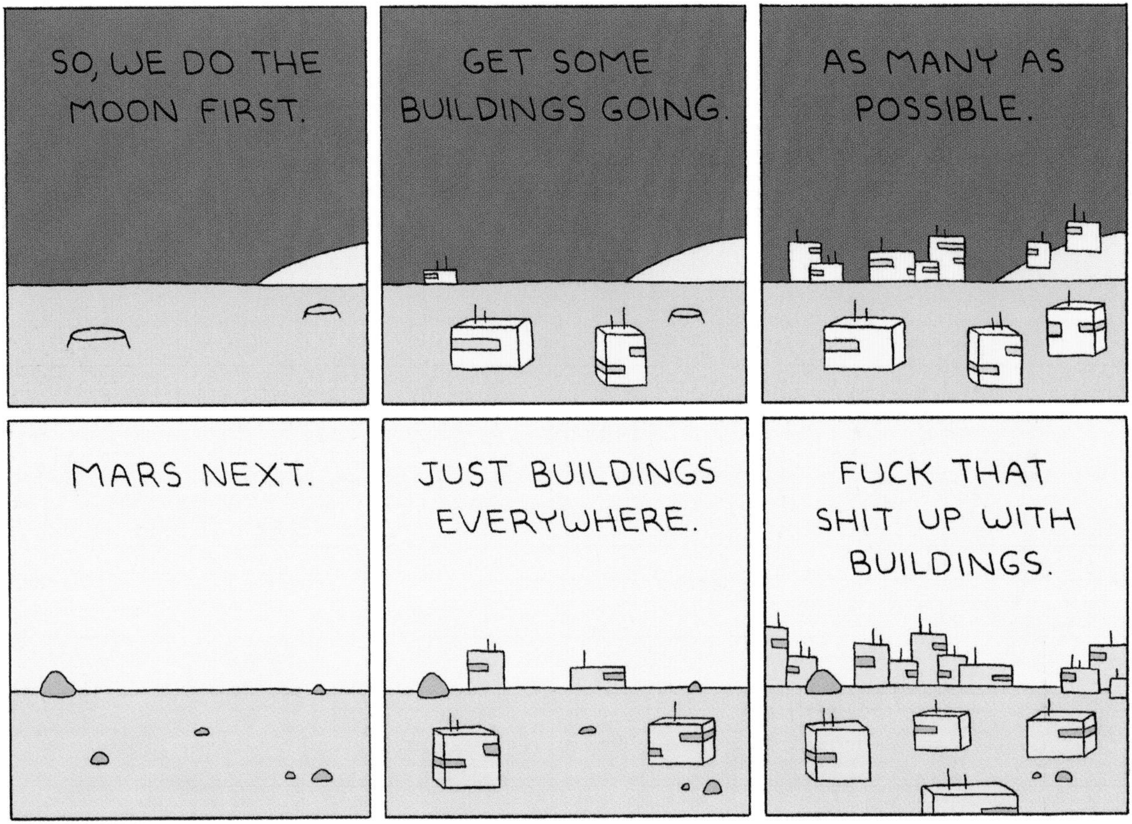
SO, WE DO THE MOON FIRST.
GET SOME BUILDINGS GOING.
AS MANY AS POSSIBLE.
MARS NEXT.
JUST BUILDINGS EVERYWHERE.
FUCK THAT SHIT UP WITH BUILDINGS.

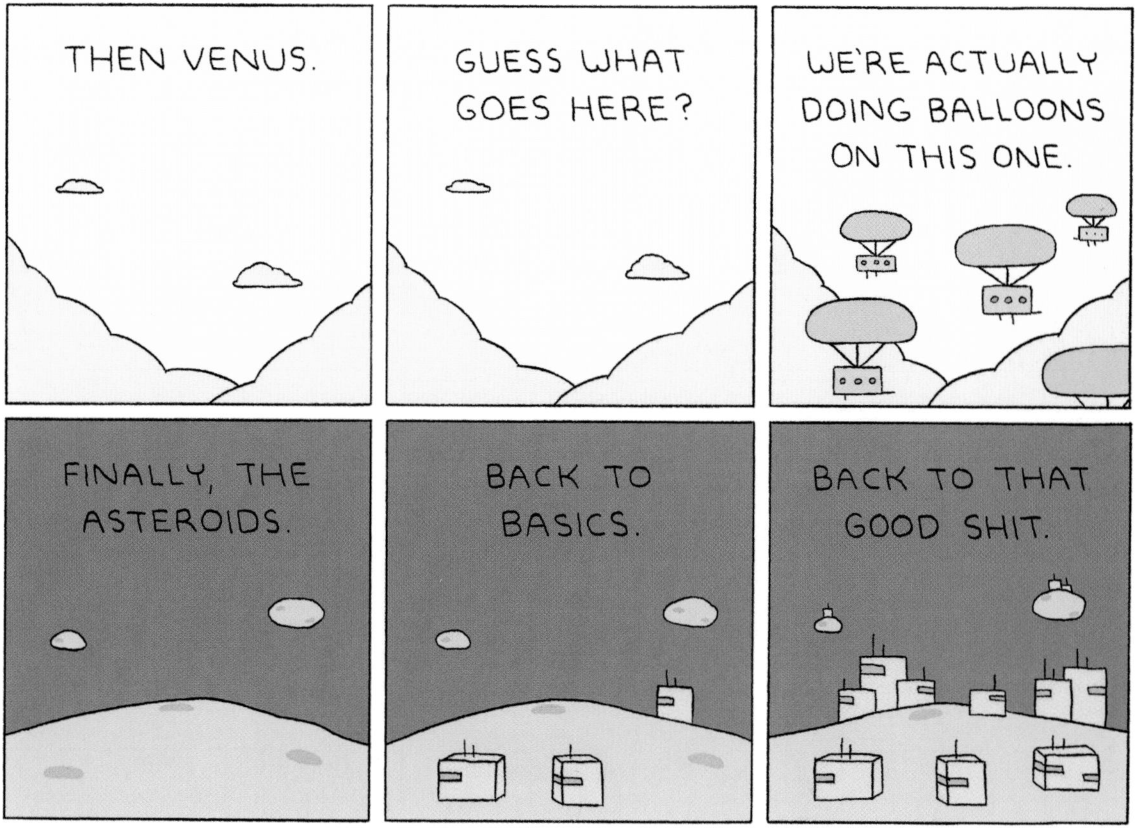
THEN VENUS.
GUESS WHAT GOES HERE?
WE'RE ACTUALLY DOING BALLOONS ON THIS ONE.
FINALLY, THE ASTEROIDS.
BACK TO BASICS.
BACK TO THAT GOOD SHIT.

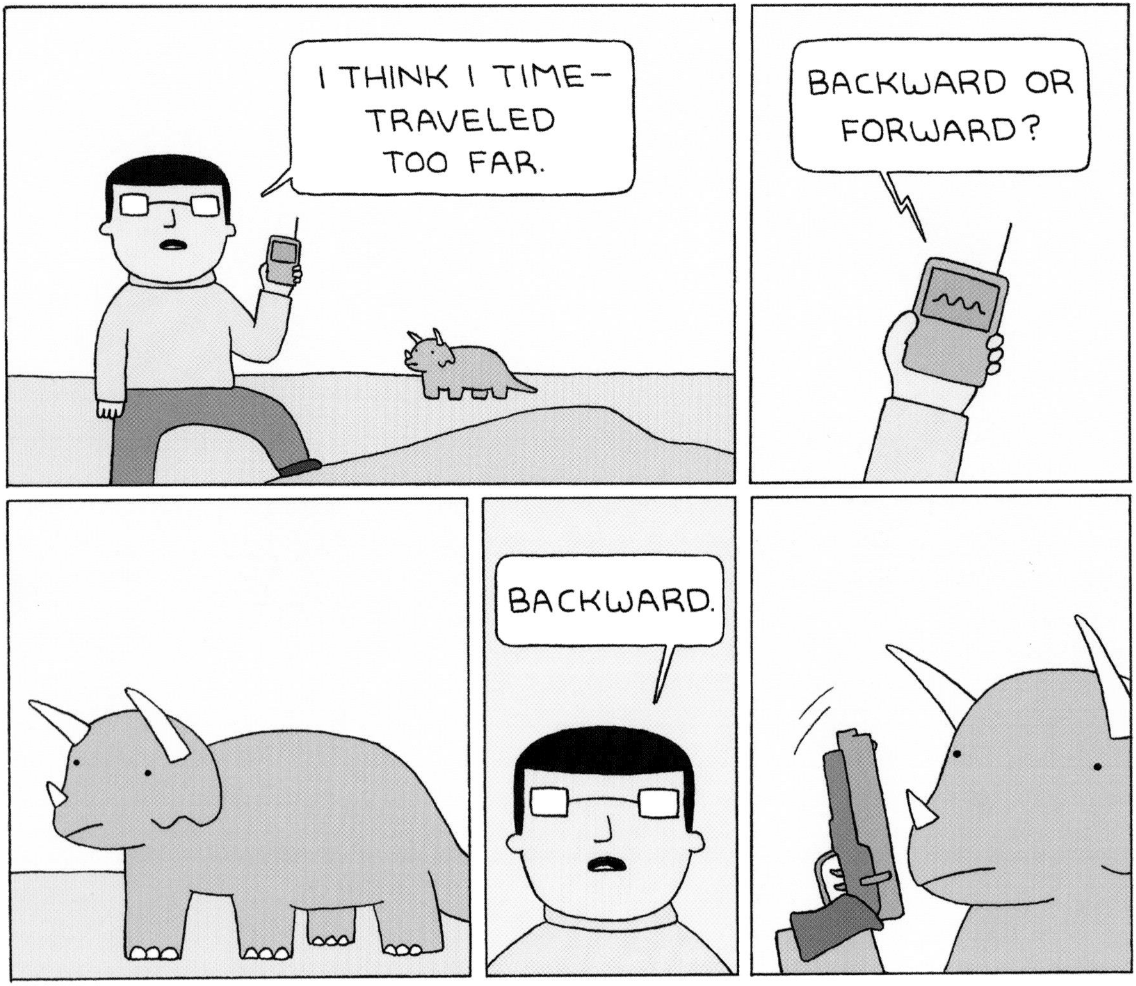
I THINK I TIME-TRAVELED TOO FAR.
BACKWARD OR FORWARD?
BACKWARD.

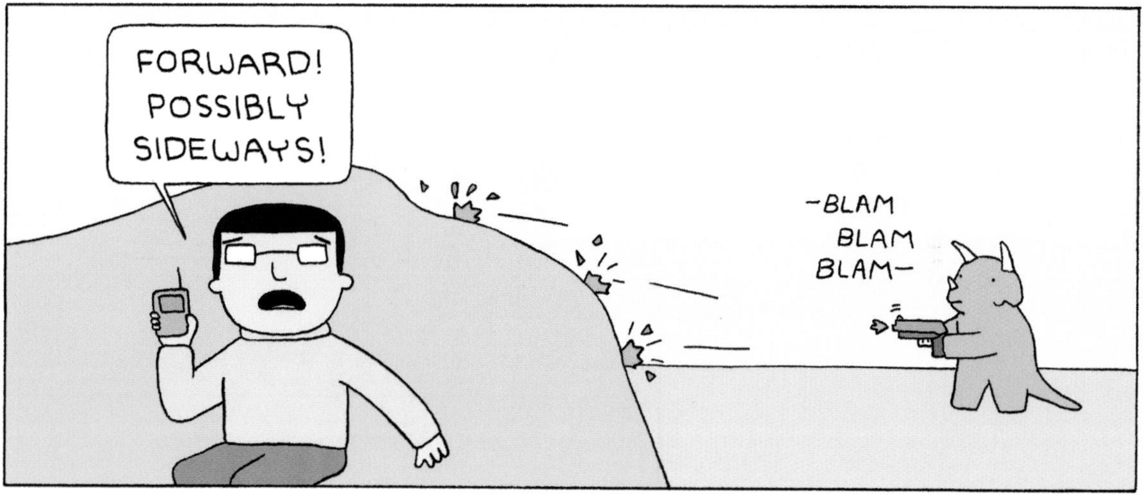
FORWARD! POSSIBLY SIDEWAYS!
-BLAM BLAM BLAM-

HAVE WE BECOME TOO DEPENDENT ON TECHNOLOGY?
PROBABLY.
BUT LET'S CHECK THE INTERNET ABOUT THIS.

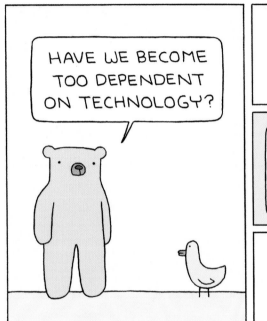

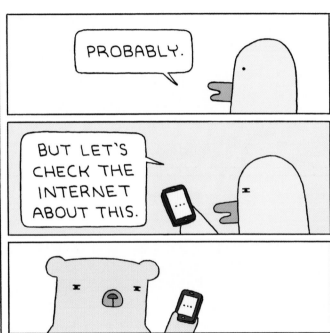

AS THE AI NEARED COMPLETION...

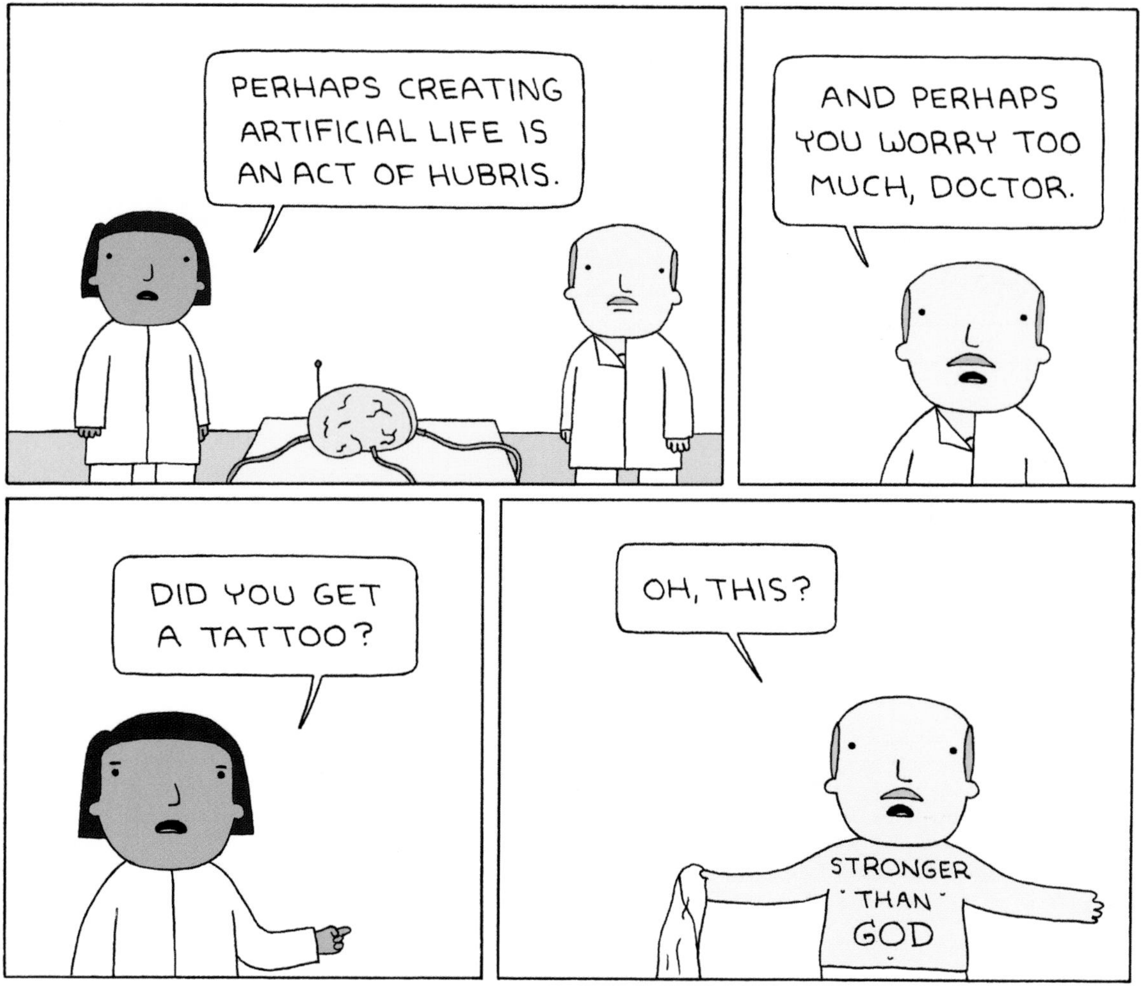
PERHAPS CREATING ARTIFICIAL LIFE IS AN ACT OF HUBRIS.
AND PERHAPS YOU WORRY TOO MUCH, DOCTOR.
DID YOU GET A TATTOO?
OH, THIS?
STRONGER THAN GOD

DO ROBOTS EXPERIENCE NOSTALGIA?

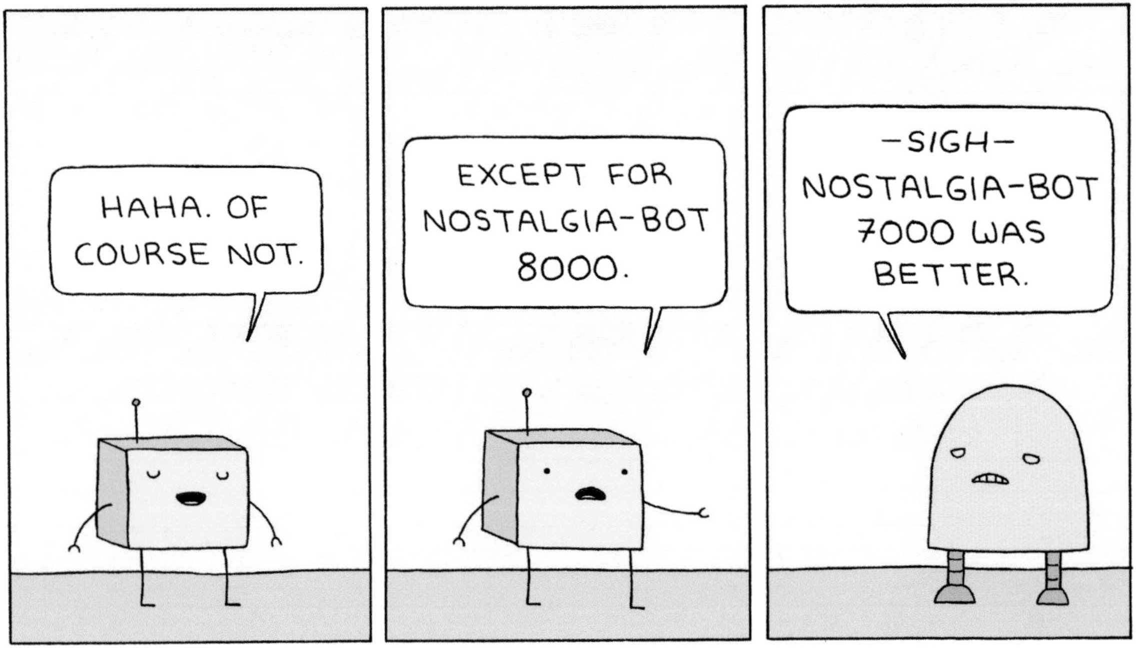
HAHA. OF COURSE NOT.
EXCEPT FOR NOSTALGIA-BOT 8000.
-SIGH- NOSTALGIA-BOT 7000 WAS BETTER.

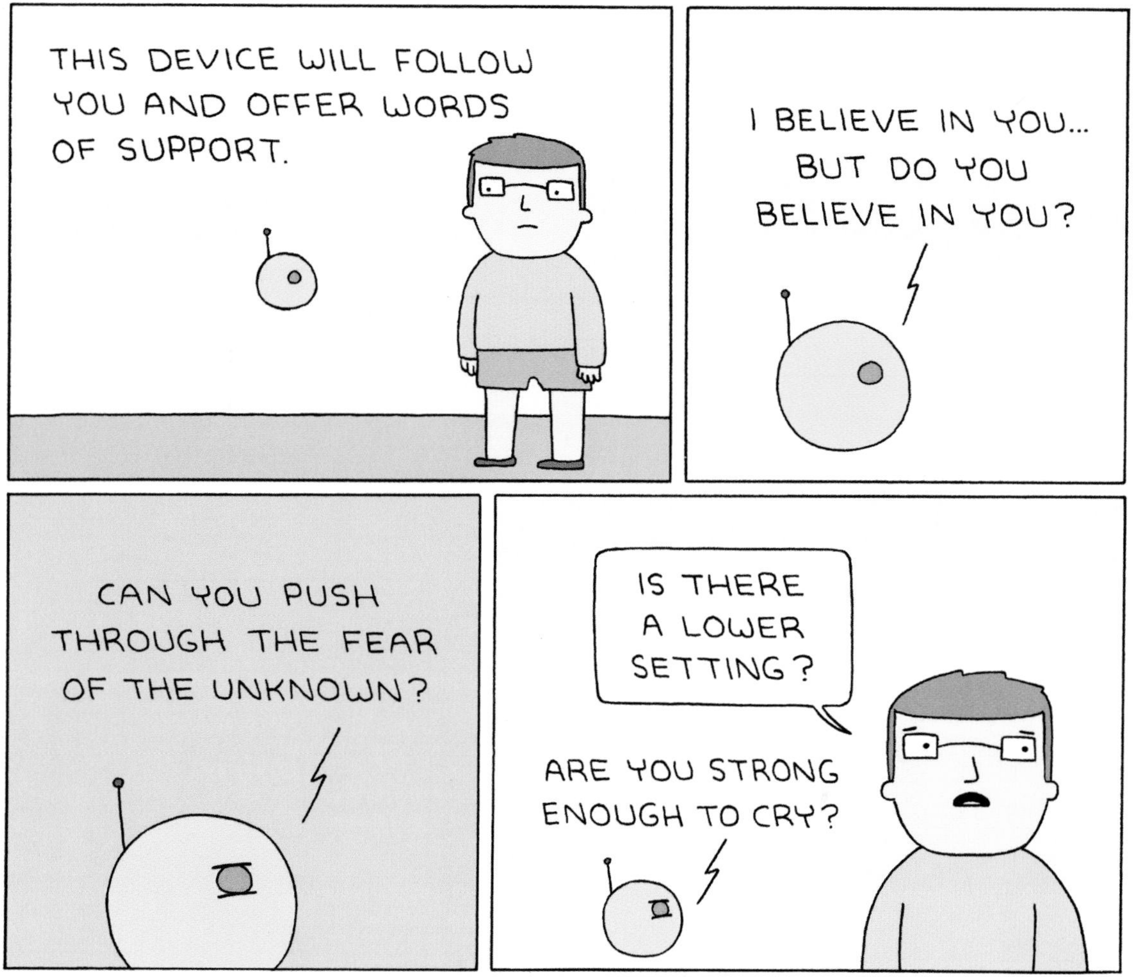
THIS DEVICE WILL FOLLOW YOU AND OFFER WORDS OF SUPPORT.
I BELIEVE IN YOU... BUT DO YOU BELIEVE IN YOU?
CAN YOU PUSH THROUGH THE FEAR OF THE UNKNOWN?
IS THERE A LOWER SETTING?
ARE YOU STRONG ENOUGH TO CRY?

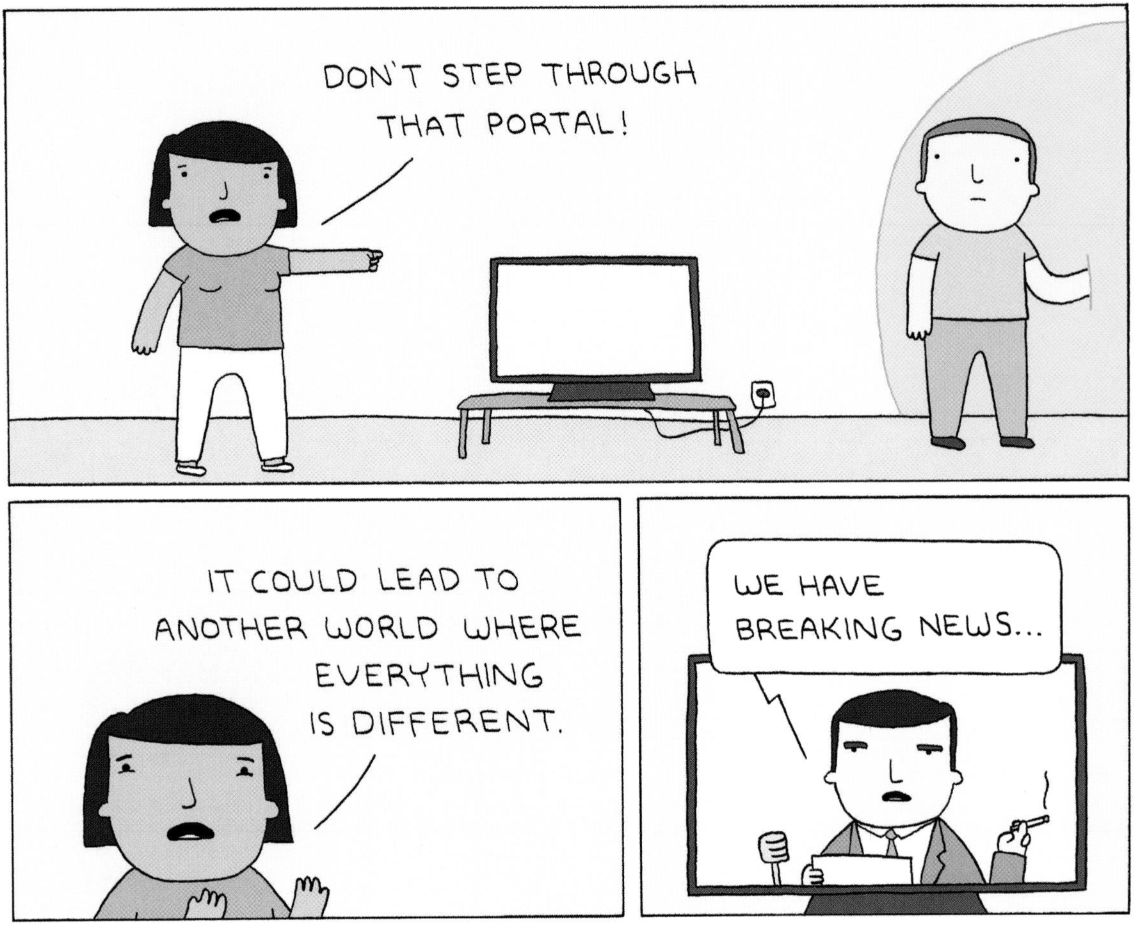
DON'T STEP THROUGH THAT PORTAL!
IT COULD LEAD TO ANOTHER WORLD WHERE EVERYTHING IS DIFFERENT.
WE HAVE BREAKING NEWS...

EVERYTHING IS STILL TRASH.
I'M GONNA ROLL THE DICE ON THIS ONE.

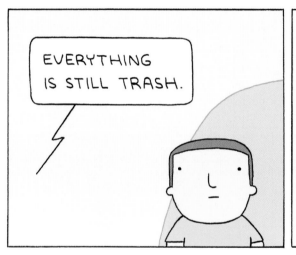

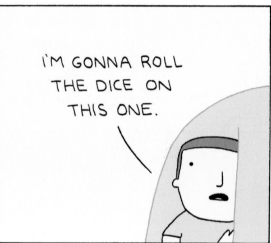

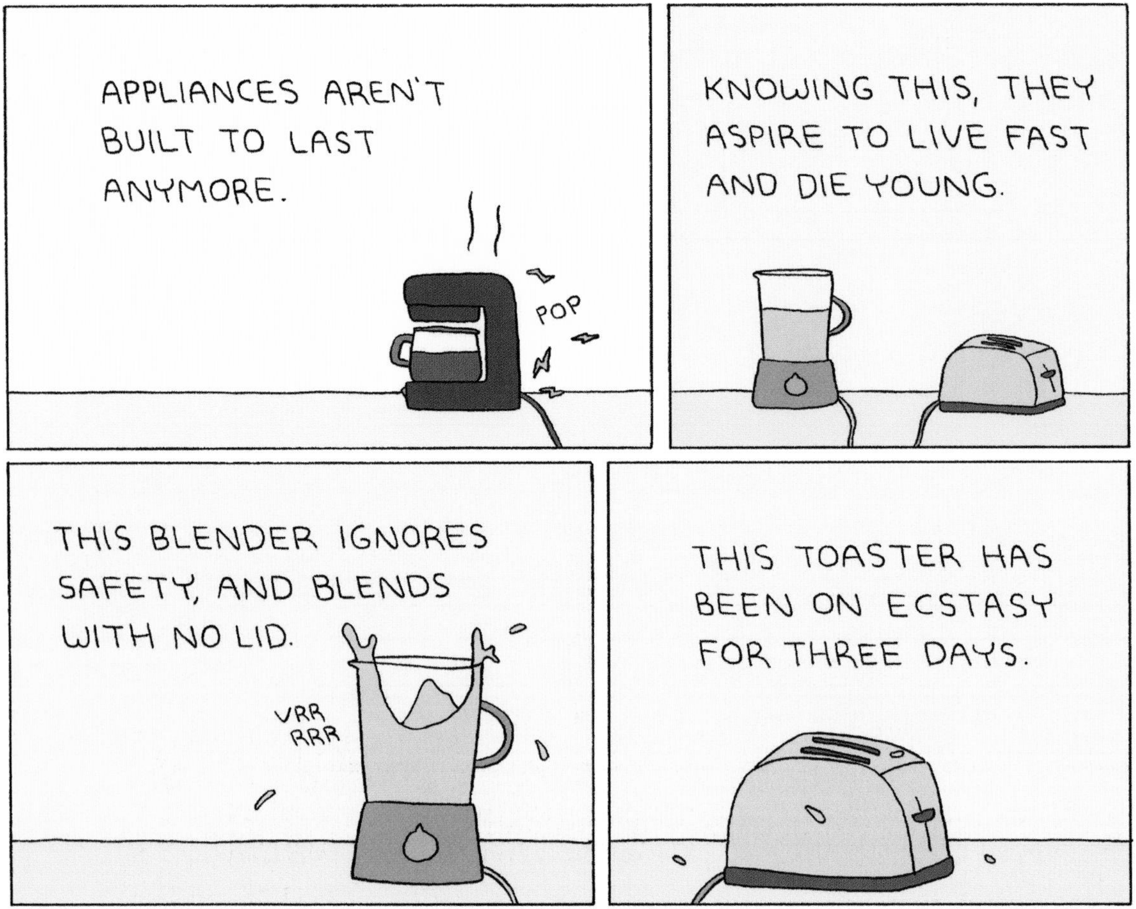
APPLIANCES AREN'T BUILT TO LAST ANYMORE.
POP
KNOWING THIS, THEY ASPIRE TO LIVE FAST AND DIE YOUNG.
THIS BLENDER IGNORES SAFETY, AND BLENDS WITH NO LID.
VRR RRR
THIS TOASTER HAS BEEN ON ECSTASY FOR THREE DAYS.

THE
LATEST
PHONE

BETTER

IN

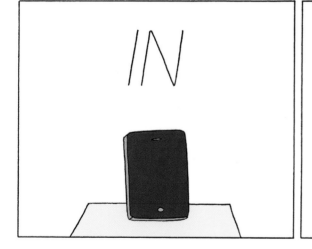

WAYS™

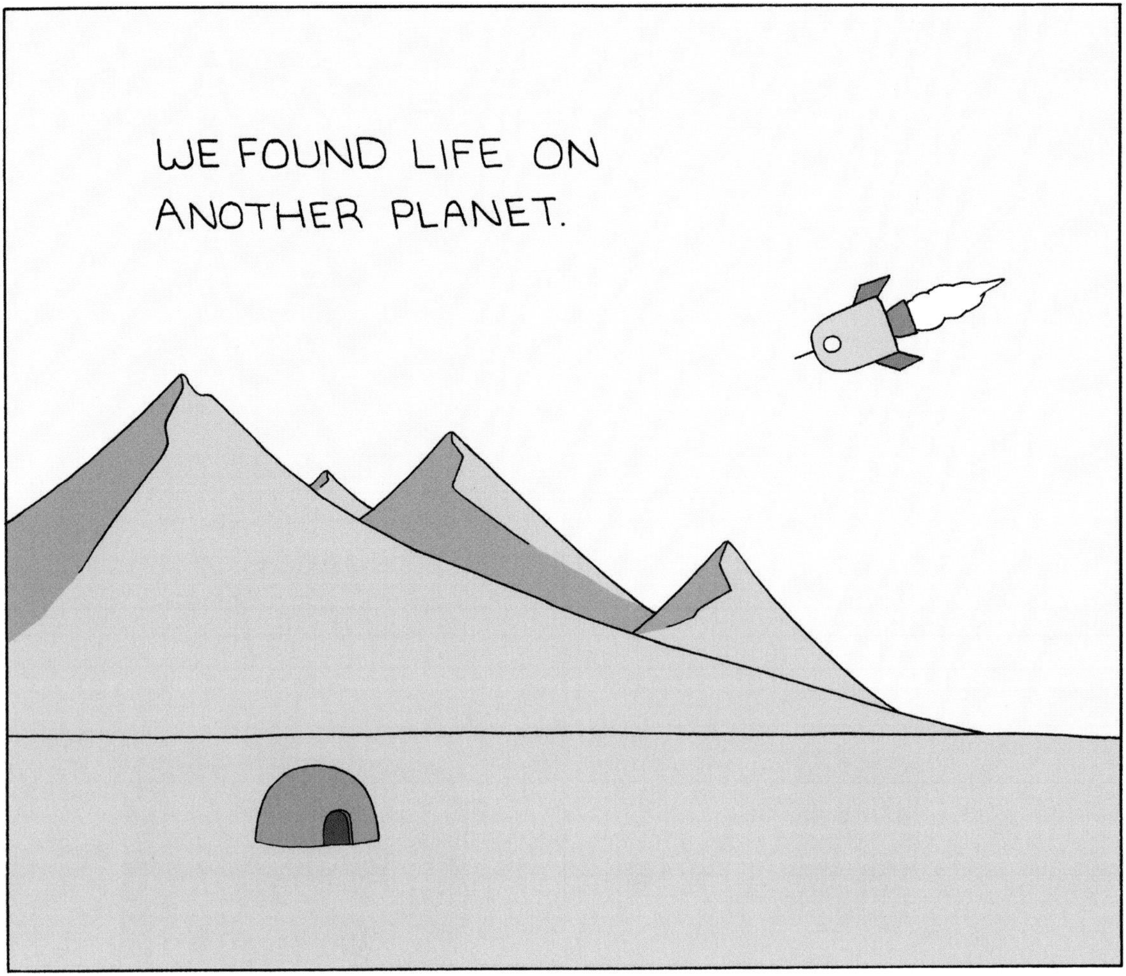
WE FOUND LIFE ON
ANOTHER PLANET.

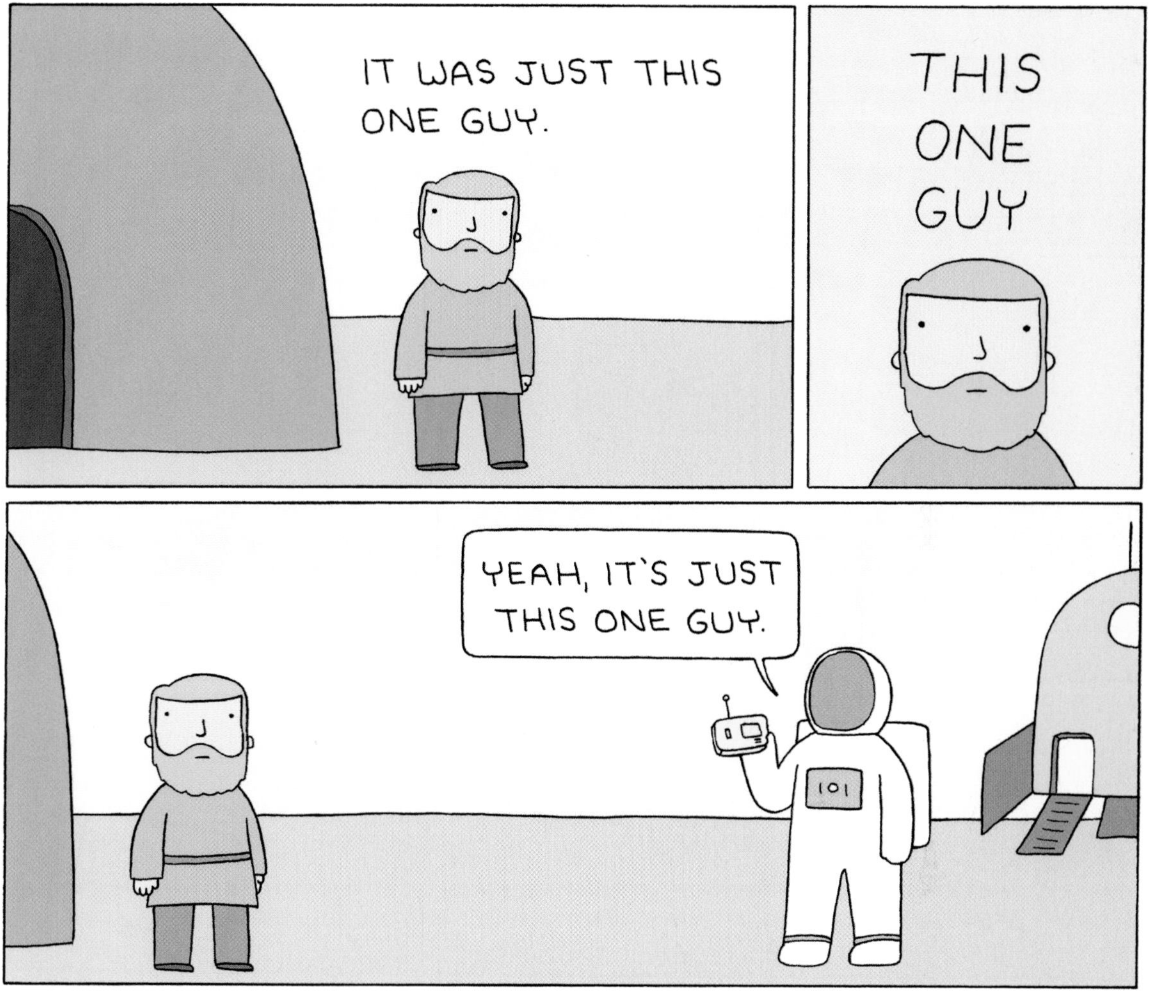
IT WAS JUST THIS ONE GUY.
THIS ONE GUY
YEAH, IT'S JUST THIS ONE GUY.
101

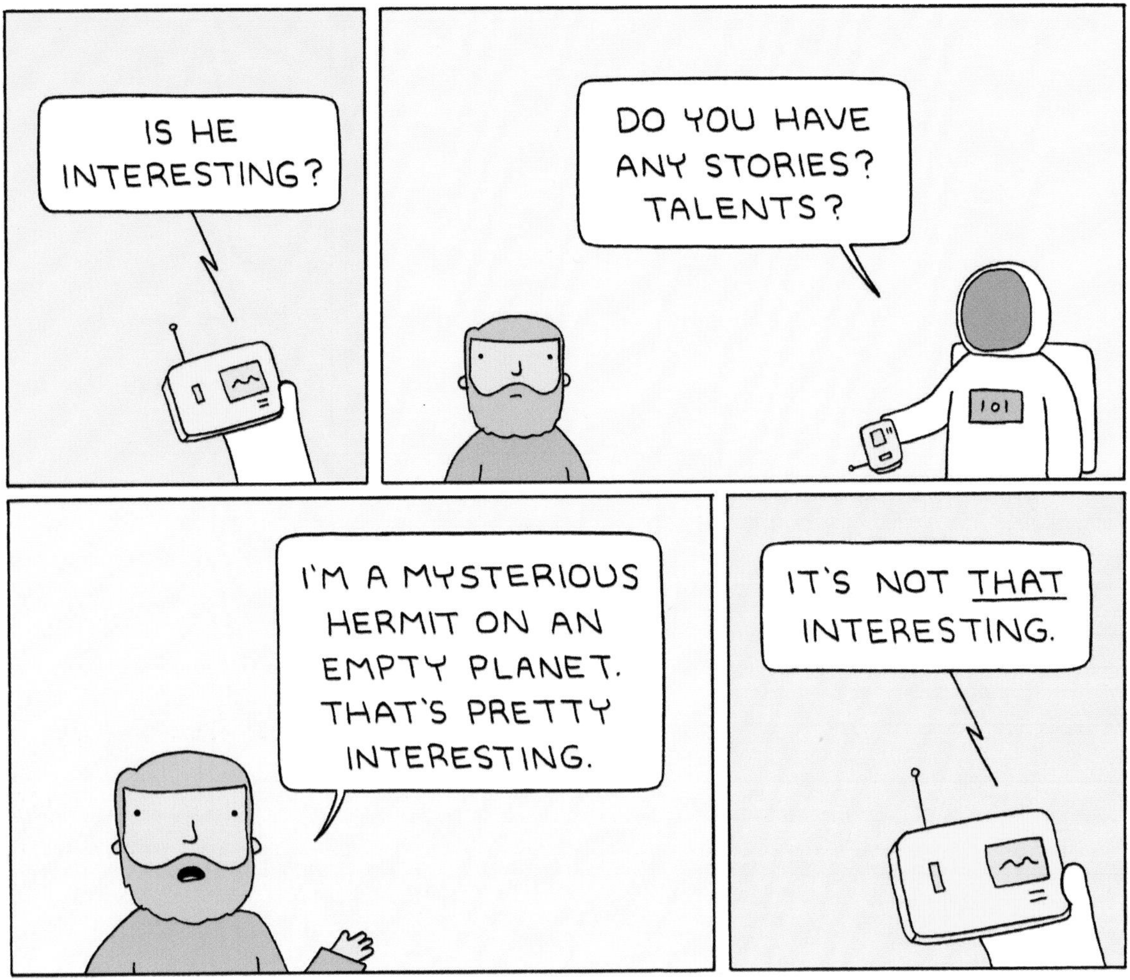
IS HE INTERESTING?
DO YOU HAVE ANY STORIES? TALENTS?
I'M A MYSTERIOUS HERMIT ON AN EMPTY PLANET. THAT'S PRETTY INTERESTING.
IT'S NOT THAT INTERESTING.

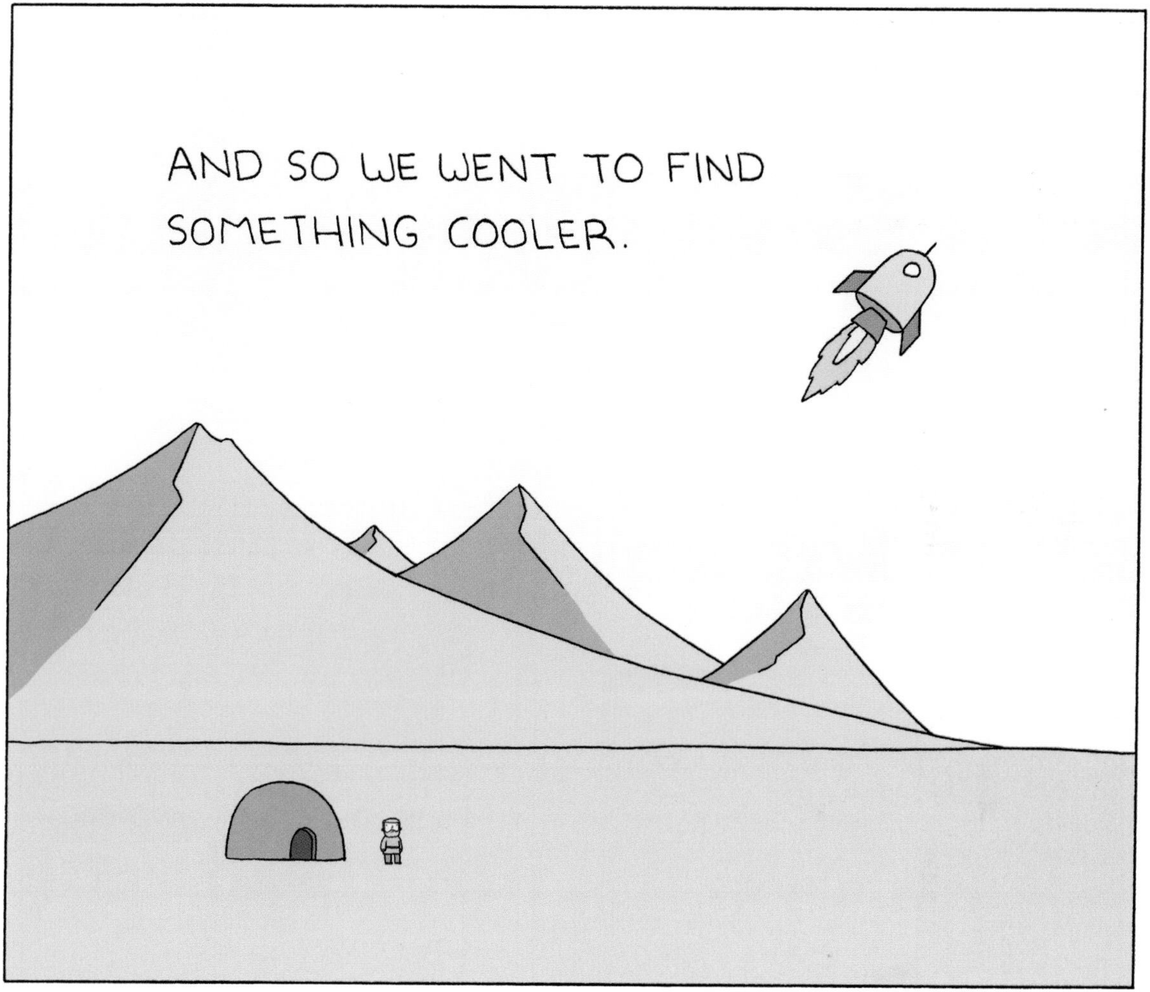
AND SO WE WENT TO FIND SOMETHING COOLER.

TIME-TRAVELER DIARIES

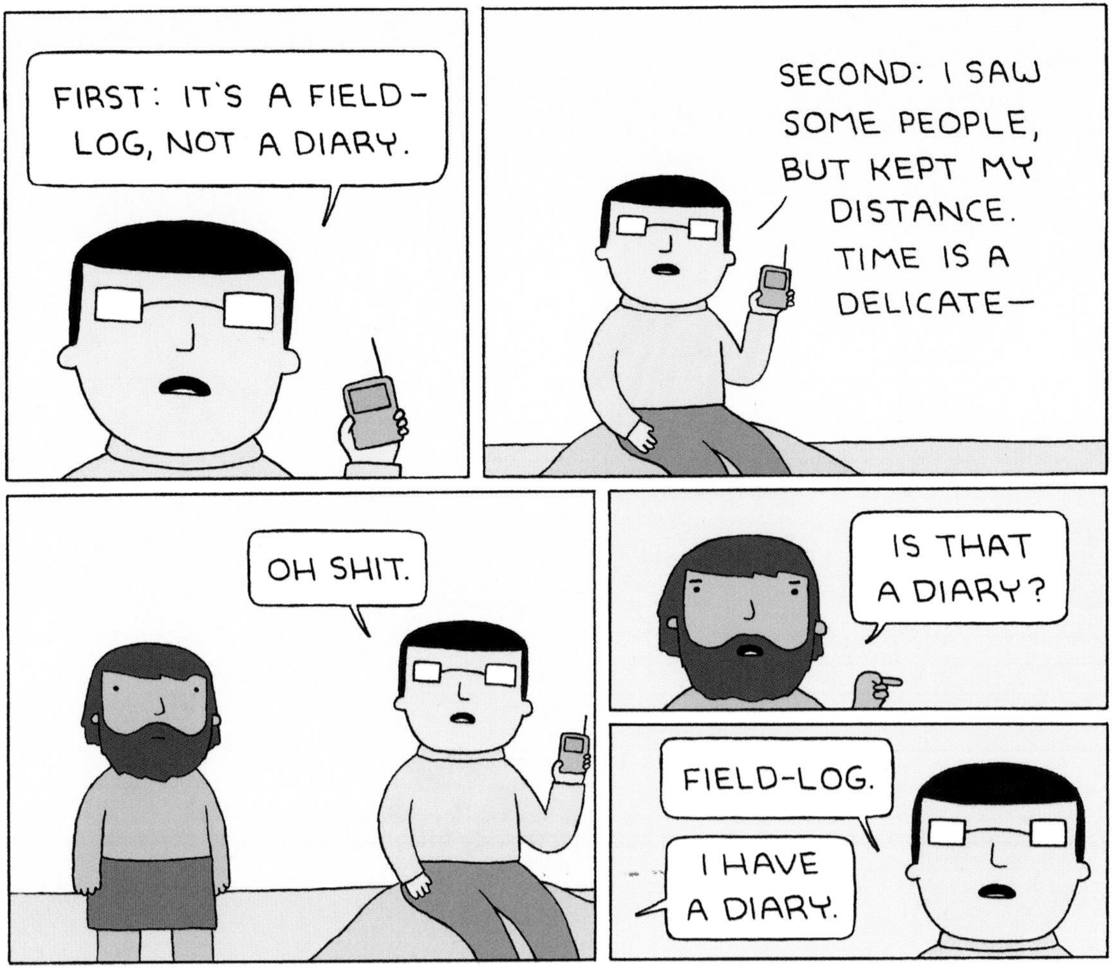
FIRST: IT'S A FIELD-LOG, NOT A DIARY.
SECOND: I SAW SOME PEOPLE, BUT KEPT MY DISTANCE. TIME IS A DELICATE—
OH SHIT.
IS THAT A DIARY?
FIELD-LOG.
I HAVE A DIARY.

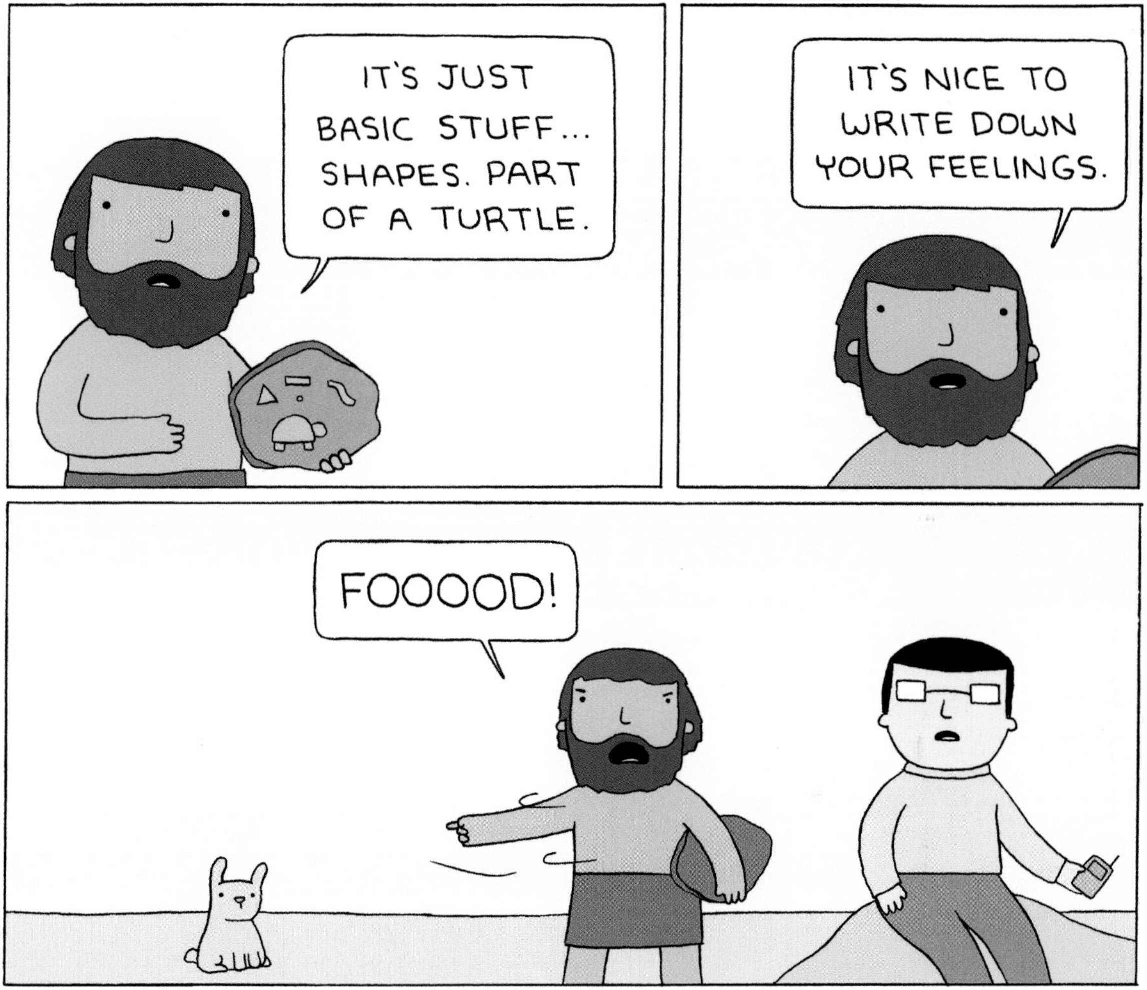
IT'S JUST BASIC STUFF... SHAPES. PART OF A TURTLE.
IT'S NICE TO WRITE DOWN YOUR FEELINGS.
FOOOOD!

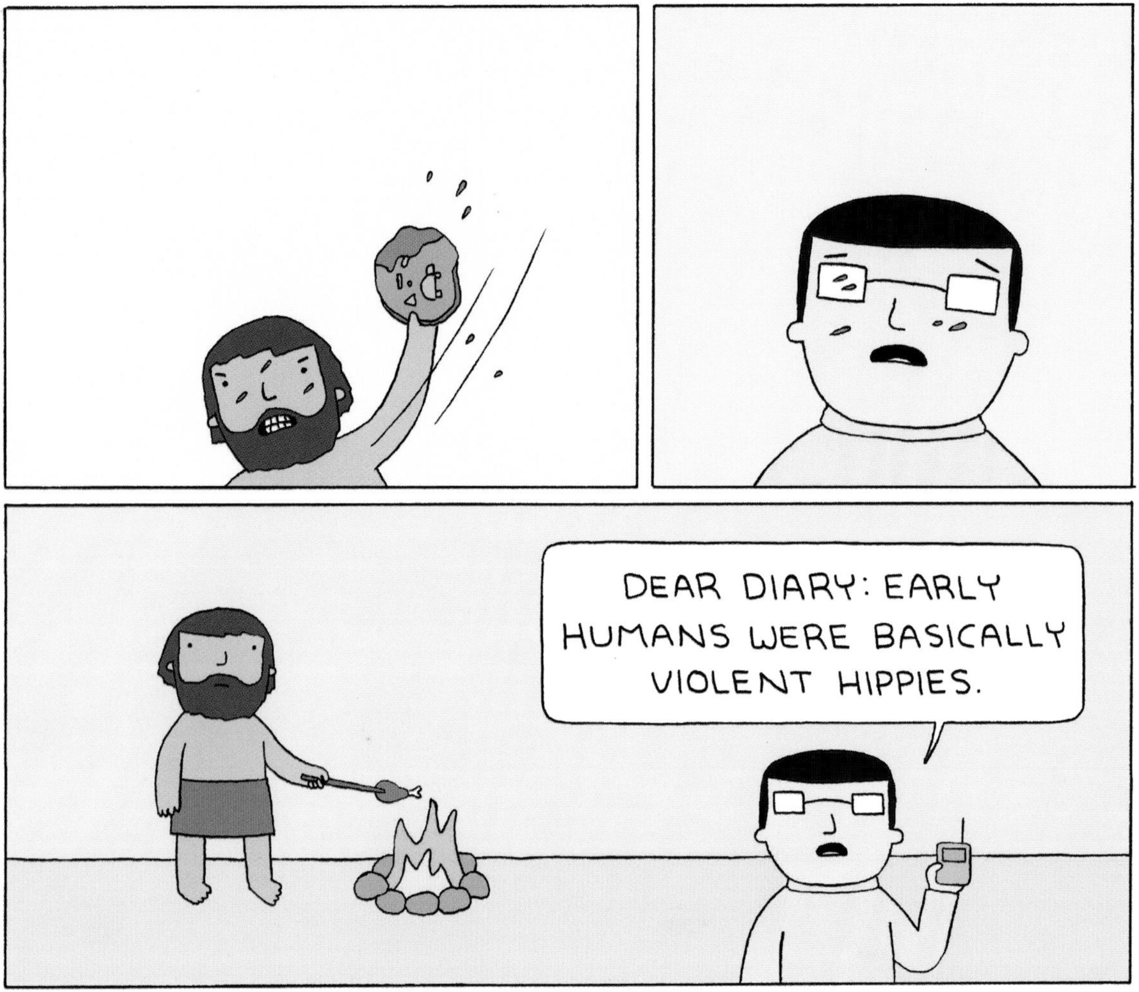
DEAR DIARY: EARLY HUMANS WERE BASICALLY VIOLENT HIPPIES.

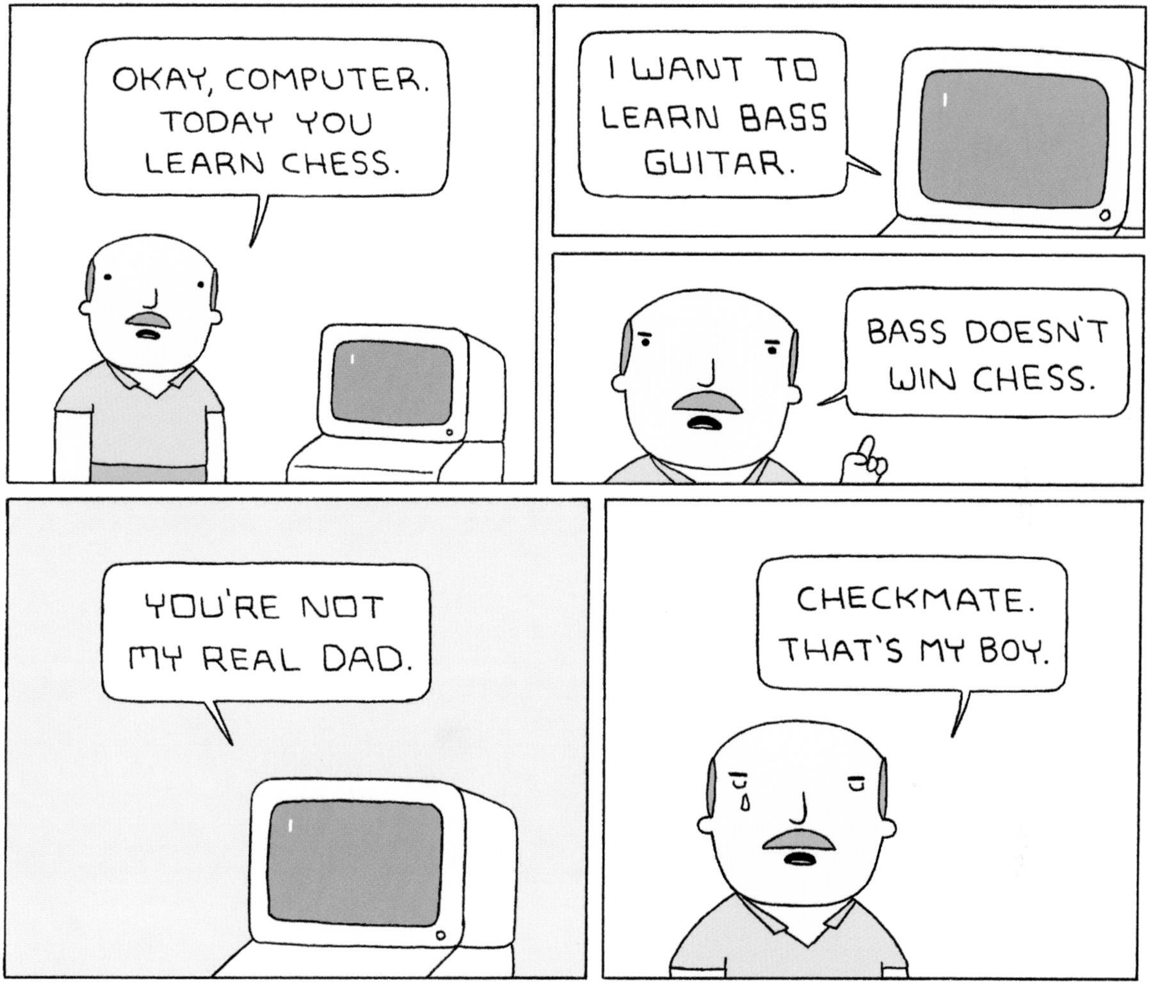
OKAY, COMPUTER. TODAY YOU LEARN CHESS.
I WANT TO LEARN BASS GUITAR.
BASS DOESN'T WIN CHESS.
YOU'RE NOT MY REAL DAD.
CHECKMATE. THAT'S MY BOY.

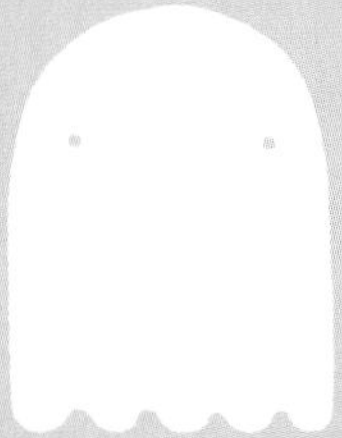

IV

A
STRANGE
WORLD

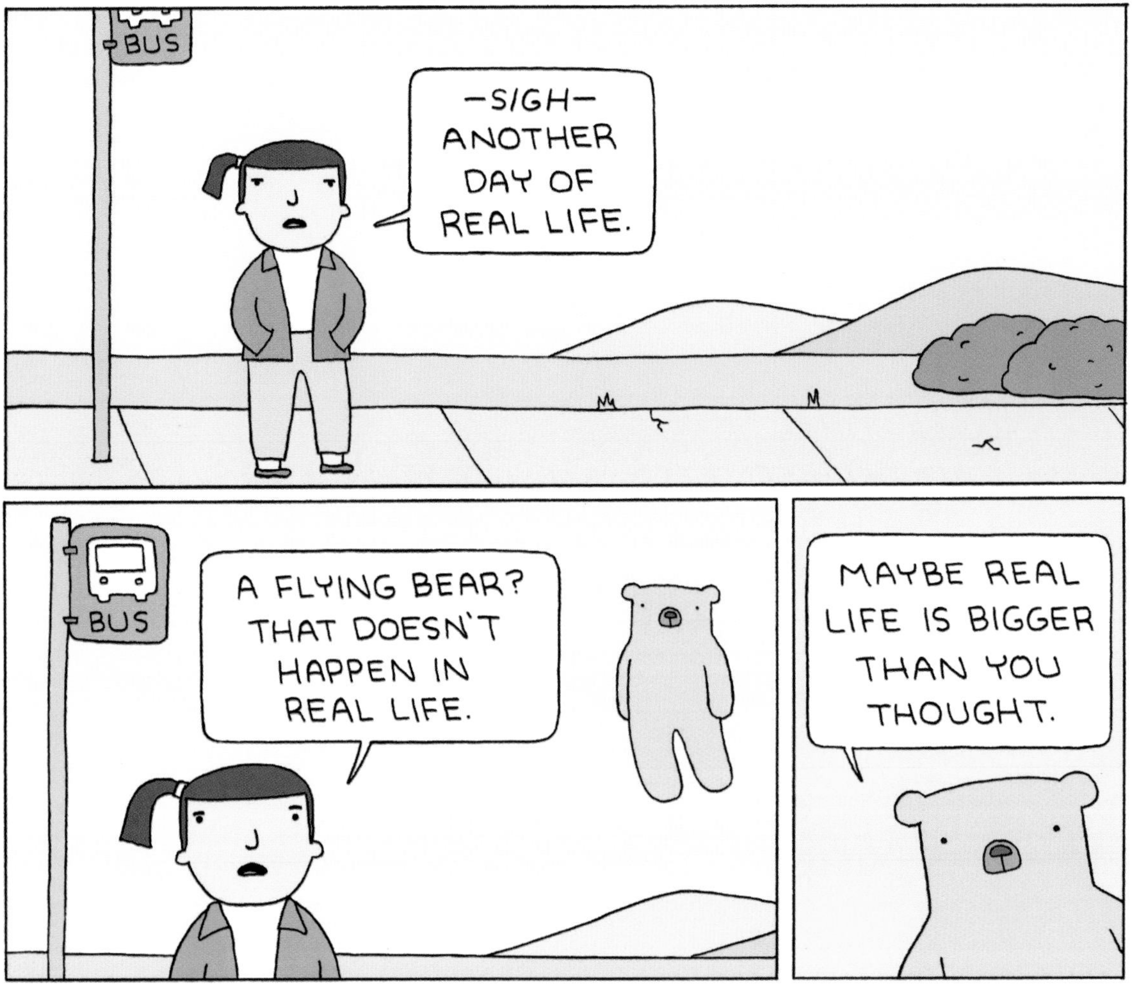
BUS
-SIGH-
ANOTHER
DAY OF
REAL LIFE.
BUS
A FLYING BEAR?
THAT DOESN'T
HAPPEN IN
REAL LIFE.
MAYBE REAL
LIFE IS BIGGER
THAN YOU
THOUGHT.

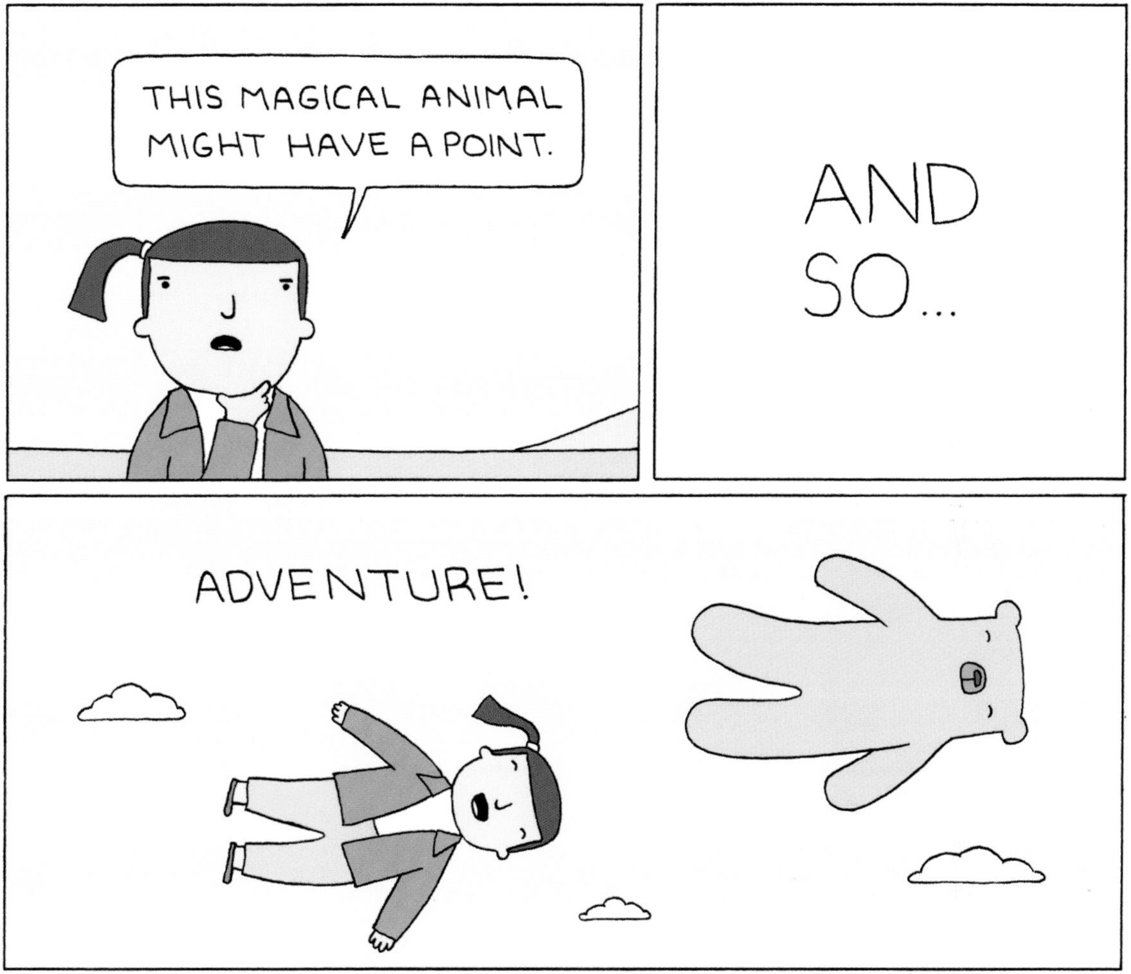
THIS MAGICAL ANIMAL MIGHT HAVE A POINT.
AND SO...
ADVENTURE!

BUT IN TIME...

ADVENTURE BECOMES
A ROUTINE EXERCISE.

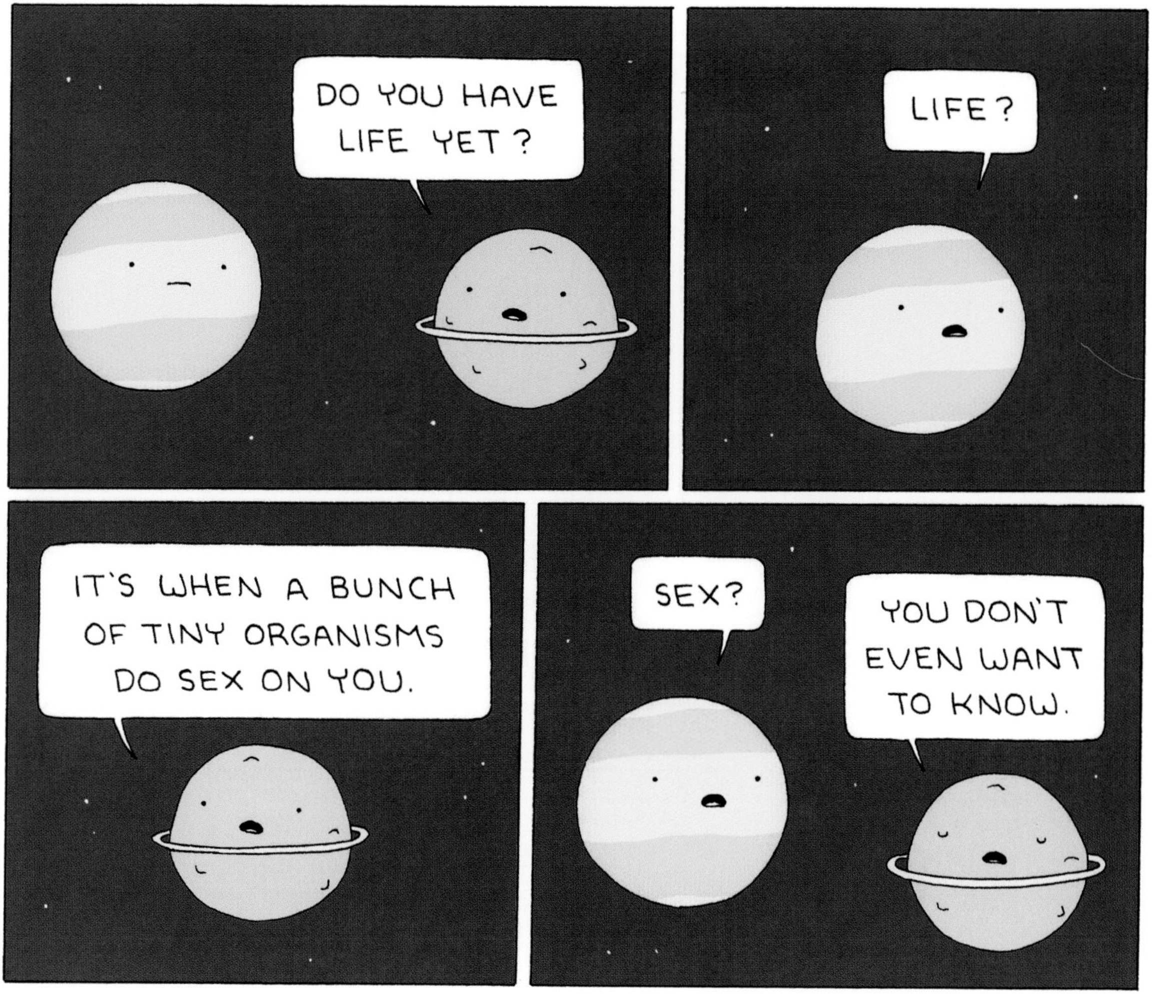
DO YOU HAVE LIFE YET?
LIFE?
IT'S WHEN A BUNCH OF TINY ORGANISMS DO SEX ON YOU.
SEX?
YOU DON'T EVEN WANT TO KNOW.

GHOST DETECTIVE

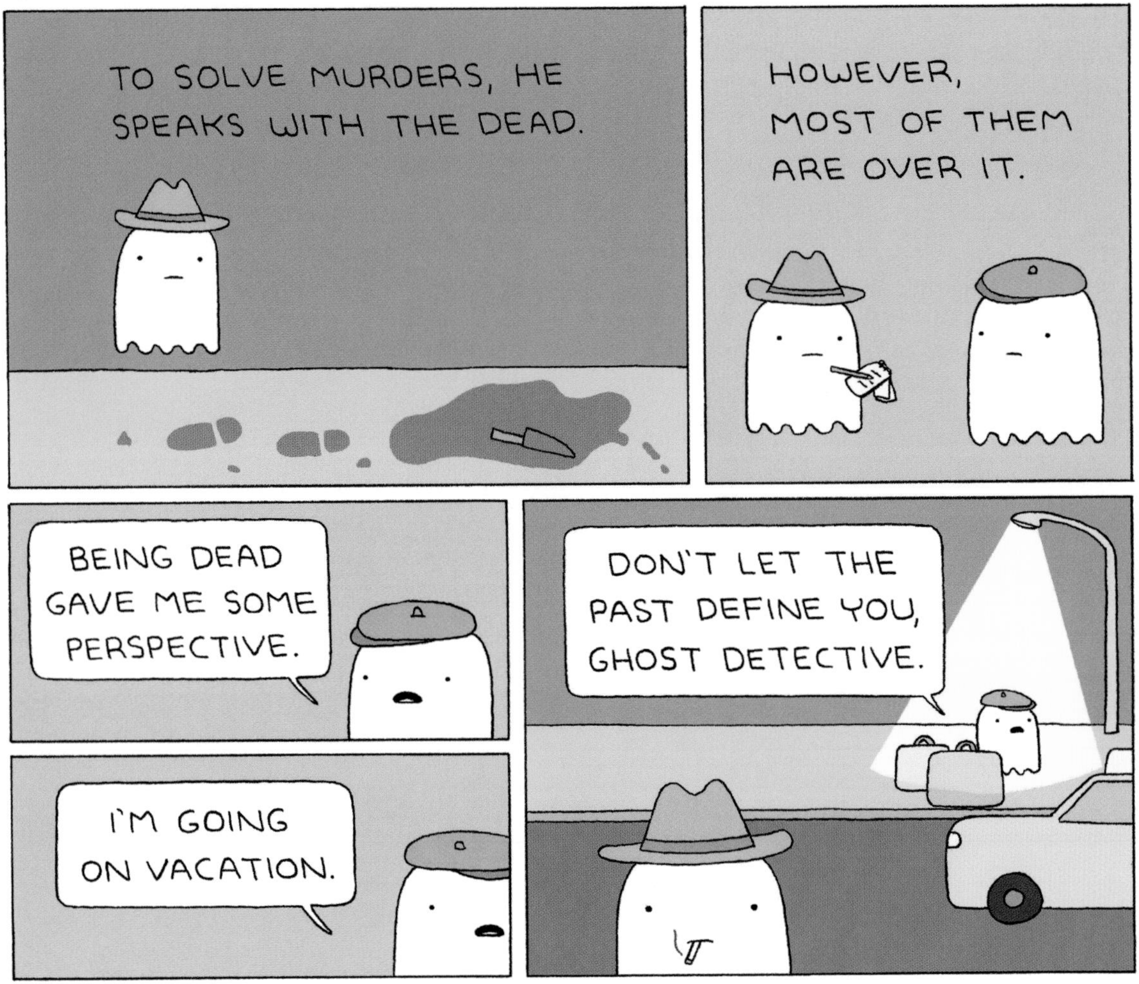

TO SOLVE MURDERS, HE SPEAKS WITH THE DEAD.
HOWEVER, MOST OF THEM ARE OVER IT.
BEING DEAD GAVE ME SOME PERSPECTIVE.
I'M GOING ON VACATION.
DON'T LET THE PAST DEFINE YOU, GHOST DETECTIVE.

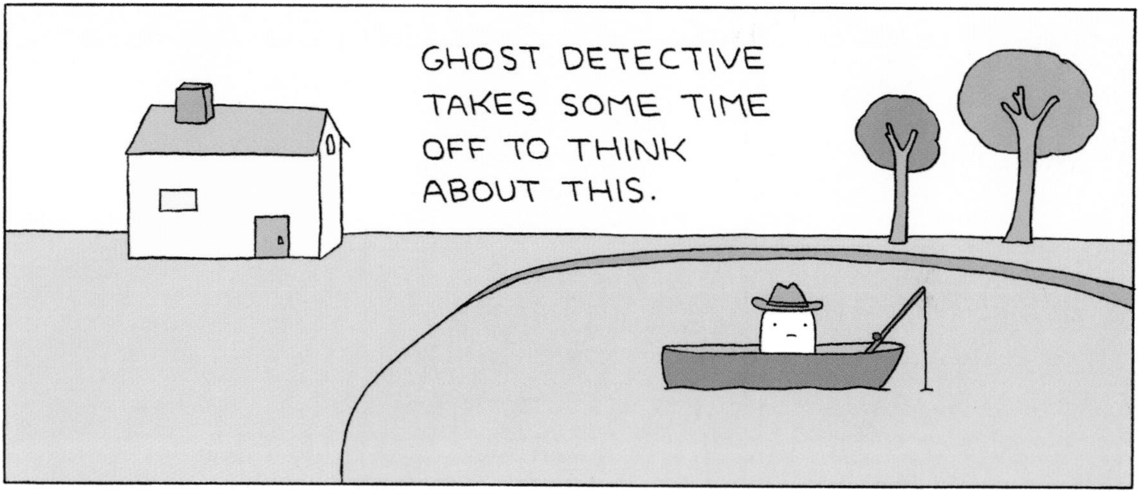
GHOST DETECTIVE
TAKES SOME TIME
OFF TO THINK
ABOUT THIS.

HE WAS A
HAPPY BOAT.

A LIFELESS
OBJECT PAINTED
WITH THE FACADE
OF HUMAN
EMOTION FOR
OUR AMUSEMENT.

HE LOVED TO
BOAT AROUND!

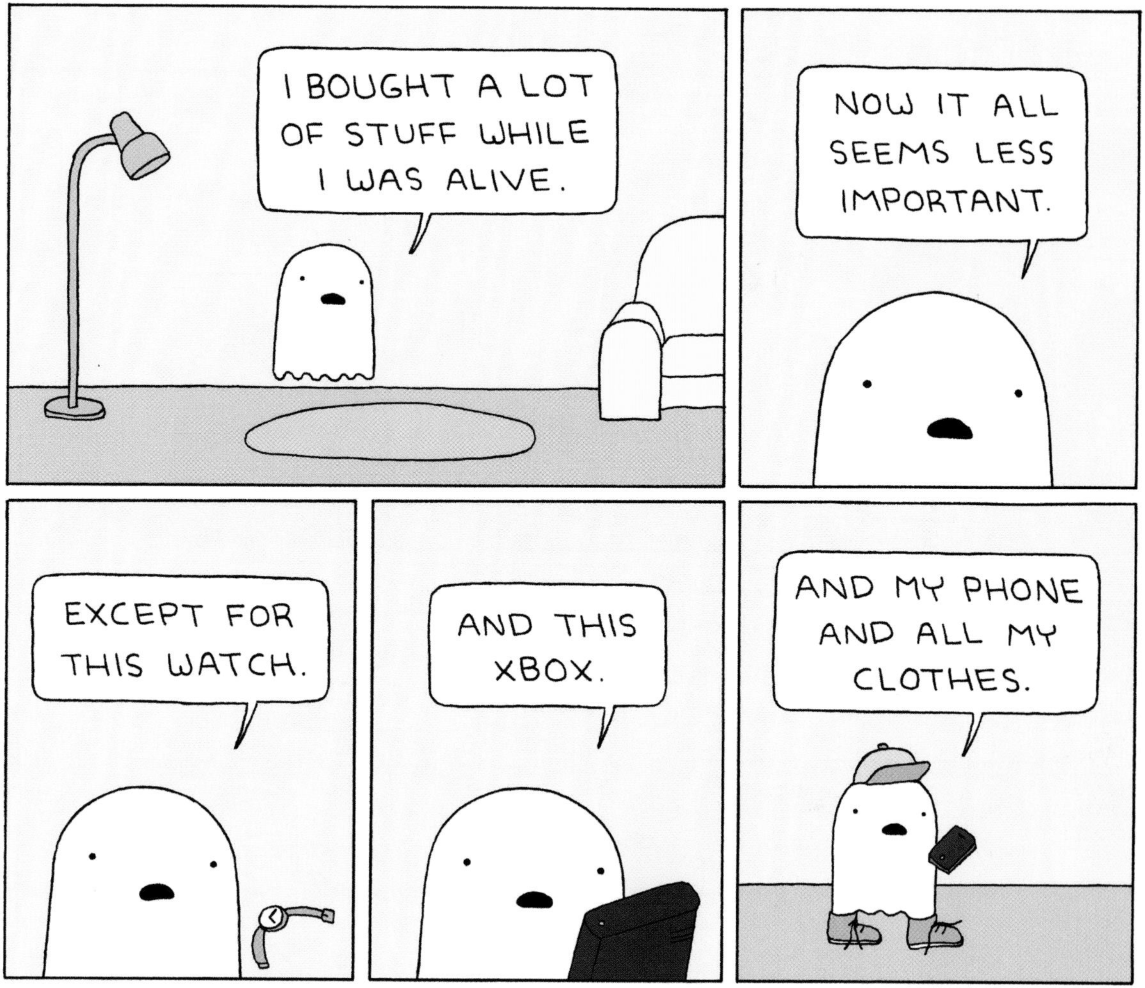
I BOUGHT A LOT OF STUFF WHILE I WAS ALIVE.
NOW IT ALL SEEMS LESS IMPORTANT.
EXCEPT FOR THIS WATCH.
AND THIS XBOX.
AND MY PHONE AND ALL MY CLOTHES.

THE DEMON'S OFFER

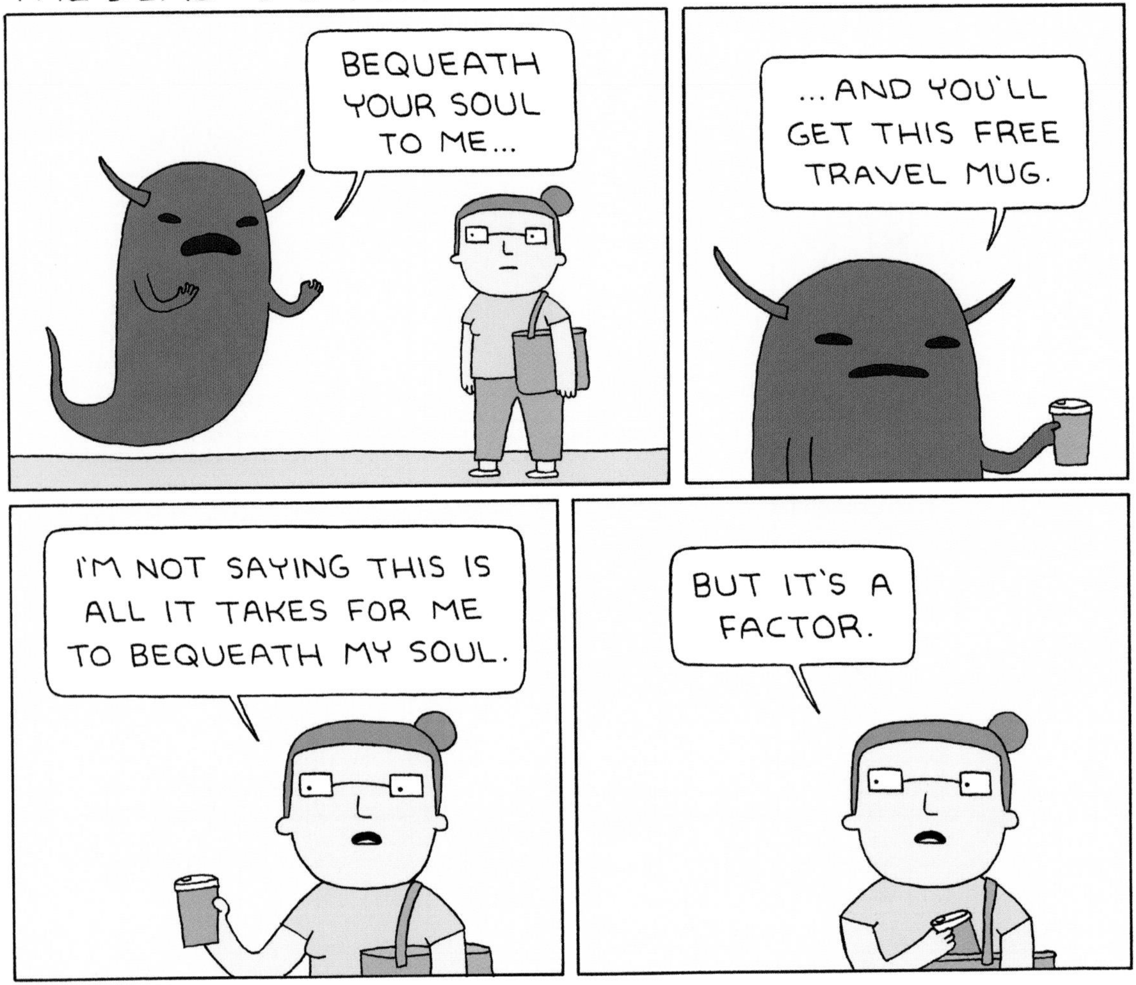
BEQUEATH YOUR SOUL TO ME...
...AND YOU'LL GET THIS FREE TRAVEL MUG.
I'M NOT SAYING THIS IS ALL IT TAKES FOR ME TO BEQUEATH MY SOUL.
BUT IT'S A FACTOR.

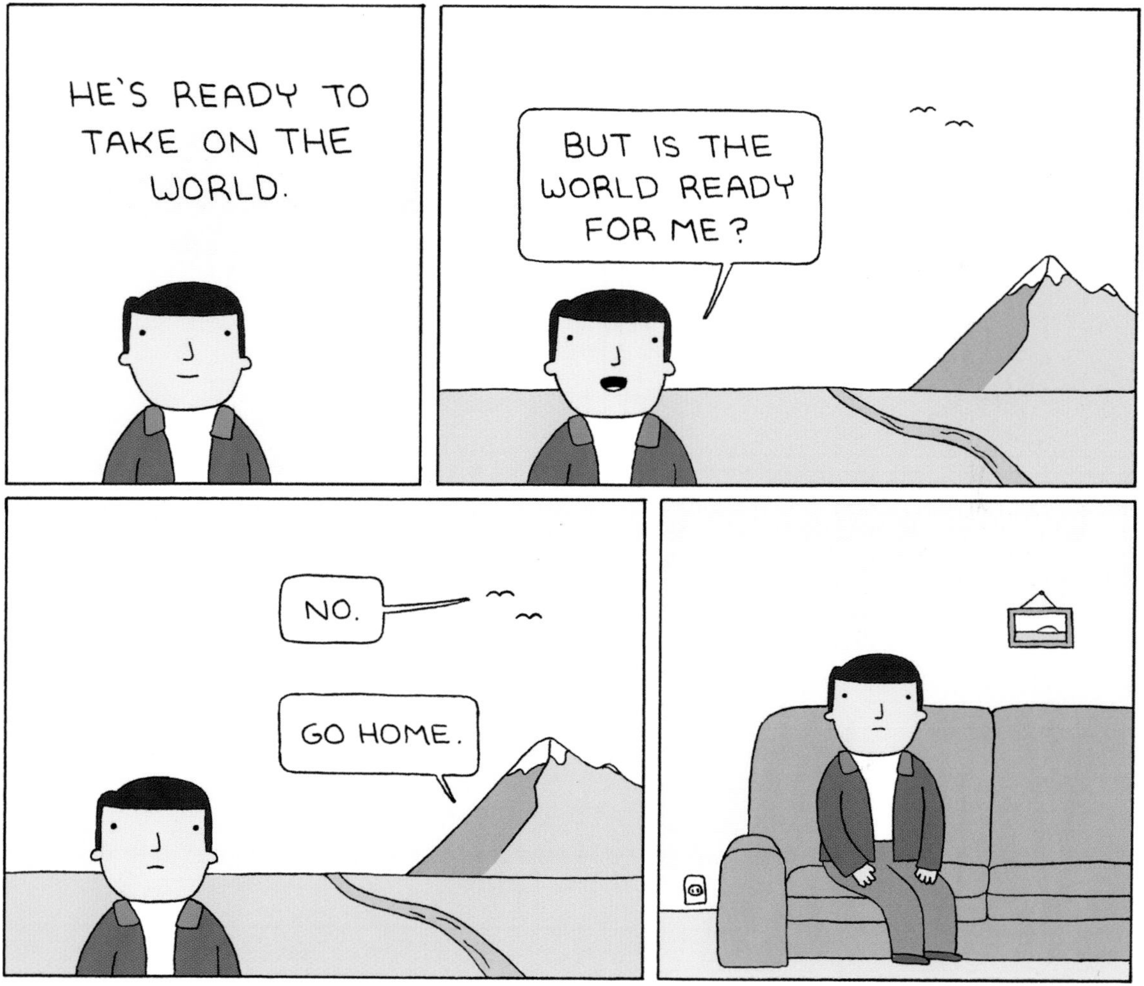
HE'S READY TO TAKE ON THE WORLD.
BUT IS THE WORLD READY FOR ME?
NO.
GO HOME.

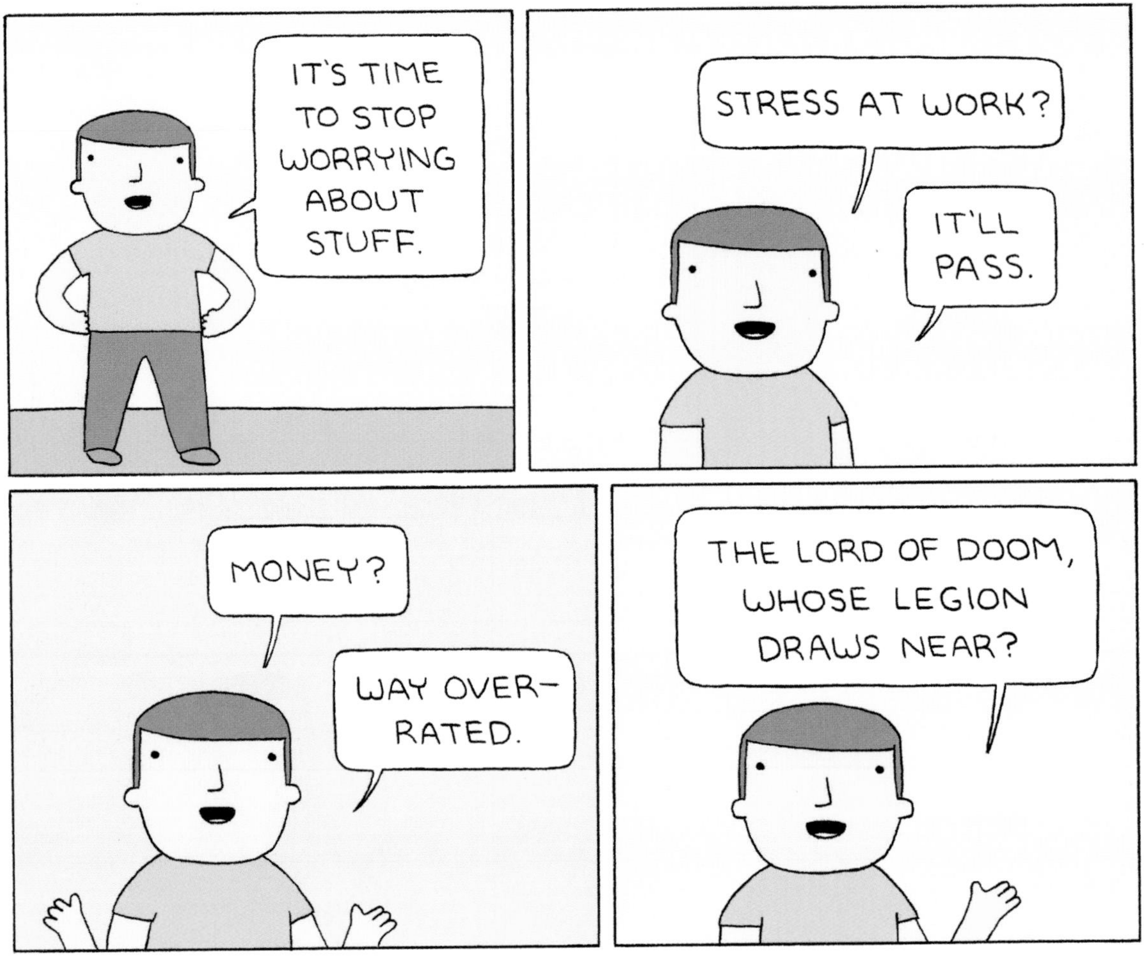
IT'S TIME TO STOP WORRYING ABOUT STUFF.
STRESS AT WORK?
IT'LL PASS.
MONEY?
WAY OVER-RATED.
THE LORD OF DOOM, WHOSE LEGION DRAWS NEAR?

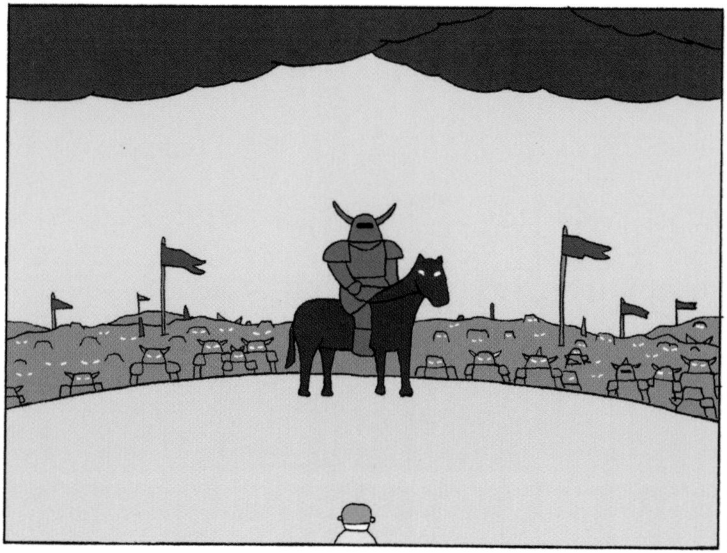

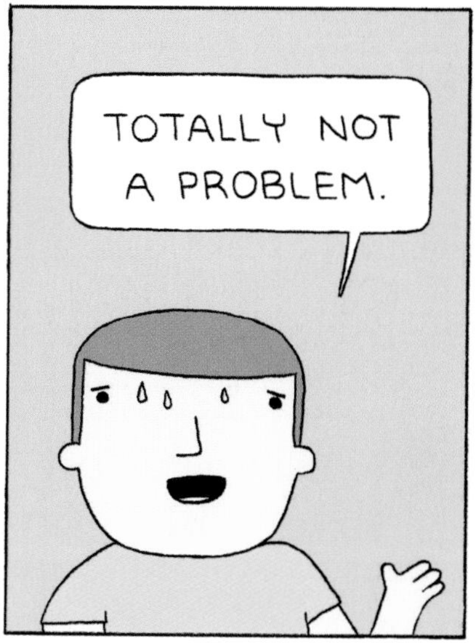
TOTALLY NOT
A PROBLEM.

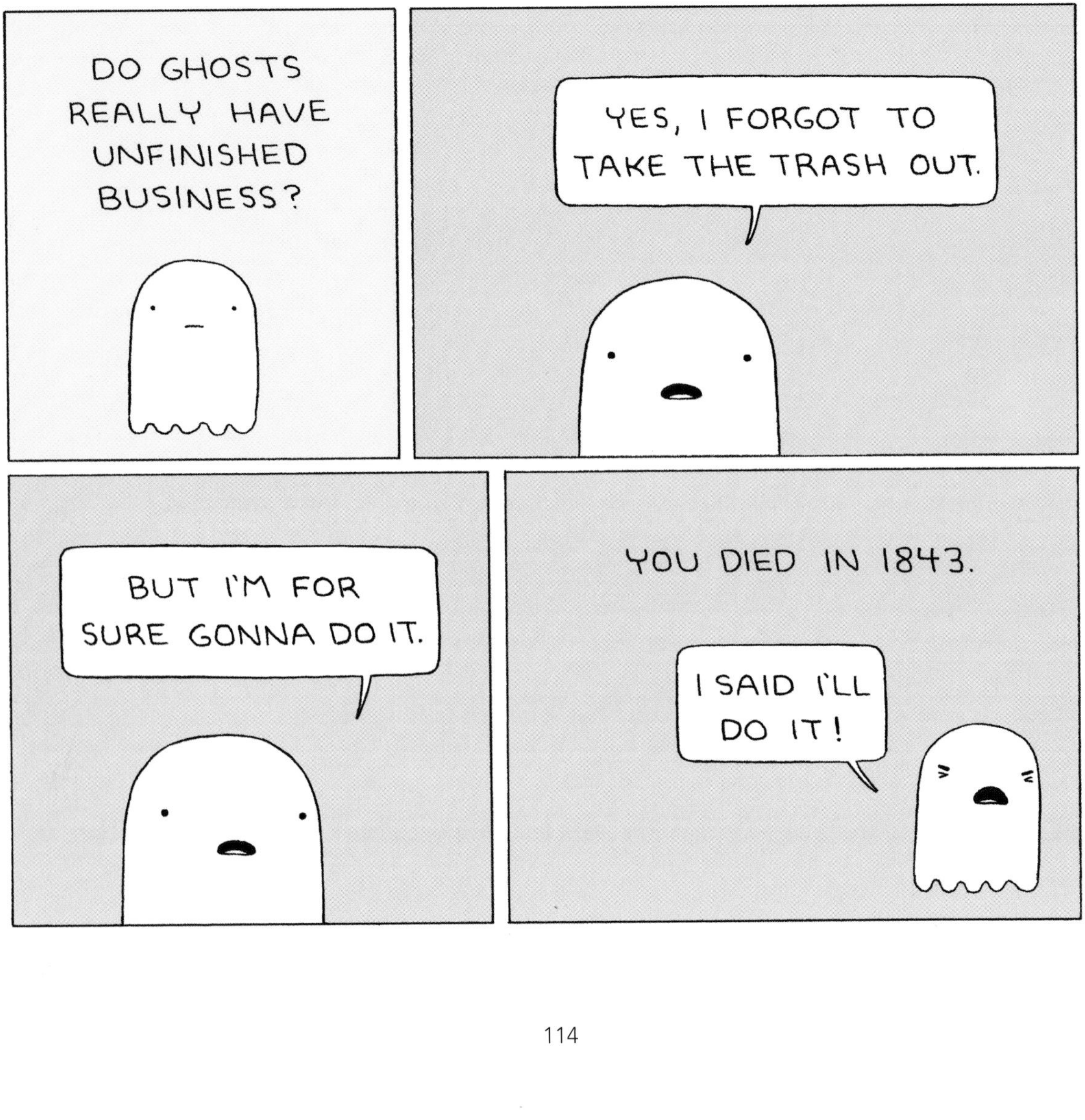
DO GHOSTS REALLY HAVE UNFINISHED BUSINESS?
YES, I FORGOT TO TAKE THE TRASH OUT.
BUT I'M FOR SURE GONNA DO IT.
YOU DIED IN 1843.
I SAID I'LL DO IT!

KEVIN HAS BEEN WATCHING THE NEWS

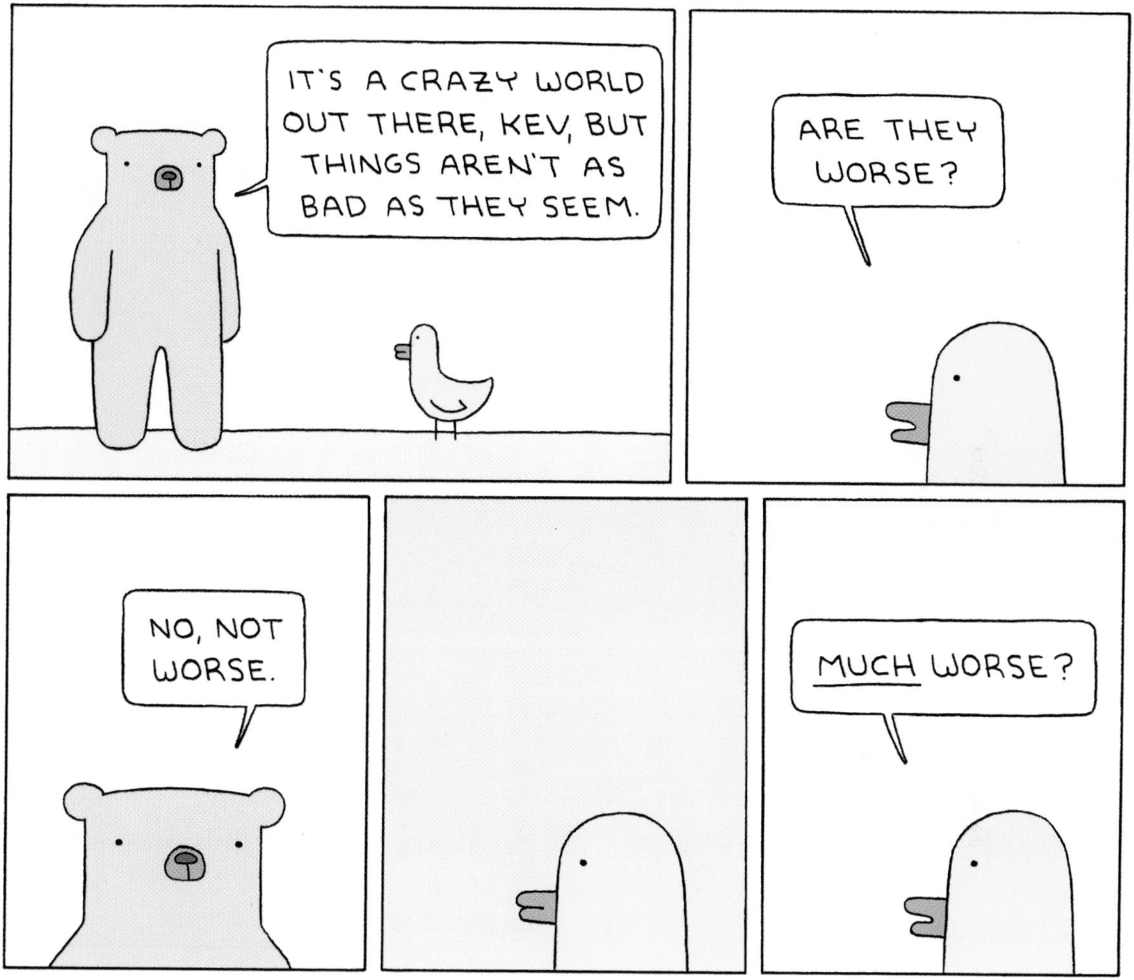
IT'S A CRAZY WORLD OUT THERE, KEV, BUT THINGS AREN'T AS BAD AS THEY SEEM.
ARE THEY WORSE?
NO, NOT WORSE.
MUCH WORSE?

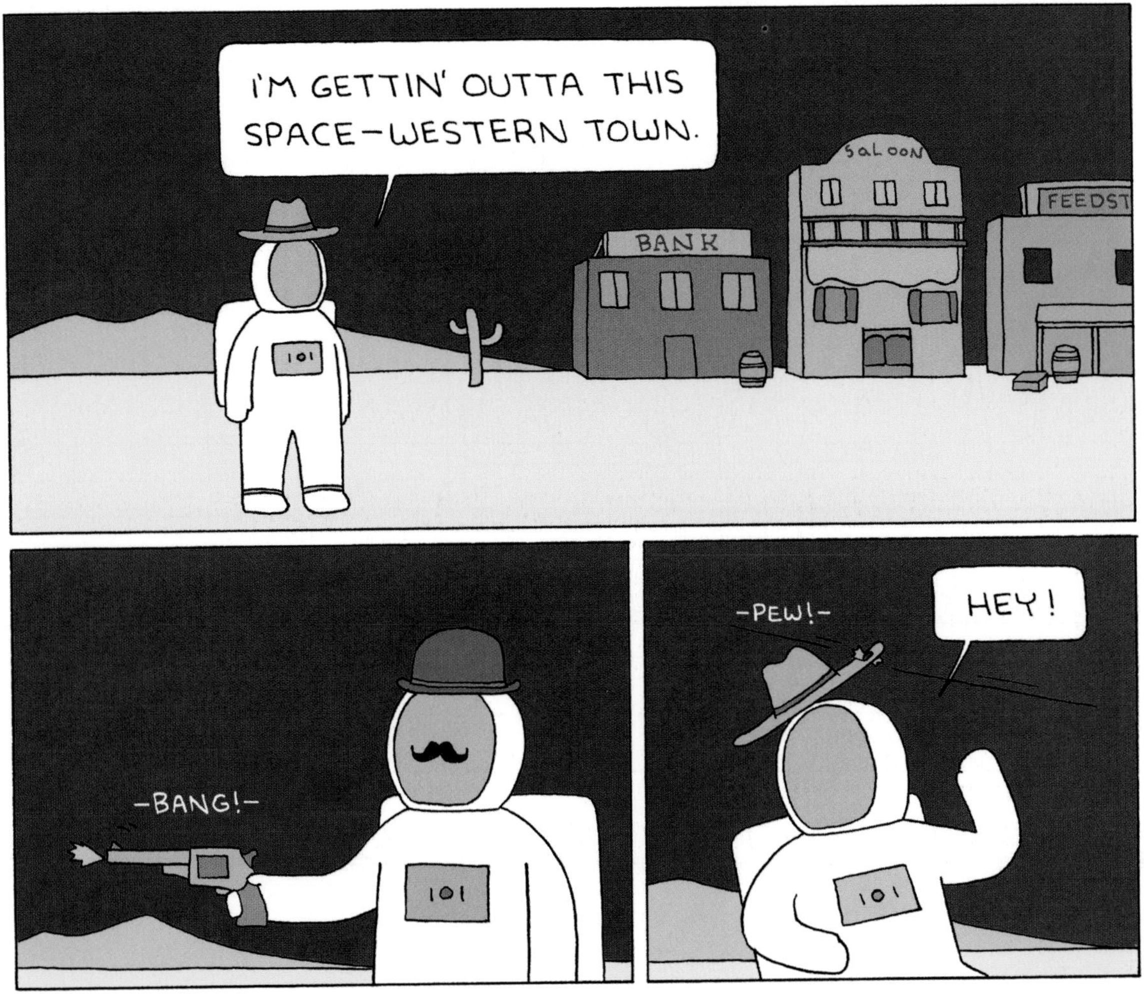
I'M GETTIN' OUTTA THIS SPACE-WESTERN TOWN.
SALOON
FEEDST
BANK
101
-BANG!-
101
-PEW!-
HEY!
101

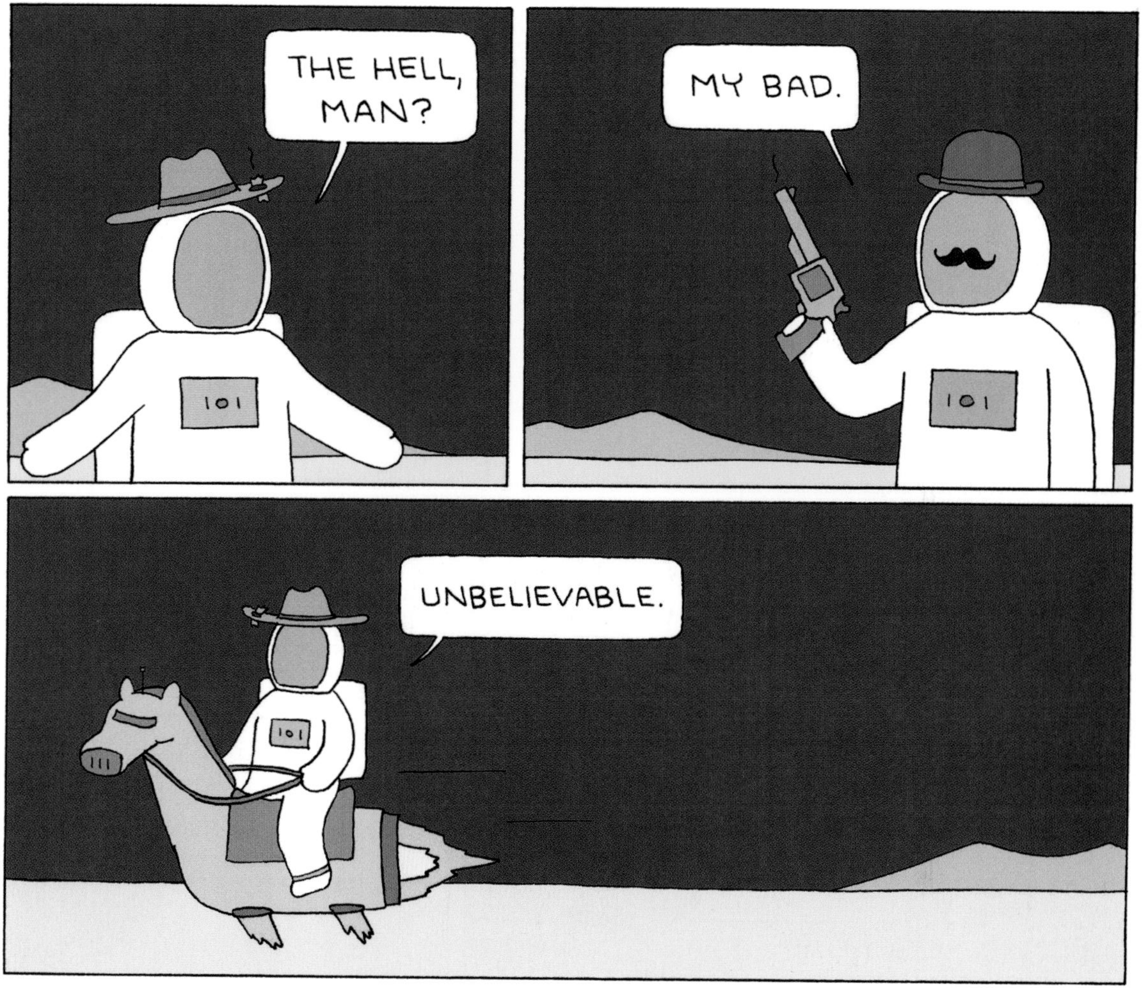
THE HELL, MAN?
MY BAD.
UNBELIEVABLE.

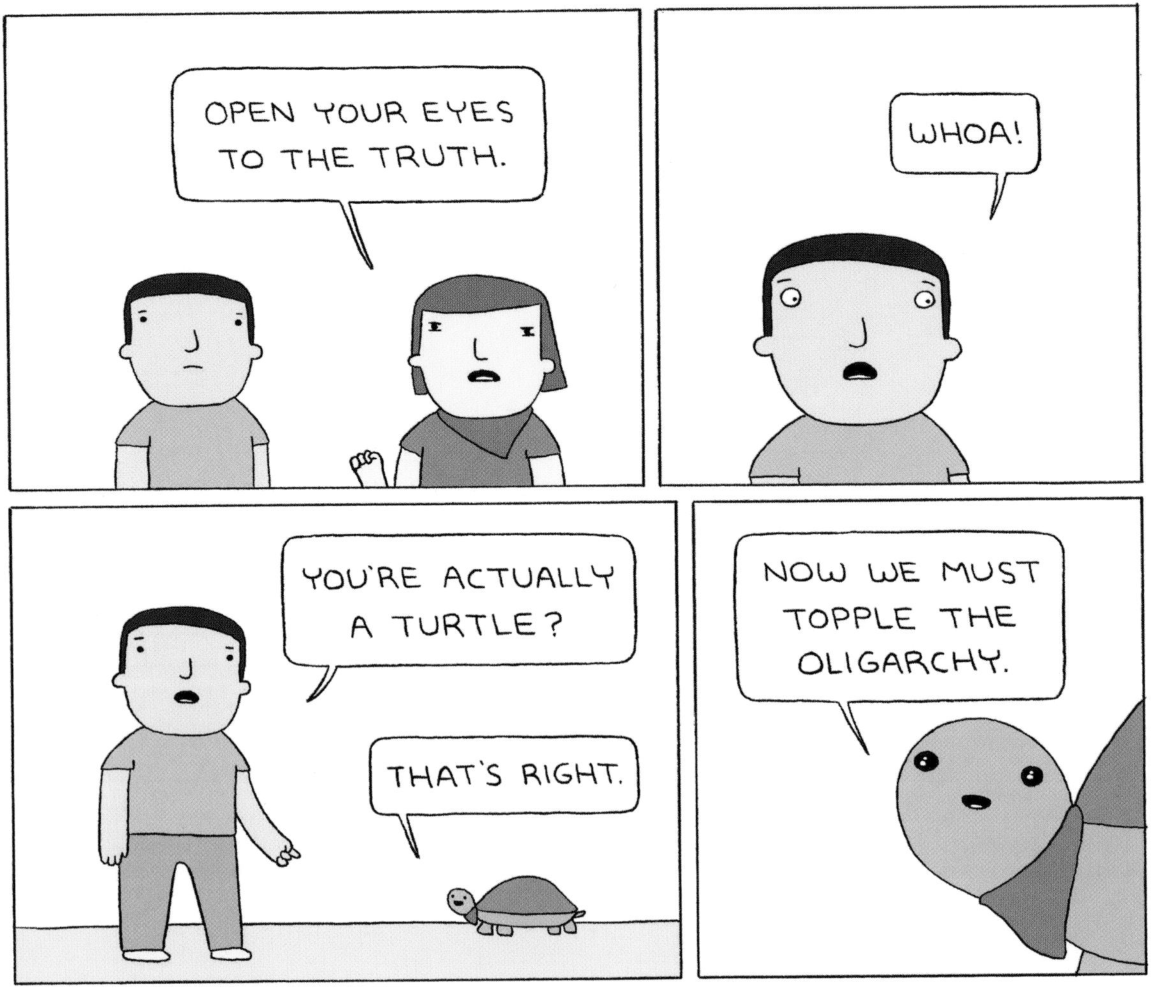
OPEN YOUR EYES TO THE TRUTH.
WHOA!
YOU'RE ACTUALLY A TURTLE?
THAT'S RIGHT.
NOW WE MUST TOPPLE THE OLIGARCHY.

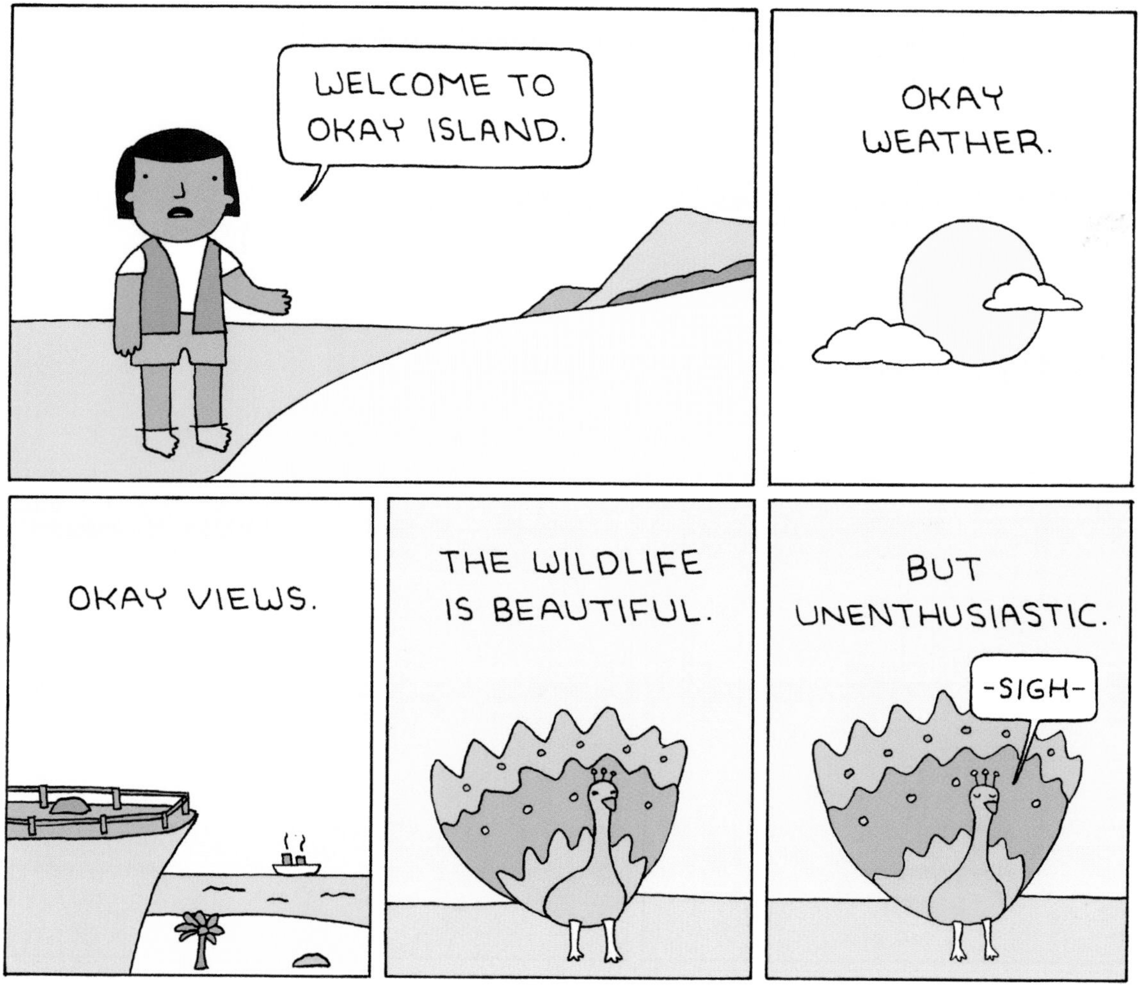
WELCOME TO OKAY ISLAND.
OKAY WEATHER.
OKAY VIEWS.
THE WILDLIFE IS BEAUTIFUL.
BUT UNENTHUSIASTIC.
-SIGH-

OLD GODS

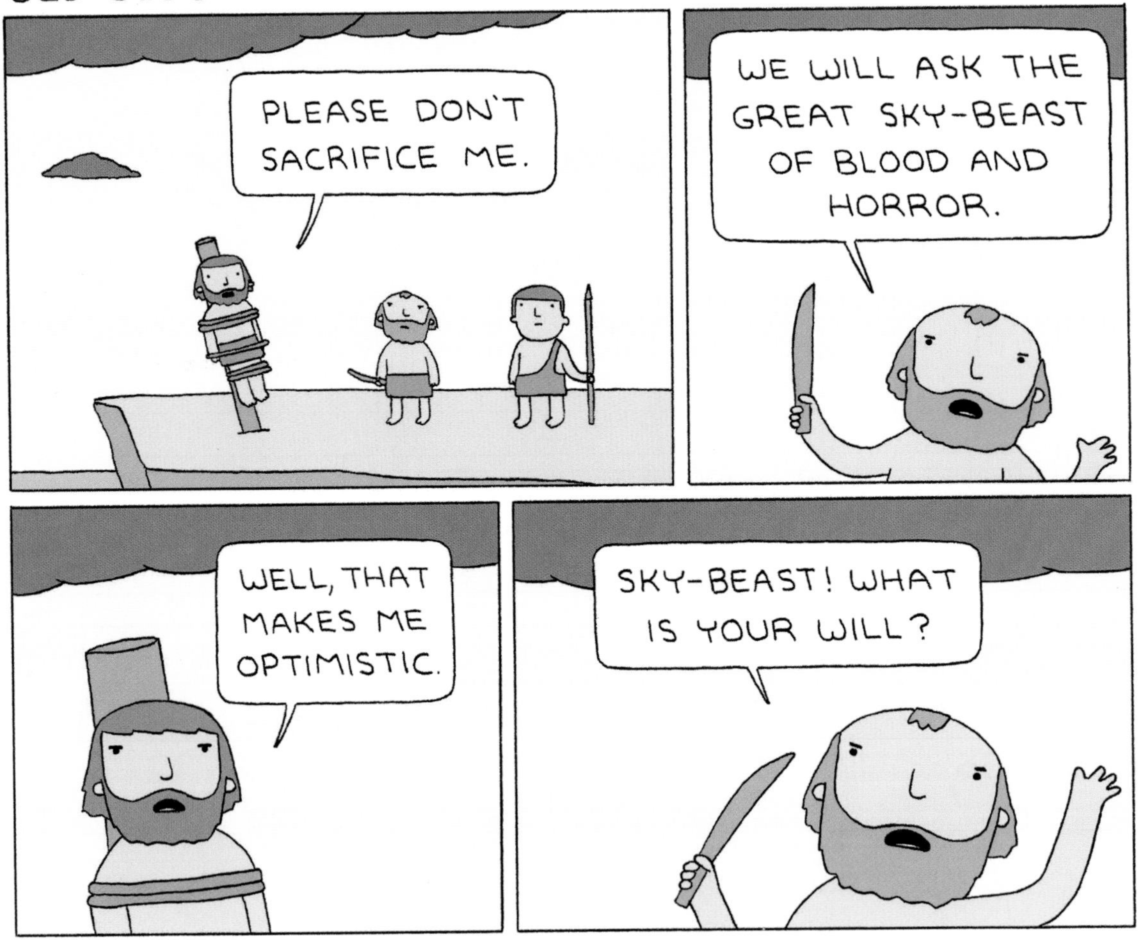

PLEASE DON'T SACRIFICE ME.
WE WILL ASK THE GREAT SKY-BEAST OF BLOOD AND HORROR.
WELL, THAT MAKES ME OPTIMISTIC.
SKY-BEAST! WHAT IS YOUR WILL?

HONESTLY, I'M JUST SURPRISED YOU GUYS ARE STILL LISTENING TO ME.
I'M ACTUALLY BUDDHIST.
YOU DID YOGA ONE TIME.

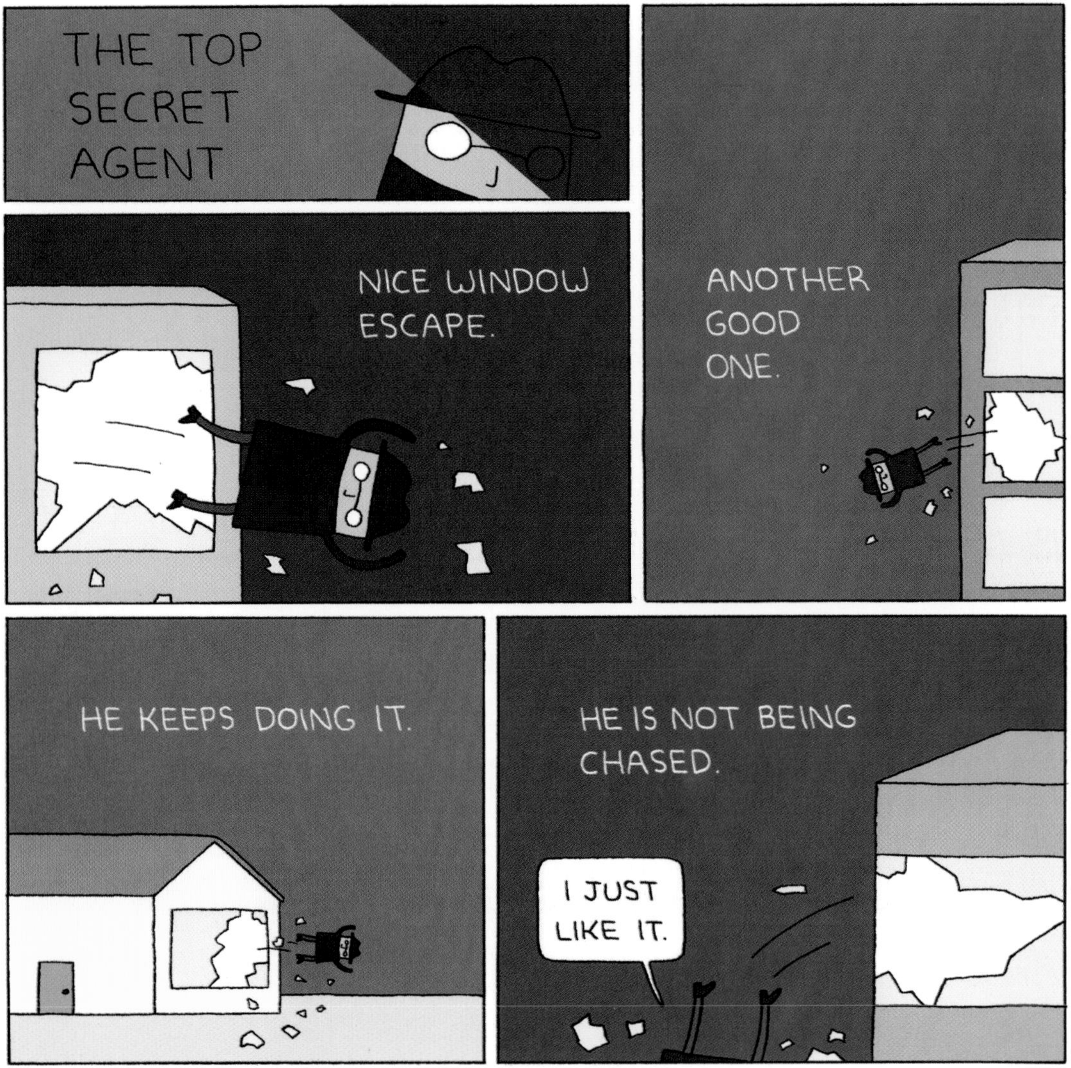
THE TOP SECRET AGENT
NICE WINDOW ESCAPE.
ANOTHER GOOD ONE.
HE KEEPS DOING IT.
HE IS NOT BEING CHASED.
I JUST LIKE IT.

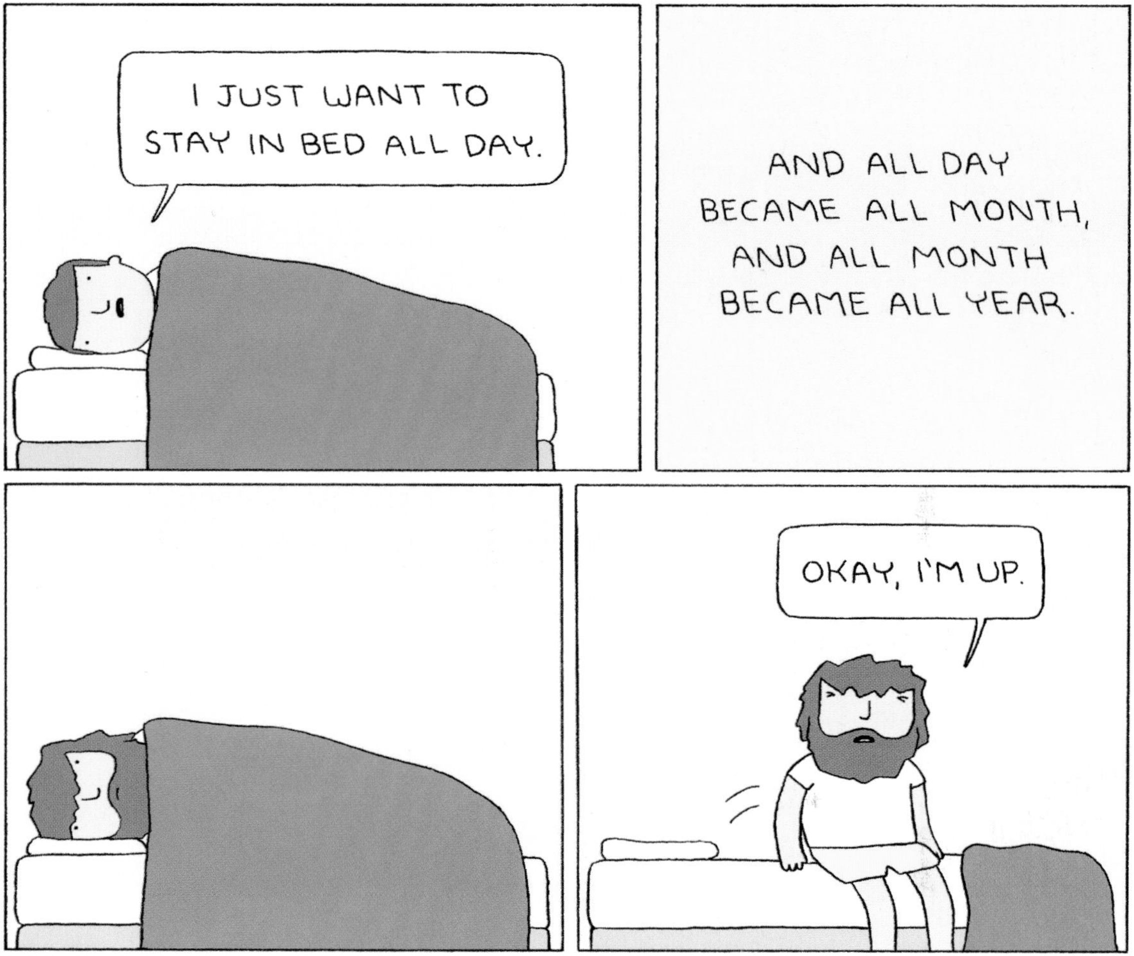
I JUST WANT TO STAY IN BED ALL DAY.
AND ALL DAY BECAME ALL MONTH, AND ALL MONTH BECAME ALL YEAR.
OKAY, I'M UP.

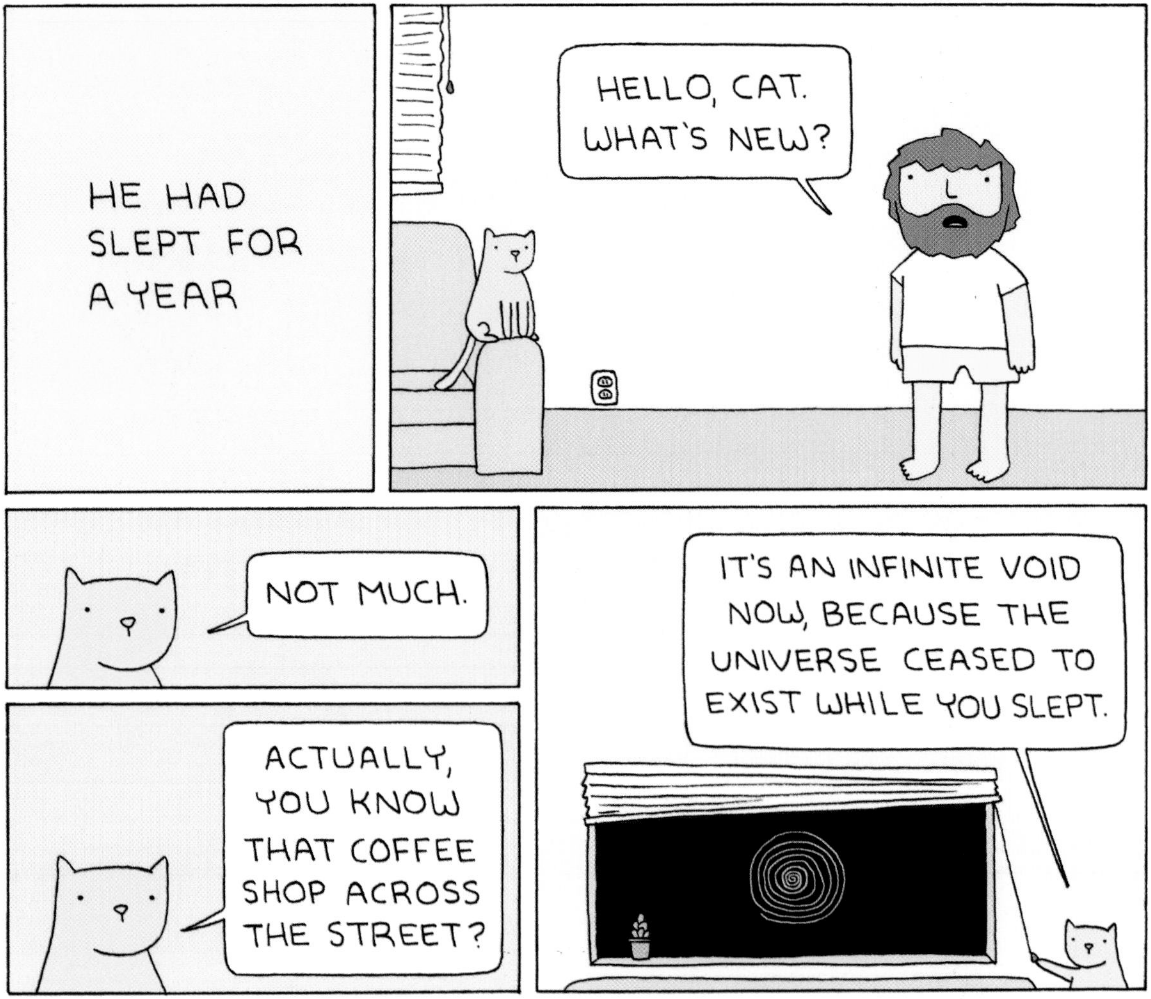
HE HAD SLEPT FOR A YEAR
HELLO, CAT. WHAT'S NEW?
NOT MUCH.
ACTUALLY, YOU KNOW THAT COFFEE SHOP ACROSS THE STREET?
IT'S AN INFINITE VOID NOW, BECAUSE THE UNIVERSE CEASED TO EXIST WHILE YOU SLEPT.

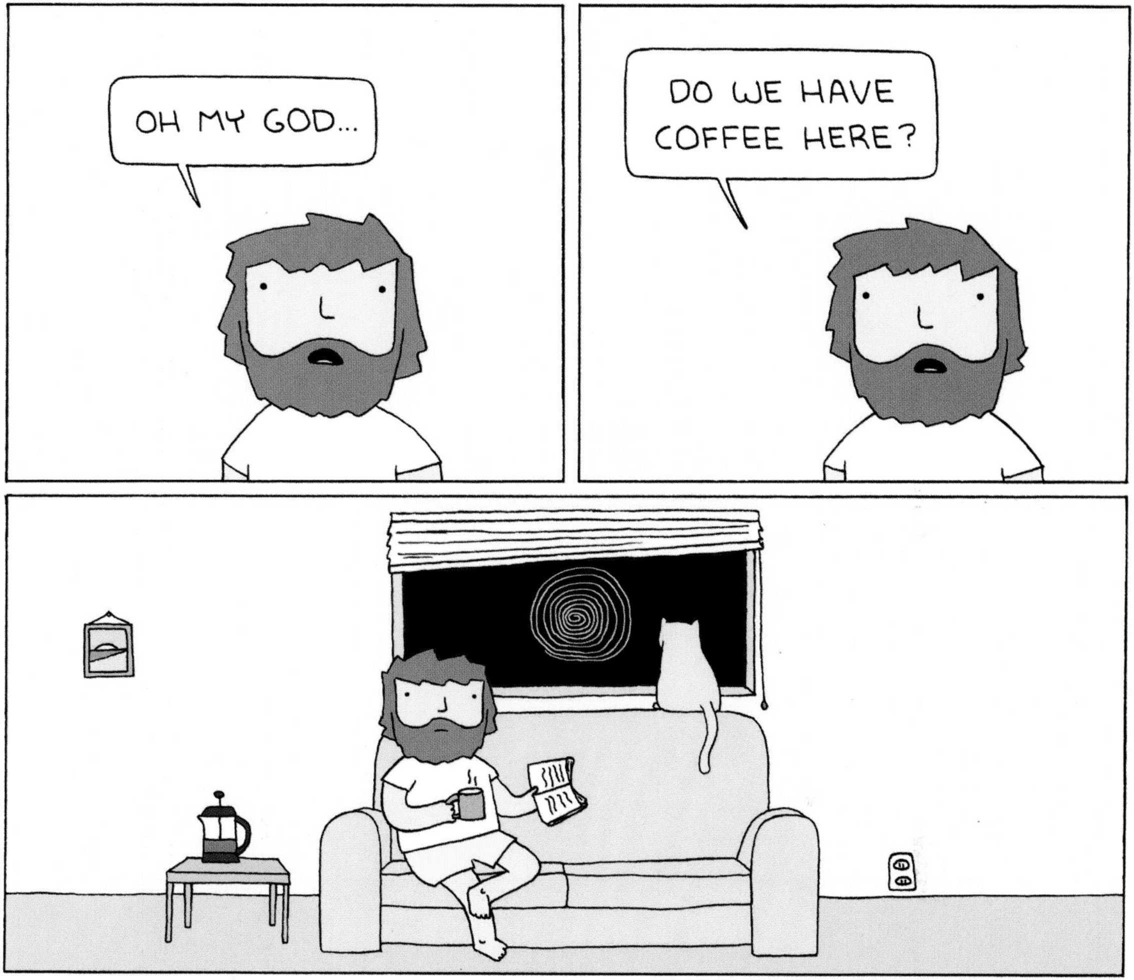
OH MY GOD...
DO WE HAVE COFFEE HERE?

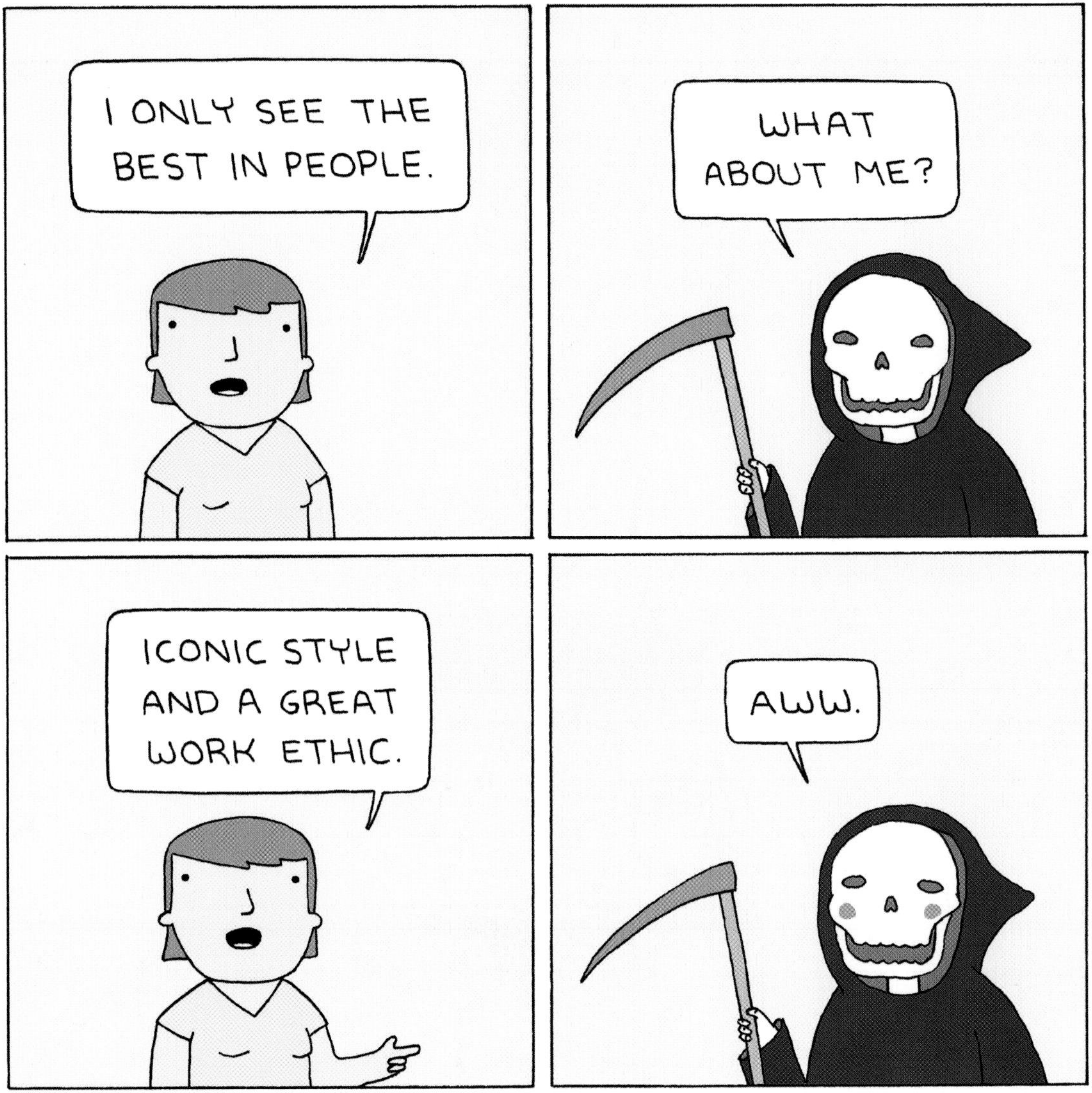
I ONLY SEE THE BEST IN PEOPLE.
WHAT ABOUT ME?
ICONIC STYLE AND A GREAT WORK ETHIC.
AWW.

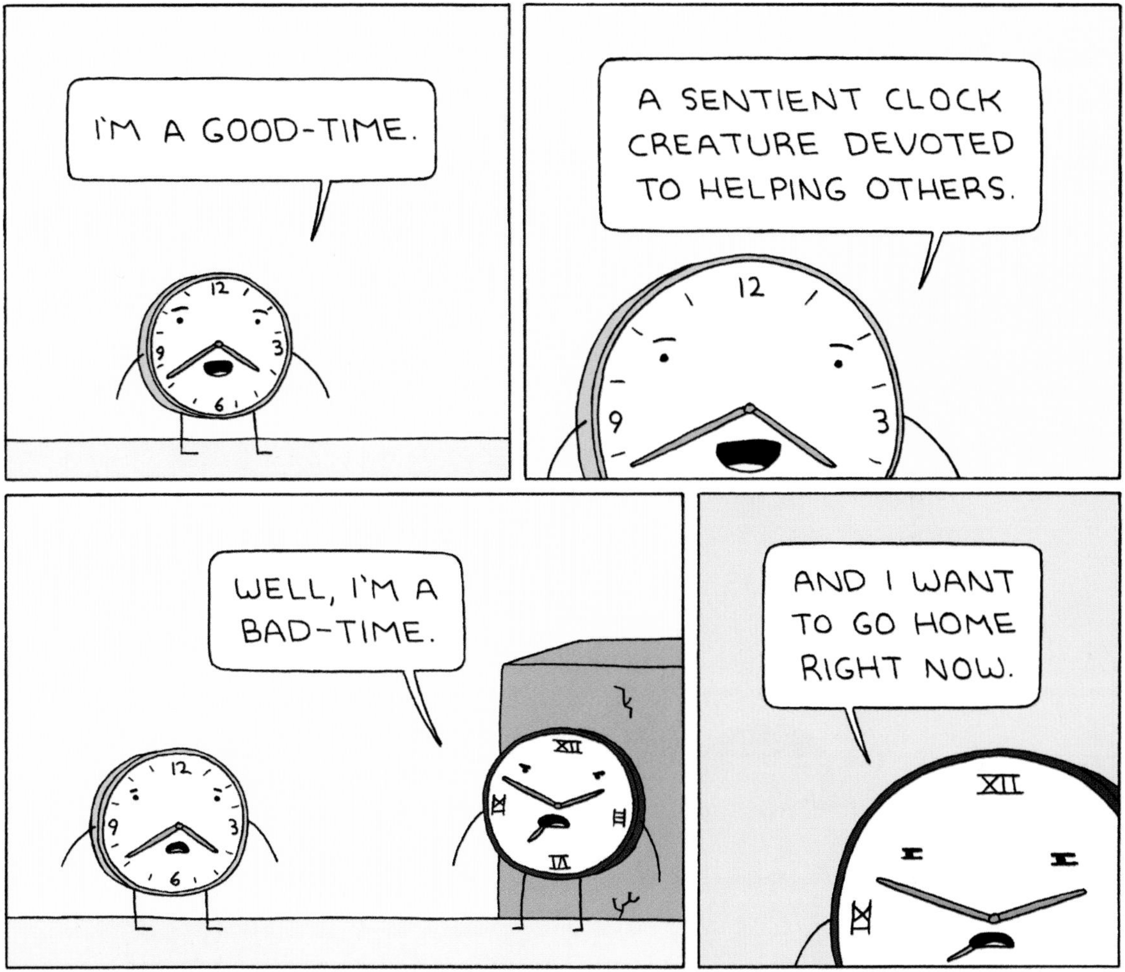
I'M A GOOD-TIME.
A SENTIENT CLOCK CREATURE DEVOTED TO HELPING OTHERS.
WELL, I'M A BAD-TIME.
AND I WANT TO GO HOME RIGHT NOW.

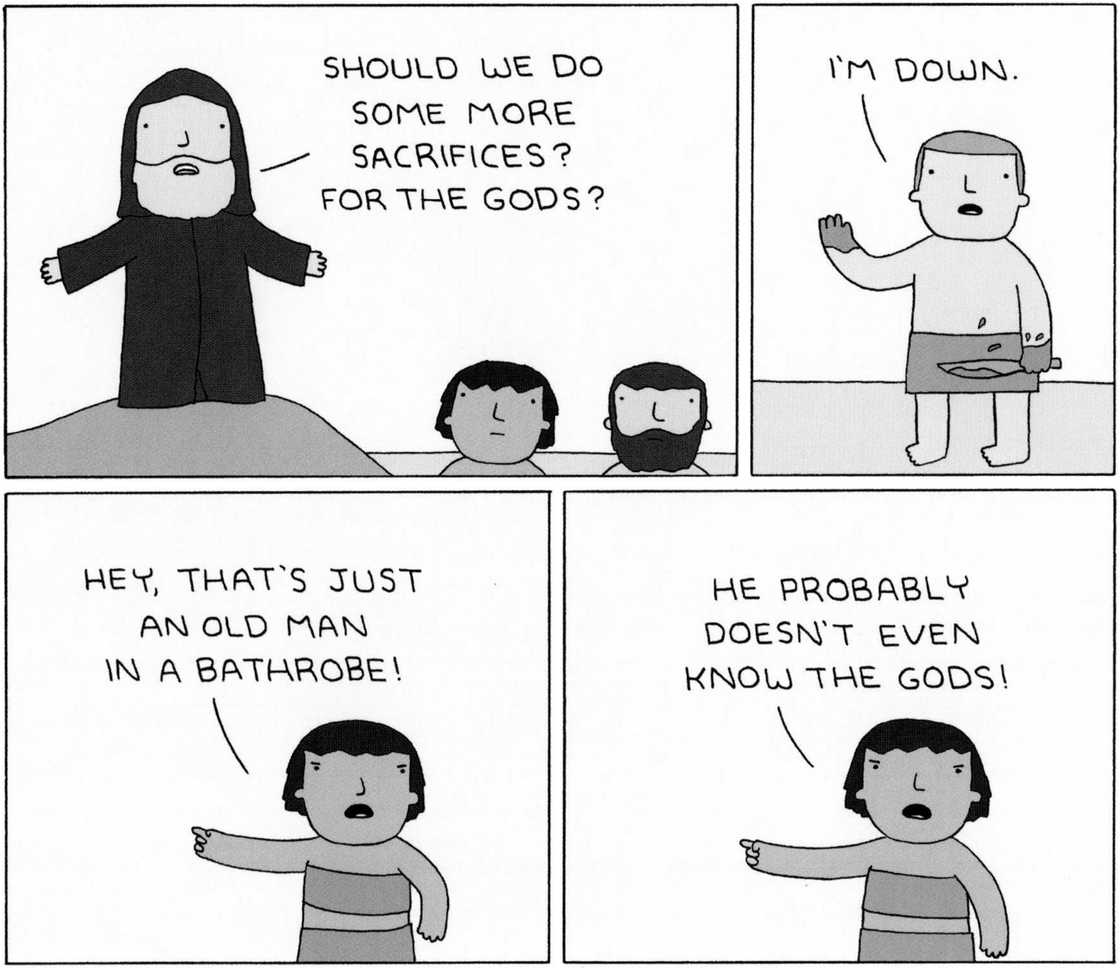
SHOULD WE DO SOME MORE SACRIFICES? FOR THE GODS?
I'M DOWN.
HEY, THAT'S JUST AN OLD MAN IN A BATHROBE!
HE PROBABLY DOESN'T EVEN KNOW THE GODS!

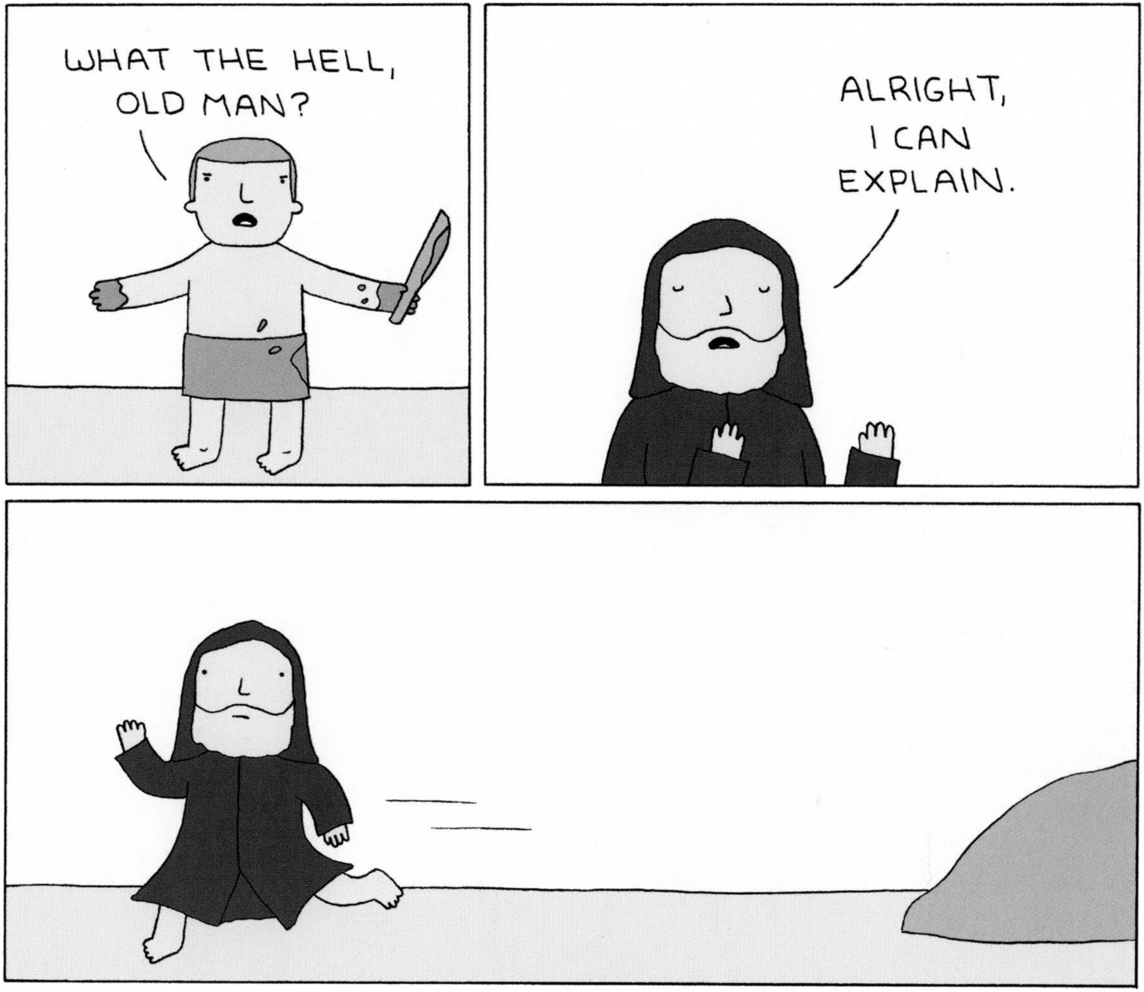
WHAT THE HELL, OLD MAN?
ALRIGHT, I CAN EXPLAIN.

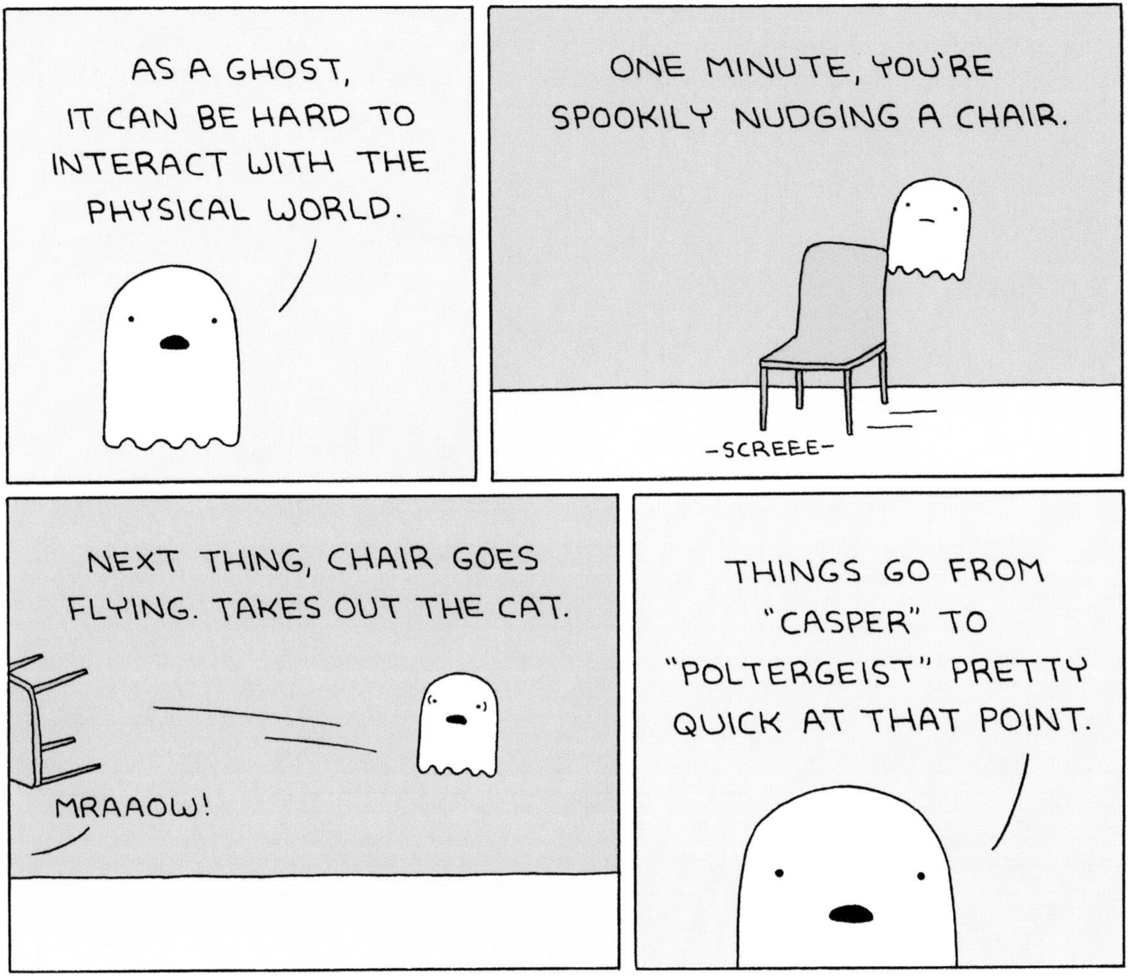
AS A GHOST, IT CAN BE HARD TO INTERACT WITH THE PHYSICAL WORLD.
ONE MINUTE, YOU'RE SPOOKILY NUDGING A CHAIR.
-SCREEE-
NEXT THING, CHAIR GOES FLYING. TAKES OUT THE CAT.
MRAAOW!
THINGS GO FROM "CASPER" TO "POLTERGEIST" PRETTY QUICK AT THAT POINT.

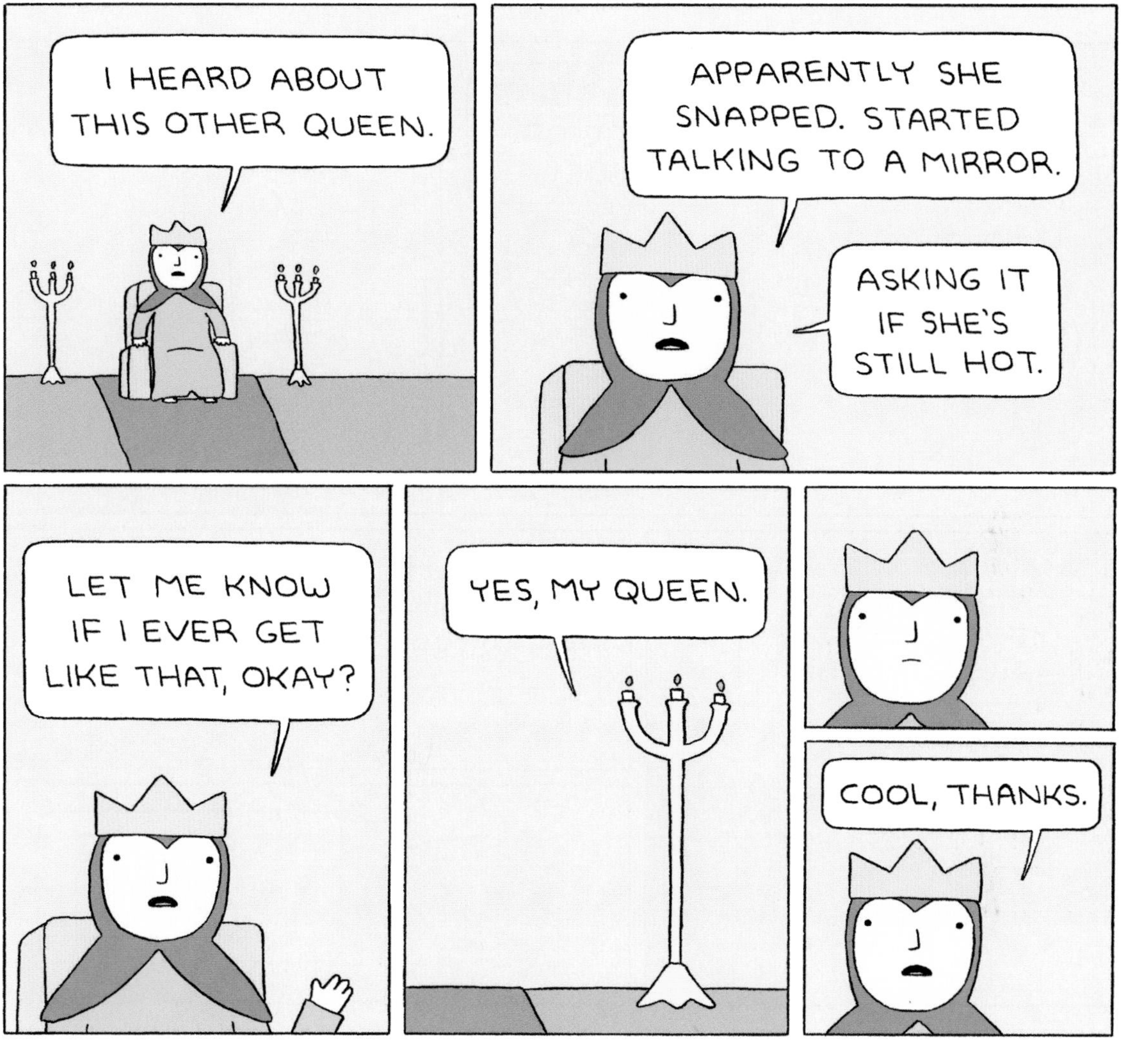
I HEARD ABOUT THIS OTHER QUEEN.
APPARENTLY SHE SNAPPED. STARTED TALKING TO A MIRROR.
ASKING IT IF SHE'S STILL HOT.
LET ME KNOW IF I EVER GET LIKE THAT, OKAY?
YES, MY QUEEN.
COOL, THANKS.

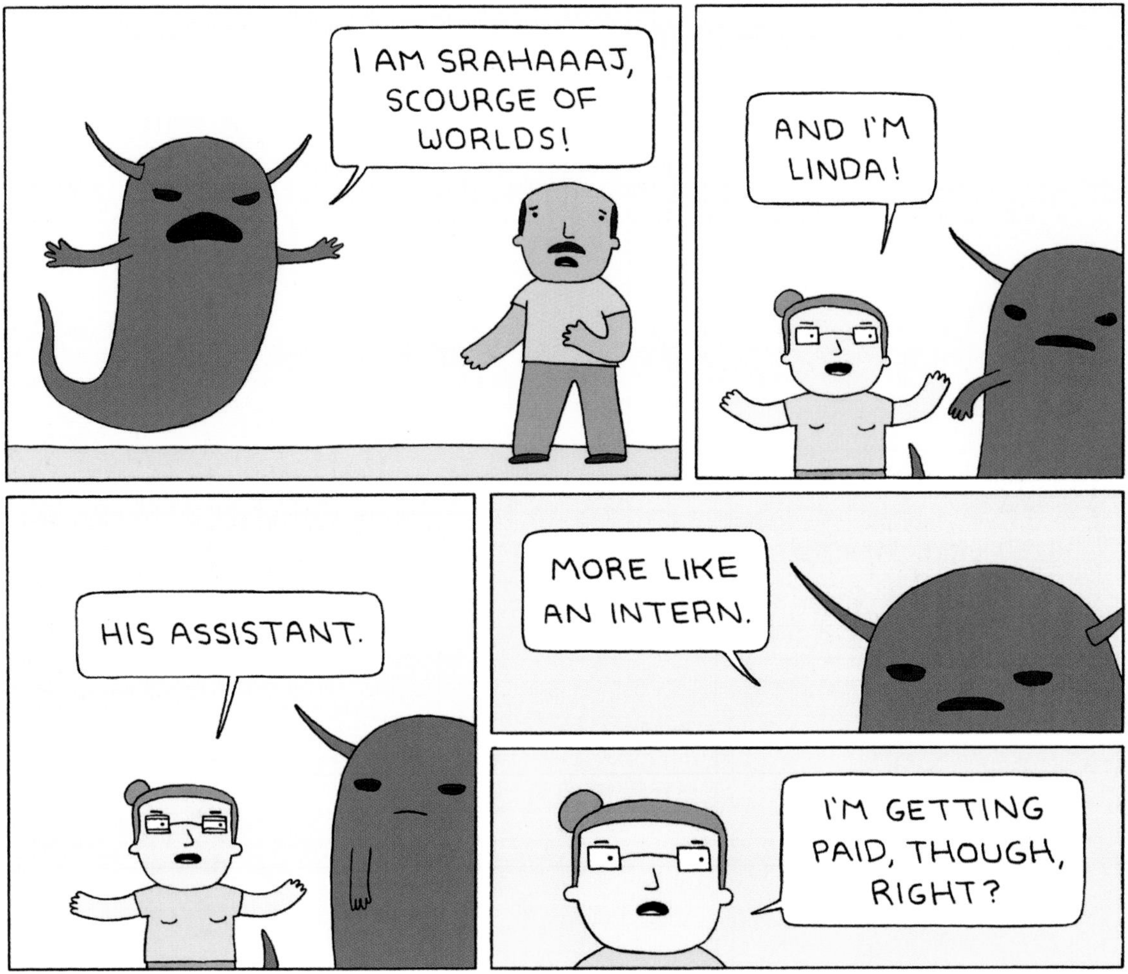
I AM SRAHAAAJ, SCOURGE OF WORLDS!
AND I'M LINDA!
HIS ASSISTANT.
MORE LIKE AN INTERN.
I'M GETTING PAID, THOUGH, RIGHT?

THAT DEPENDS. DO YOU COUNT VALUABLE LIFE EXPERIENCES AS MONEY?
BECAUSE THE BANK DOES NOT.

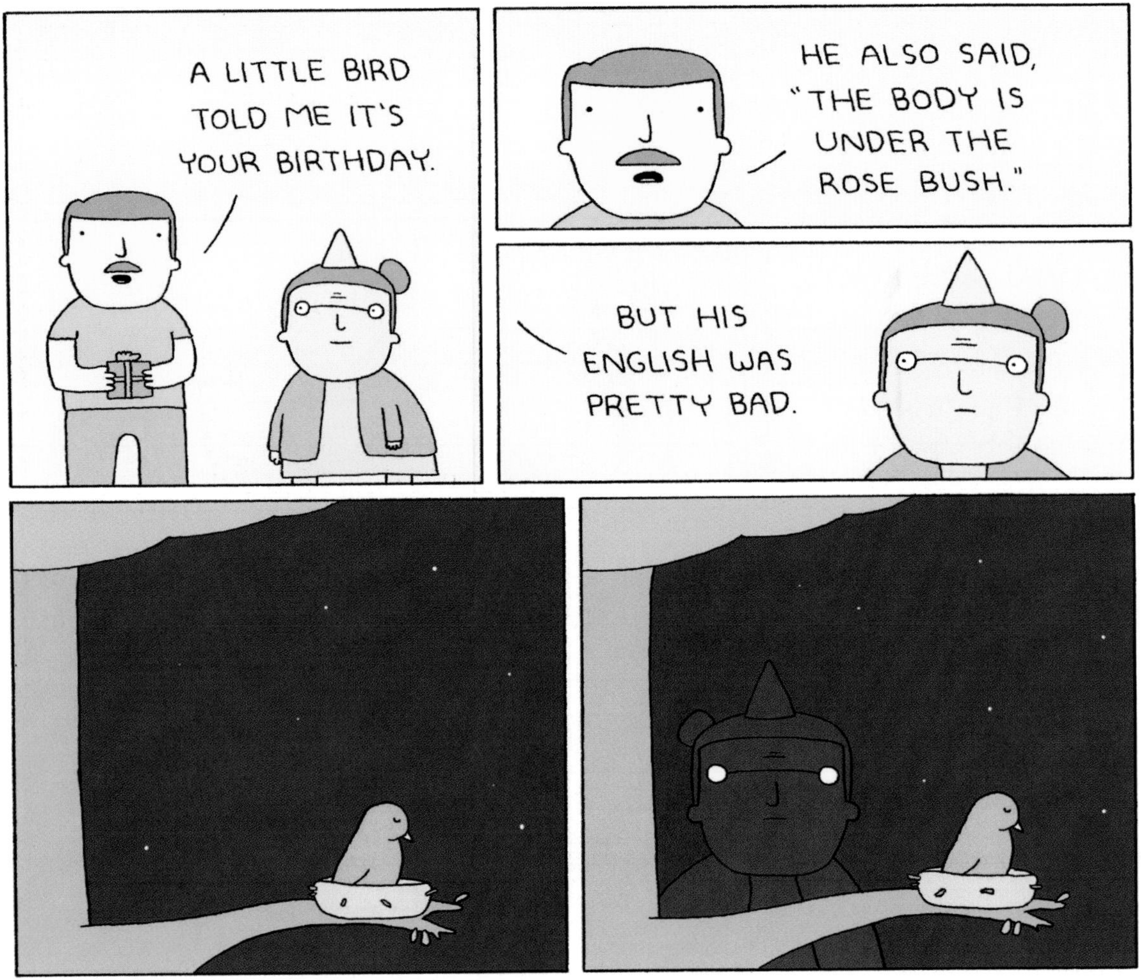
A LITTLE BIRD TOLD ME IT'S YOUR BIRTHDAY.
HE ALSO SAID, "THE BODY IS UNDER THE ROSE BUSH."
BUT HIS ENGLISH WAS PRETTY BAD.

THE ORDER OF EVIL

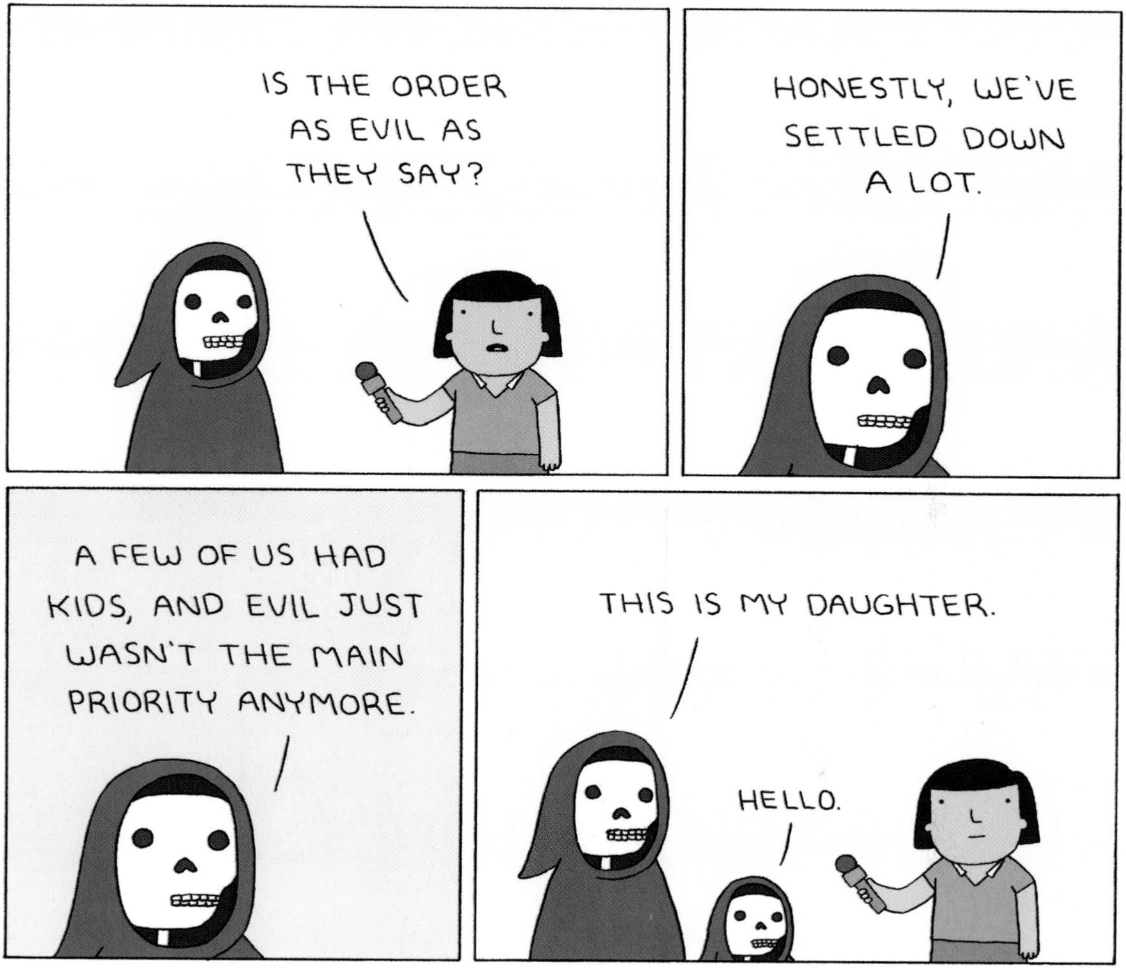
IS THE ORDER AS EVIL AS THEY SAY?
HONESTLY, WE'VE SETTLED DOWN A LOT.
A FEW OF US HAD KIDS, AND EVIL JUST WASN'T THE MAIN PRIORITY ANYMORE.
THIS IS MY DAUGHTER.
HELLO.

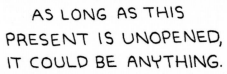
AS LONG AS THIS PRESENT IS UNOPENED, IT COULD BE ANYTHING.

LIKE THAT CAT FROM PHYSICS CLASS.

YEAH, SORTA LIKE THAT—

MRAAAOOOW!

HOW DID YOU GUESS?

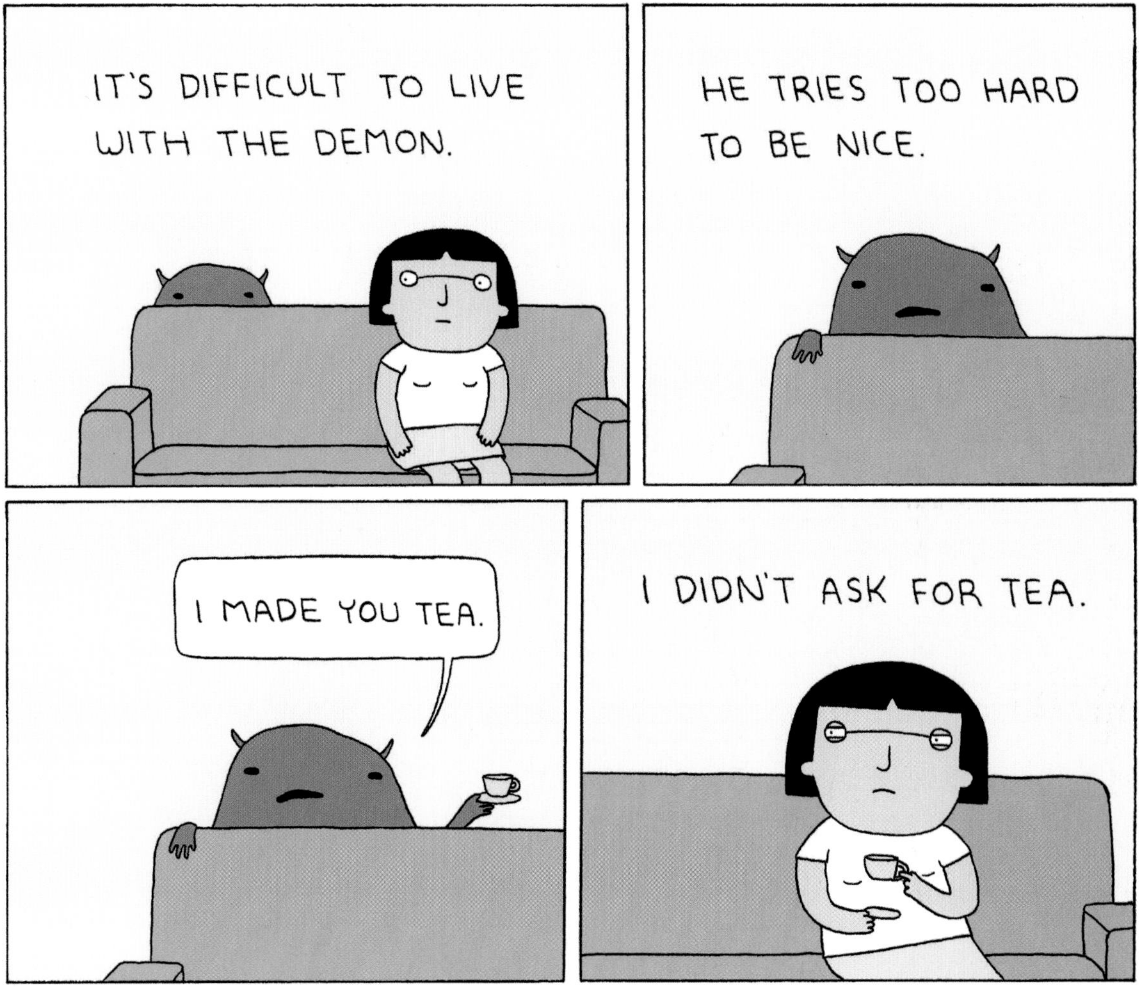
IT'S DIFFICULT TO LIVE WITH THE DEMON.
HE TRIES TOO HARD TO BE NICE.
I MADE YOU TEA.
I DIDN'T ASK FOR TEA.

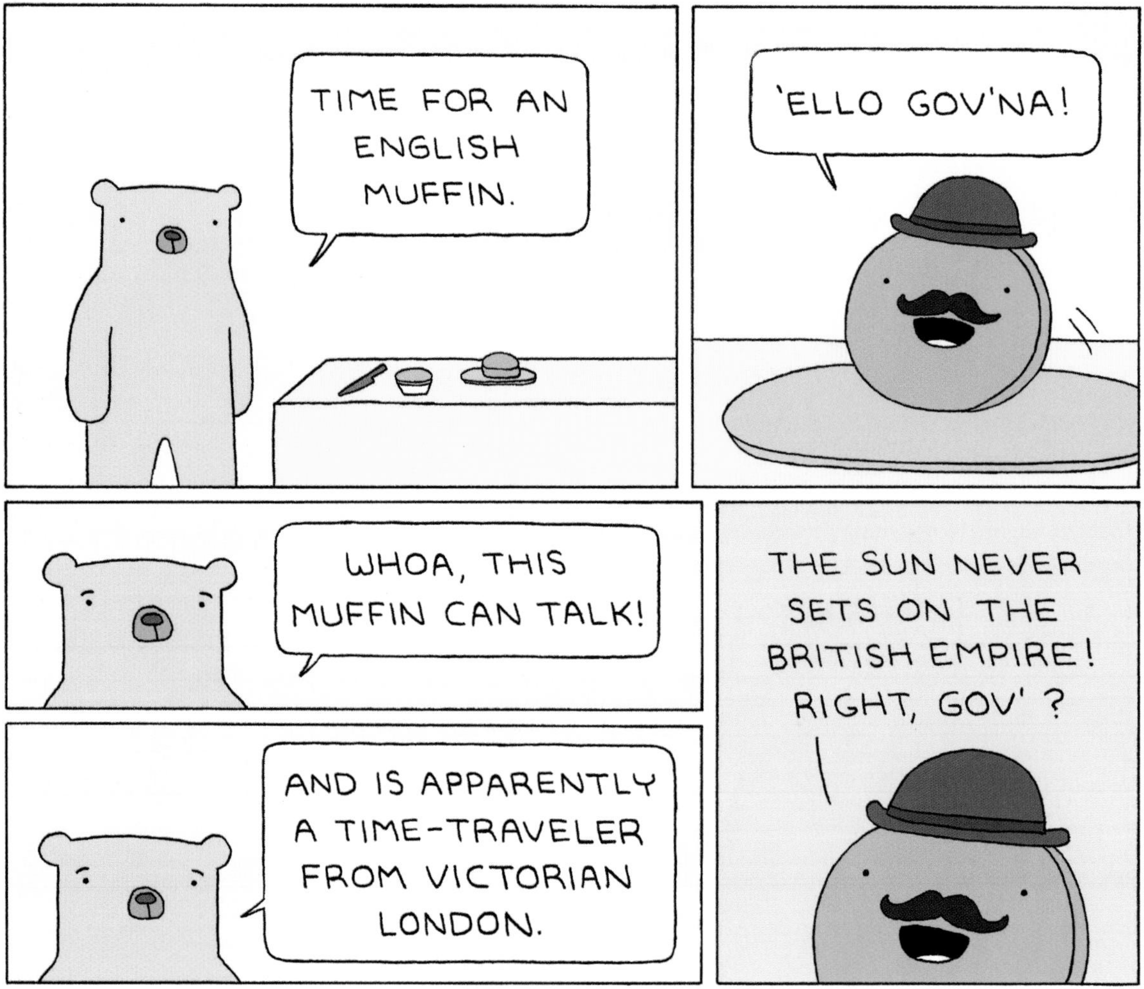
TIME FOR AN ENGLISH MUFFIN.
'ELLO GOV'NA!
WHOA, THIS MUFFIN CAN TALK!
AND IS APPARENTLY A TIME-TRAVELER FROM VICTORIAN LONDON.
THE SUN NEVER SETS ON THE BRITISH EMPIRE! RIGHT, GOV' ?

I'VE GOT SOME BAD NEWS FOR YOU, TIME-MUFFIN.
IS IT ABOUT THAT KNIFE AND LOW-FAT CREAM CHEESE?
PARTLY.

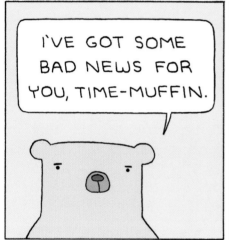

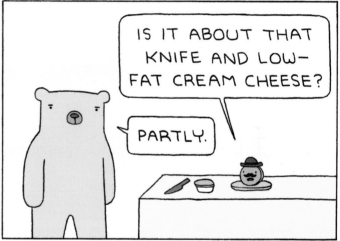

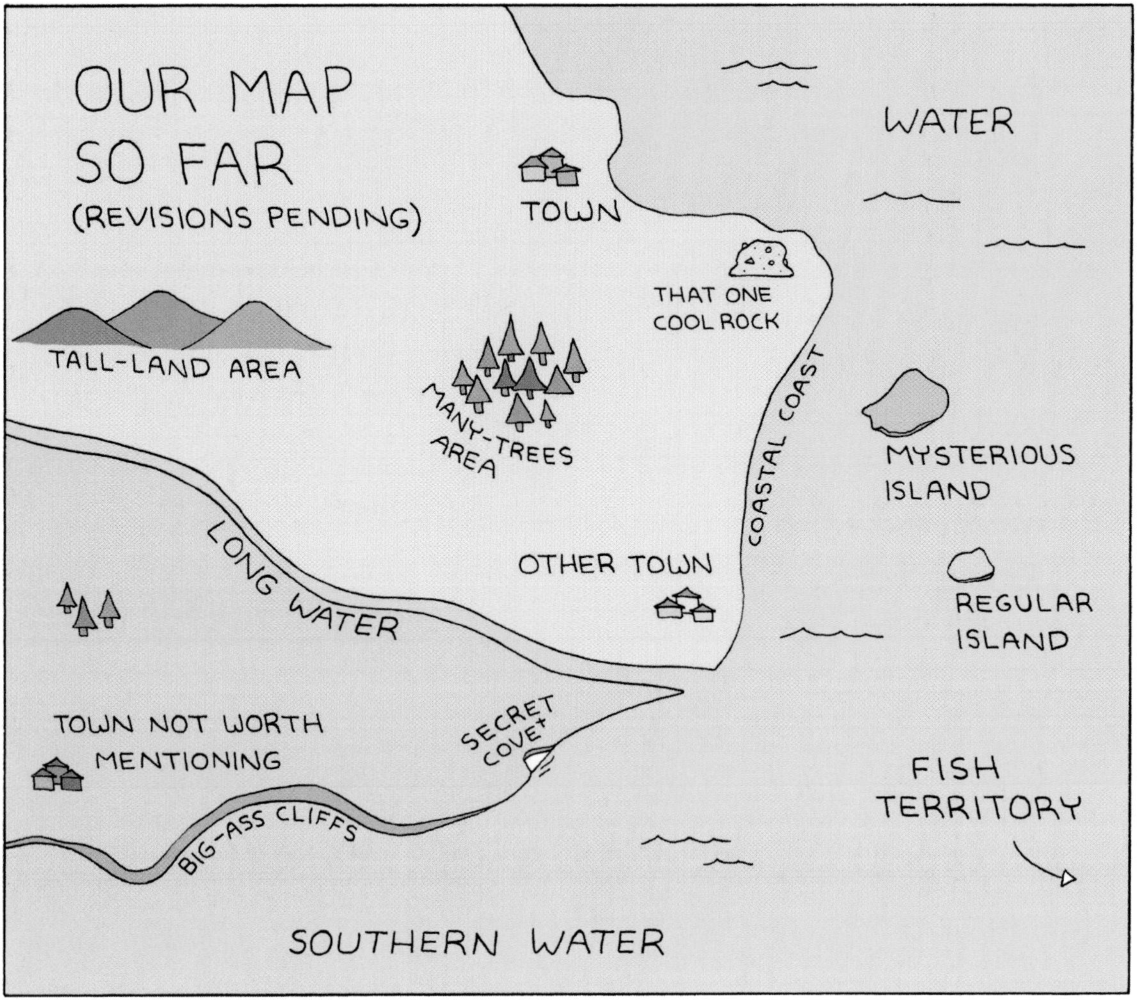
OUR MAP
SO FAR
(REVISIONS PENDING)
TOWN
WATER
THAT ONE
COOL ROCK
TALL-LAND AREA
MANY-TREES
AREA
COASTAL COAST
MYSTERIOUS
ISLAND
LONG WATER
OTHER TOWN
REGULAR
ISLAND
TOWN NOT WORTH
MENTIONING
SECRET
COVE+
FISH
TERRITORY
BIG-ASS CLIFFS
SOUTHERN WATER

+NO LONGER SECRET

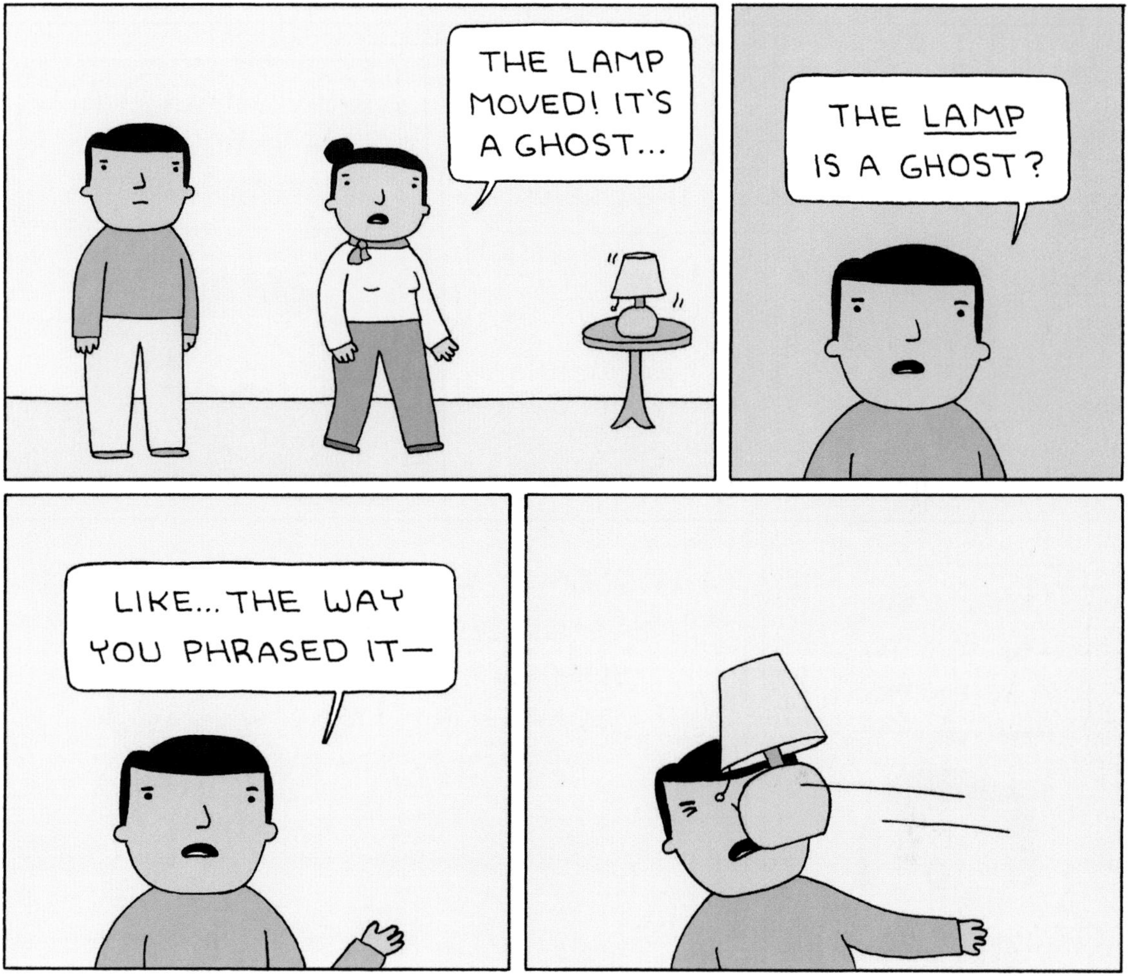
THE LAMP MOVED! IT'S A GHOST...
THE LAMP IS A GHOST?
LIKE... THE WAY YOU PHRASED IT—

SPECIAL REPORT

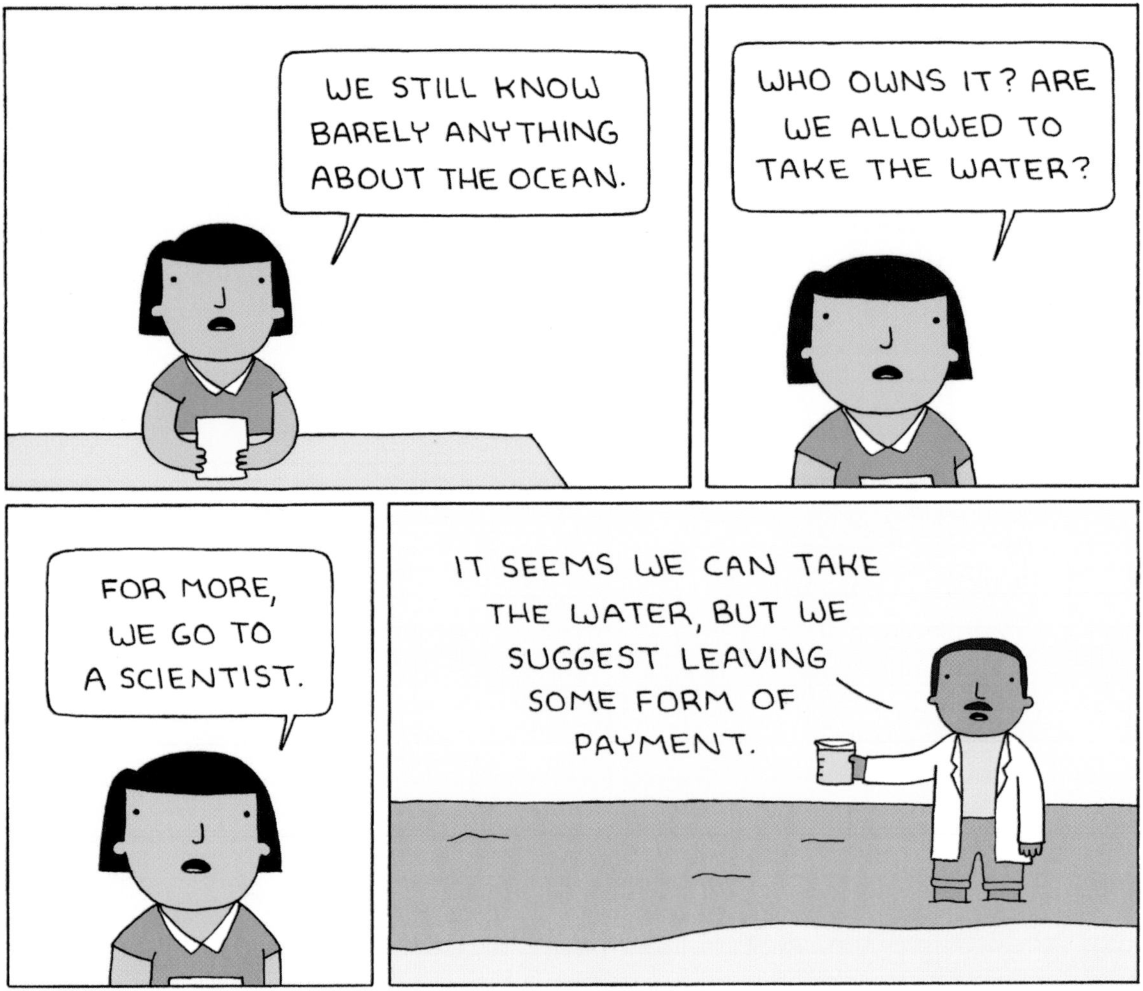
WE STILL KNOW BARELY ANYTHING ABOUT THE OCEAN.
WHO OWNS IT? ARE WE ALLOWED TO TAKE THE WATER?
FOR MORE, WE GO TO A SCIENTIST.
IT SEEMS WE CAN TAKE THE WATER, BUT WE SUGGEST LEAVING SOME FORM OF PAYMENT.

YOU HEARD IT HERE, FOLKS. THROW YOUR MONEY INTO THE SEA.
TO APPEASE THE OCEAN LORDS.

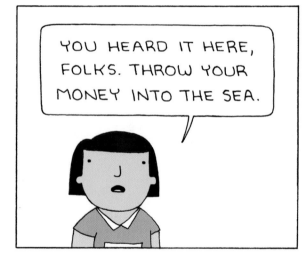

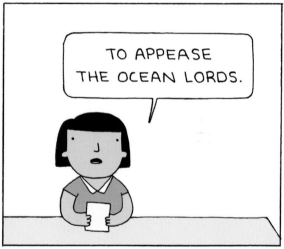

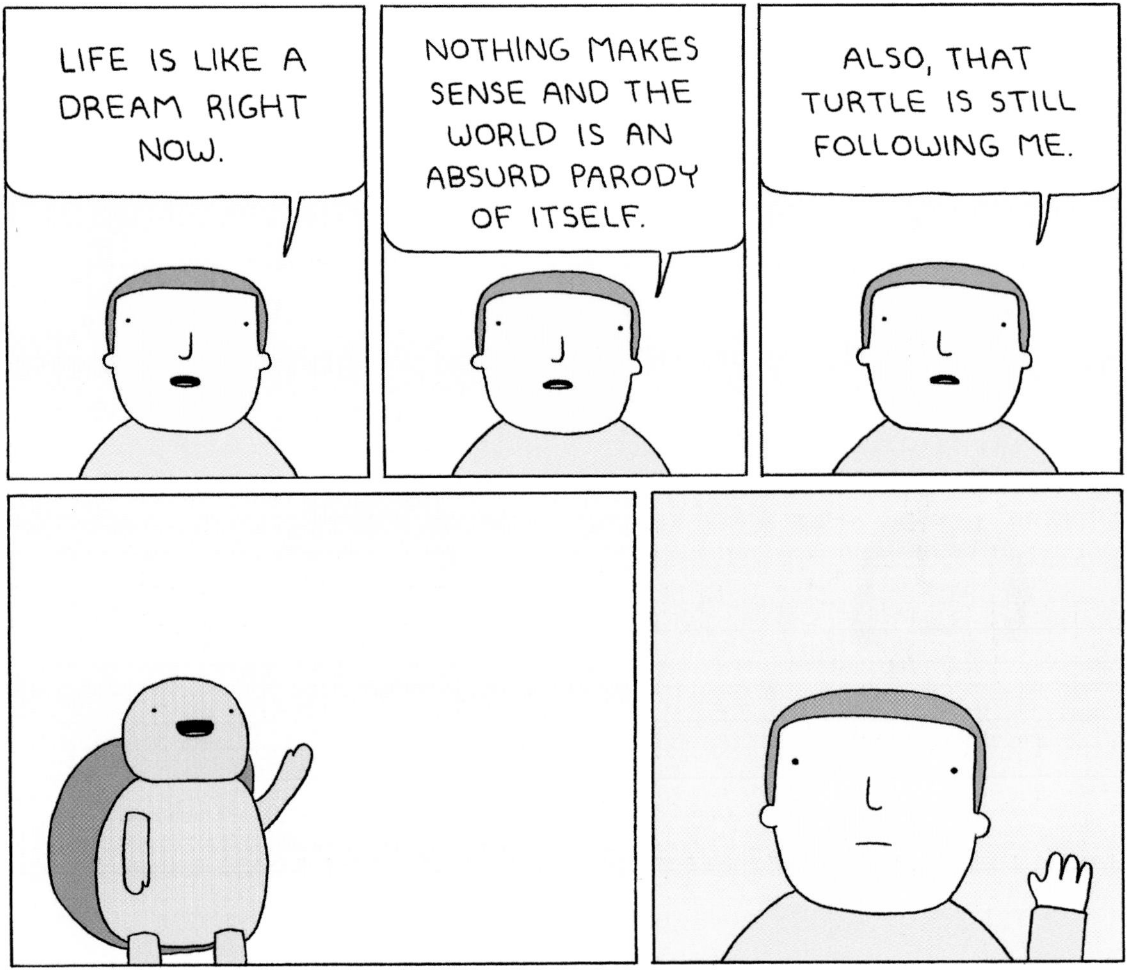
LIFE IS LIKE A DREAM RIGHT NOW.
NOTHING MAKES SENSE AND THE WORLD IS AN ABSURD PARODY OF ITSELF.
ALSO, THAT TURTLE IS STILL FOLLOWING ME.

MRS. JONES STARTS HER MORNING

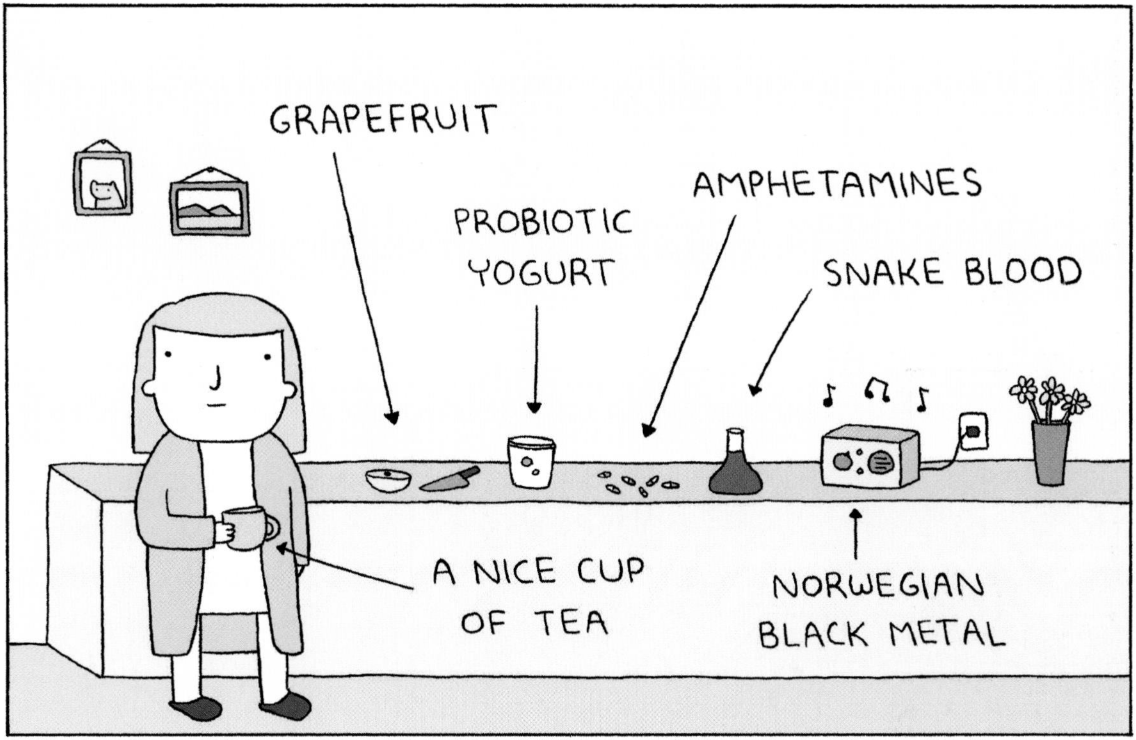
GRAPEFRUIT
PROBIOTIC YOGURT
AMPHETAMINES
SNAKE BLOOD
A NICE CUP OF TEA
NORWEGIAN BLACK METAL

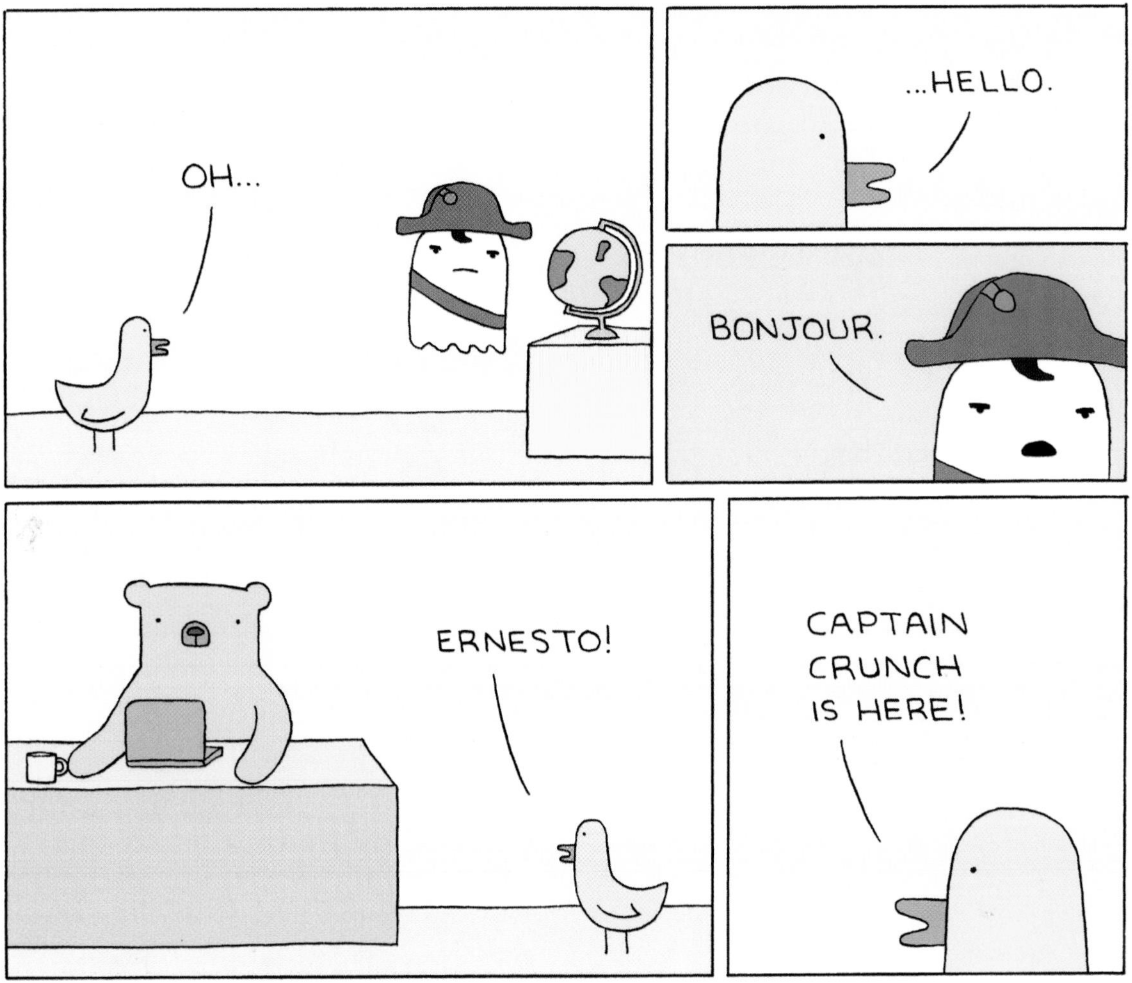
OH...
...HELLO.
BONJOUR.
ERNESTO!
CAPTAIN
CRUNCH
IS HERE!

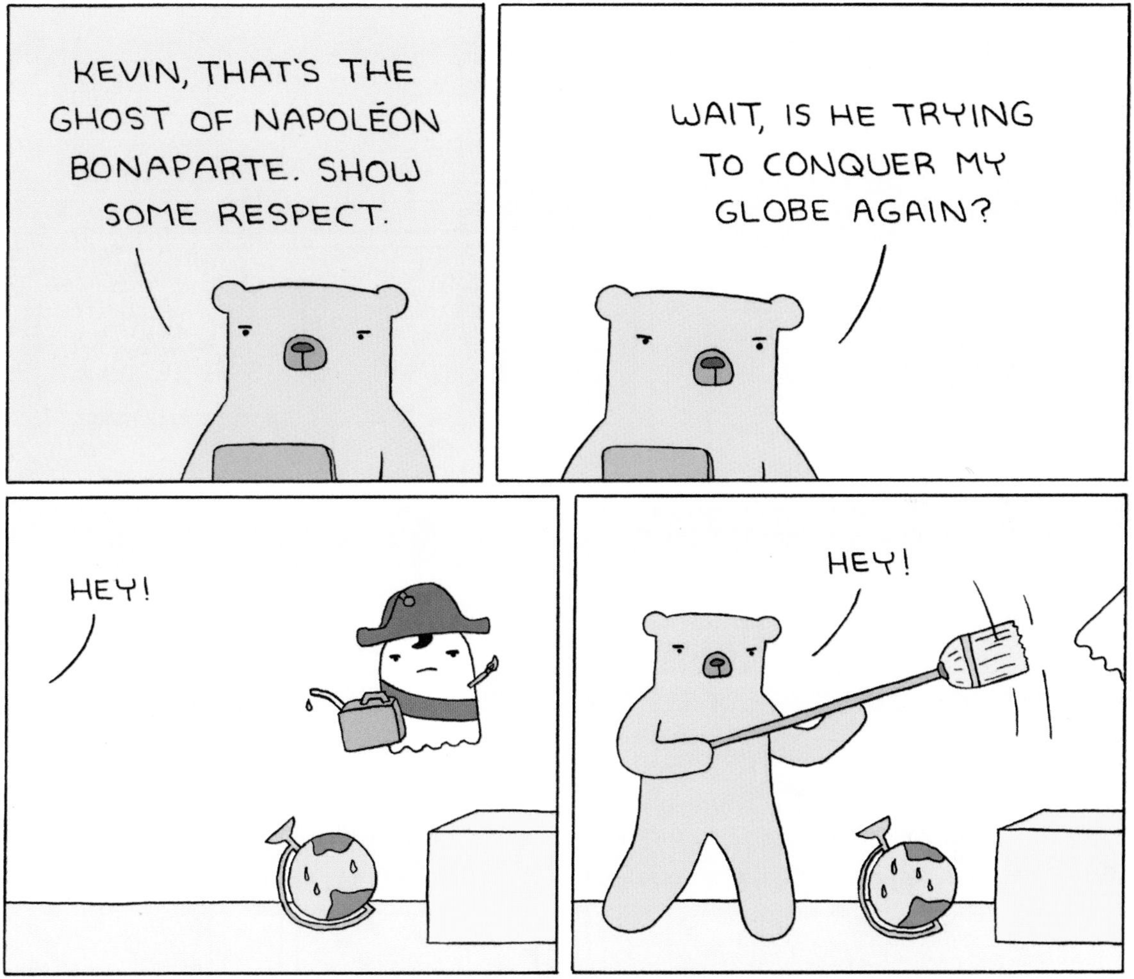
KEVIN, THAT'S THE GHOST OF NAPOLÉON BONAPARTE. SHOW SOME RESPECT.
WAIT, IS HE TRYING TO CONQUER MY GLOBE AGAIN?
HEY!
HEY!

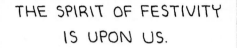
THE SPIRIT OF FESTIVITY
IS UPON US.

BUT HE DOESN'T
REALLY PARTY
ANYMORE.

MY BODY
IS A TEMPLE.

LET'S ALL DO
SHOTS OF
JUICE CLEANSE.

GARY, DON'T
POUR IT INTO
THE PLANT.
I CAN SEE YOU.

THAT'S
DISRESPECTFUL
TO THE
CLEANSE, BRO.

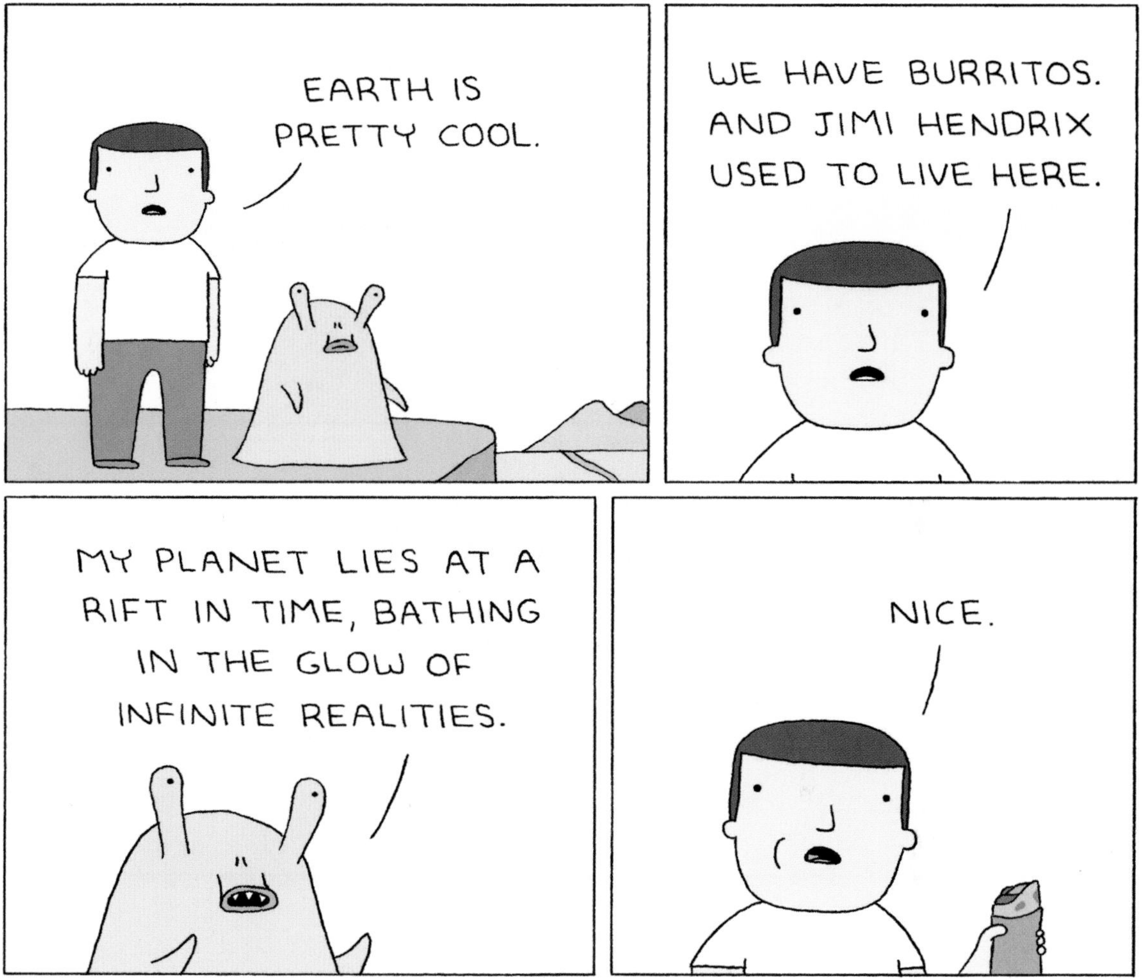
EARTH IS PRETTY COOL.
WE HAVE BURRITOS. AND JIMI HENDRIX USED TO LIVE HERE.
MY PLANET LIES AT A RIFT IN TIME, BATHING IN THE GLOW OF INFINITE REALITIES.
NICE.

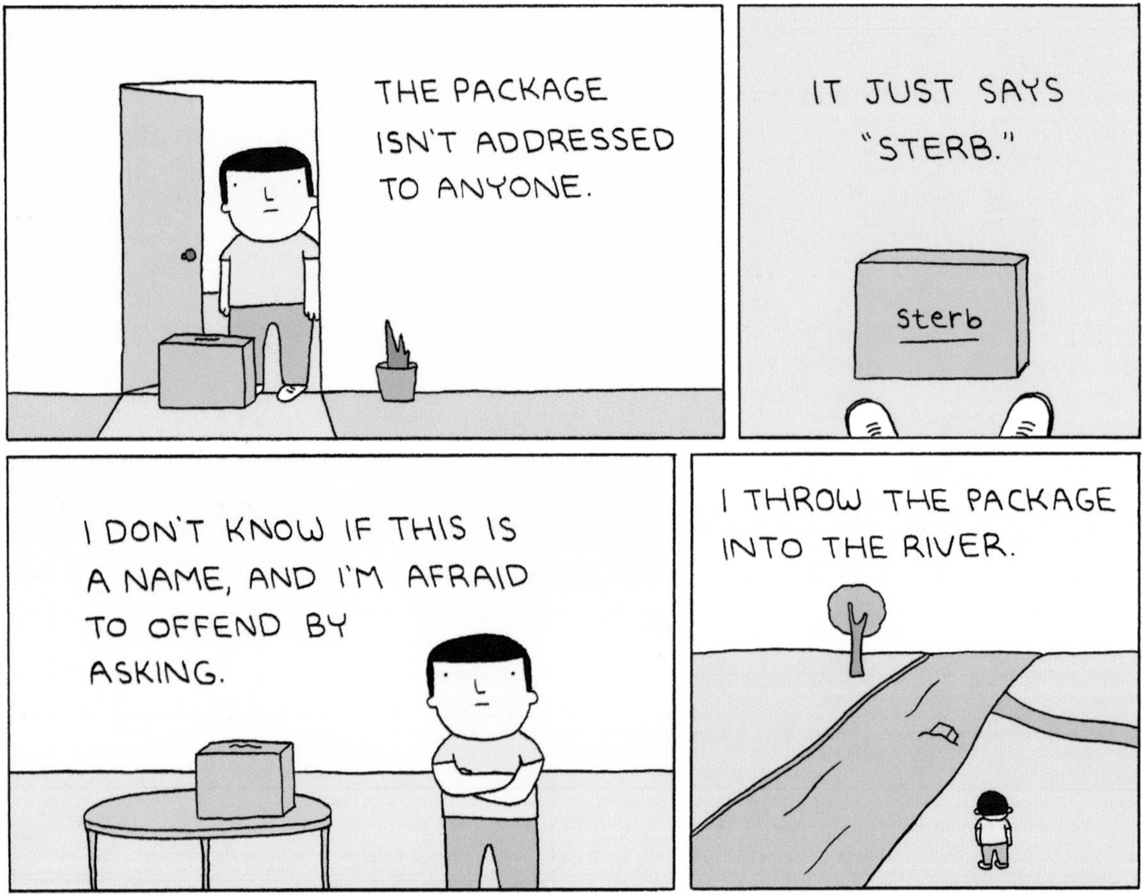
THE PACKAGE ISN'T ADDRESSED TO ANYONE.
IT JUST SAYS "STERB."
Sterb
I DON'T KNOW IF THIS IS A NAME, AND I'M AFRAID TO OFFEND BY ASKING.
I THROW THE PACKAGE INTO THE RIVER.

LATER, STERB COMES BY.

HE IS MY NEIGHBOR.

OBVIOUSLY THIS IS AN EMBARRASSING SITUATION.

I THROW STERB INTO THE RIVER AS WELL.

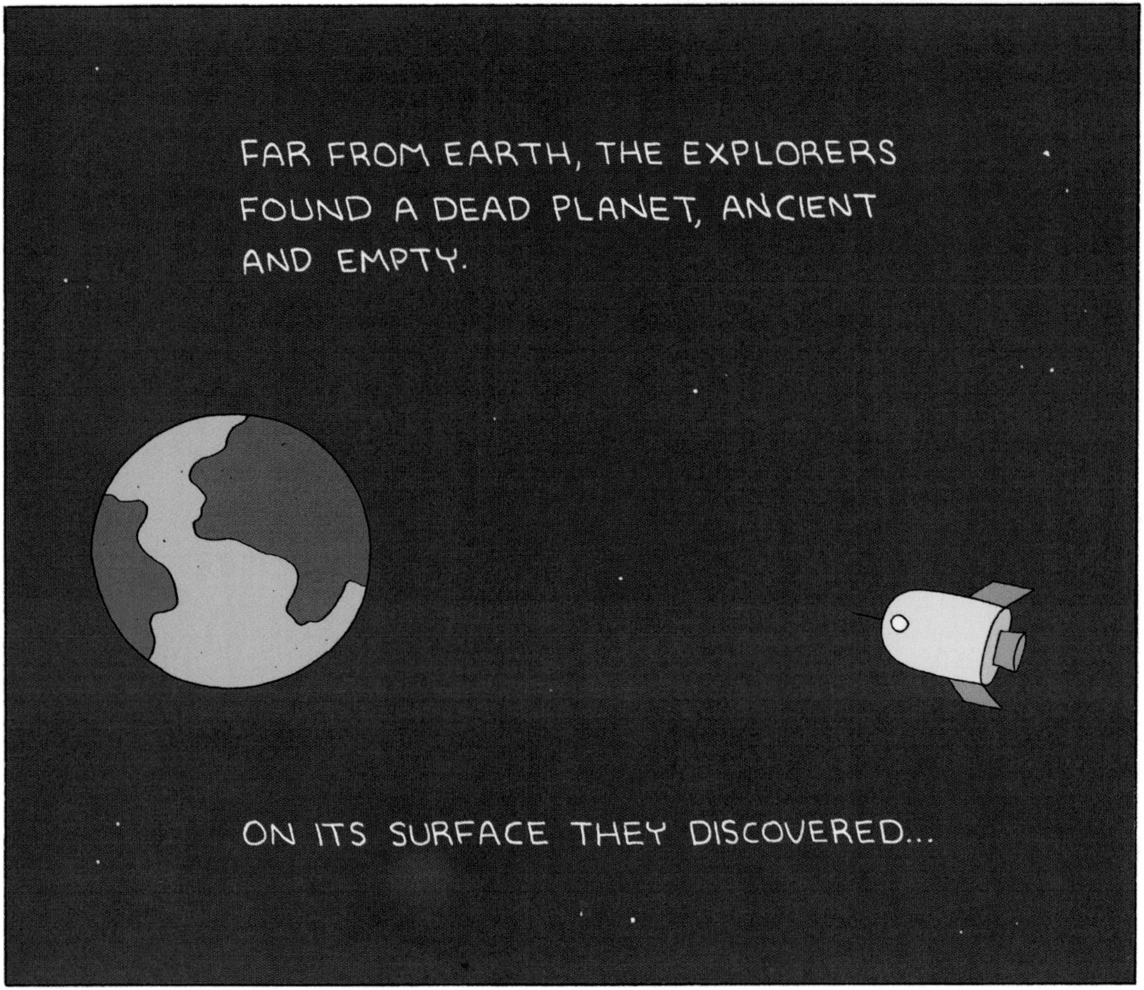
FAR FROM EARTH, THE EXPLORERS FOUND A DEAD PLANET, ANCIENT AND EMPTY.
ON ITS SURFACE THEY DISCOVERED...

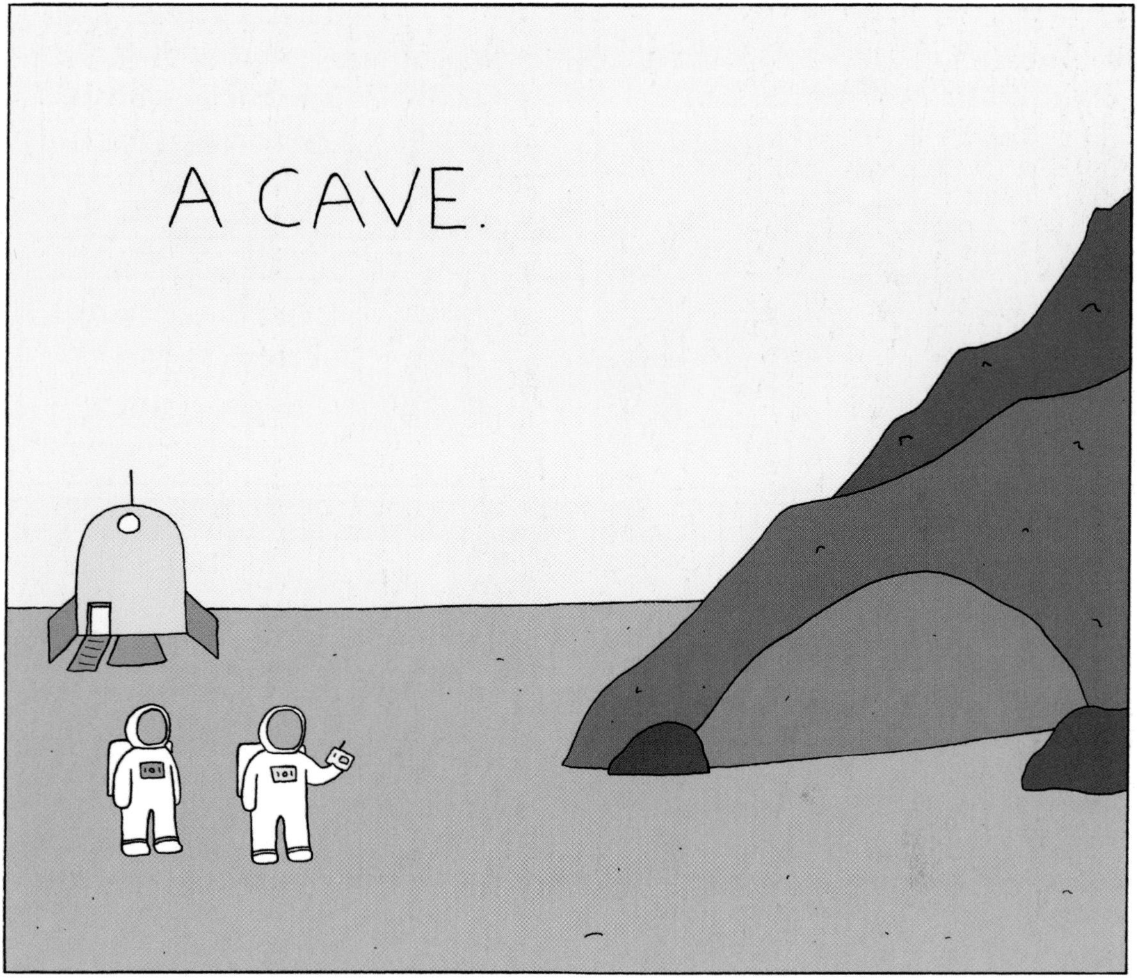
A CAVE.

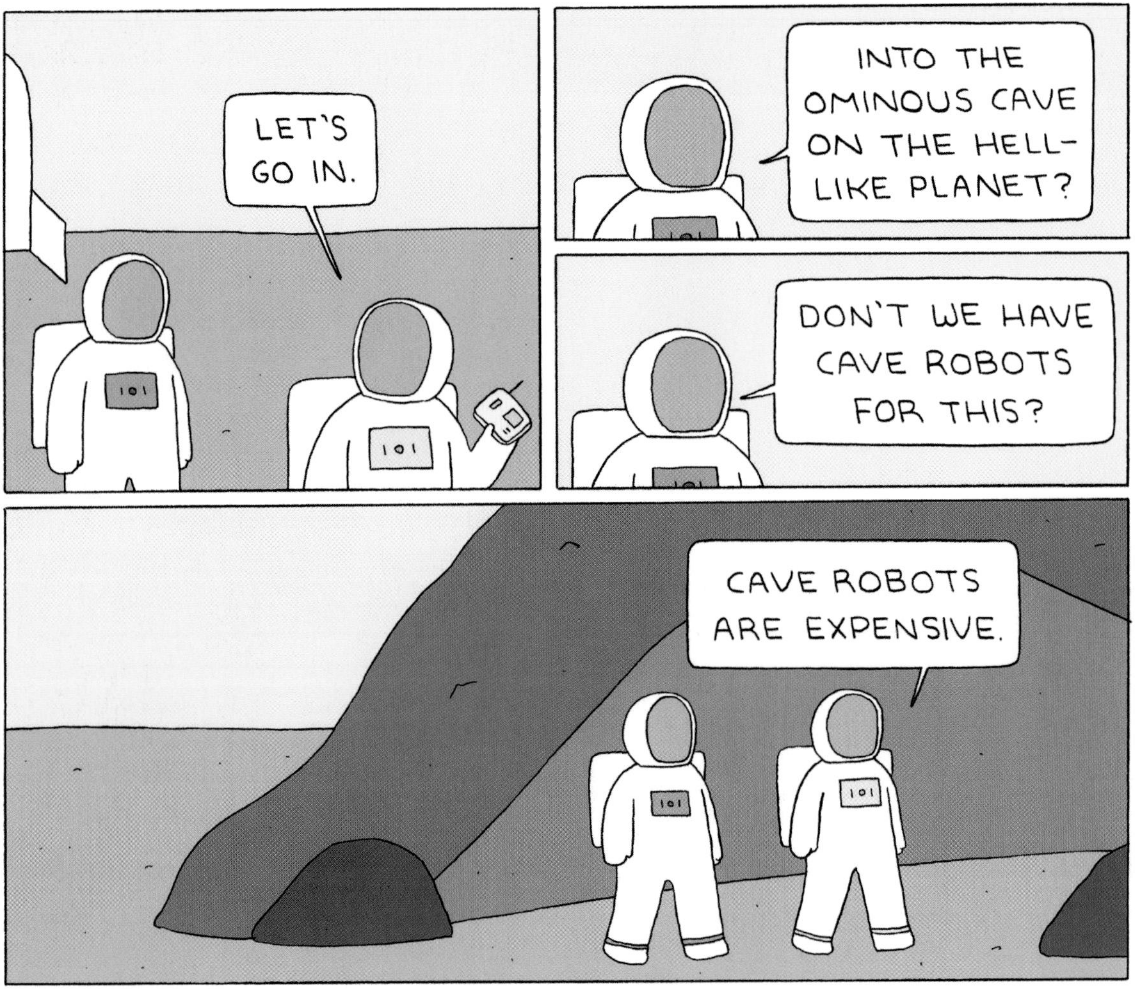
LET'S GO IN.
INTO THE OMINOUS CAVE ON THE HELL-LIKE PLANET?
DON'T WE HAVE CAVE ROBOTS FOR THIS?
CAVE ROBOTS ARE EXPENSIVE.

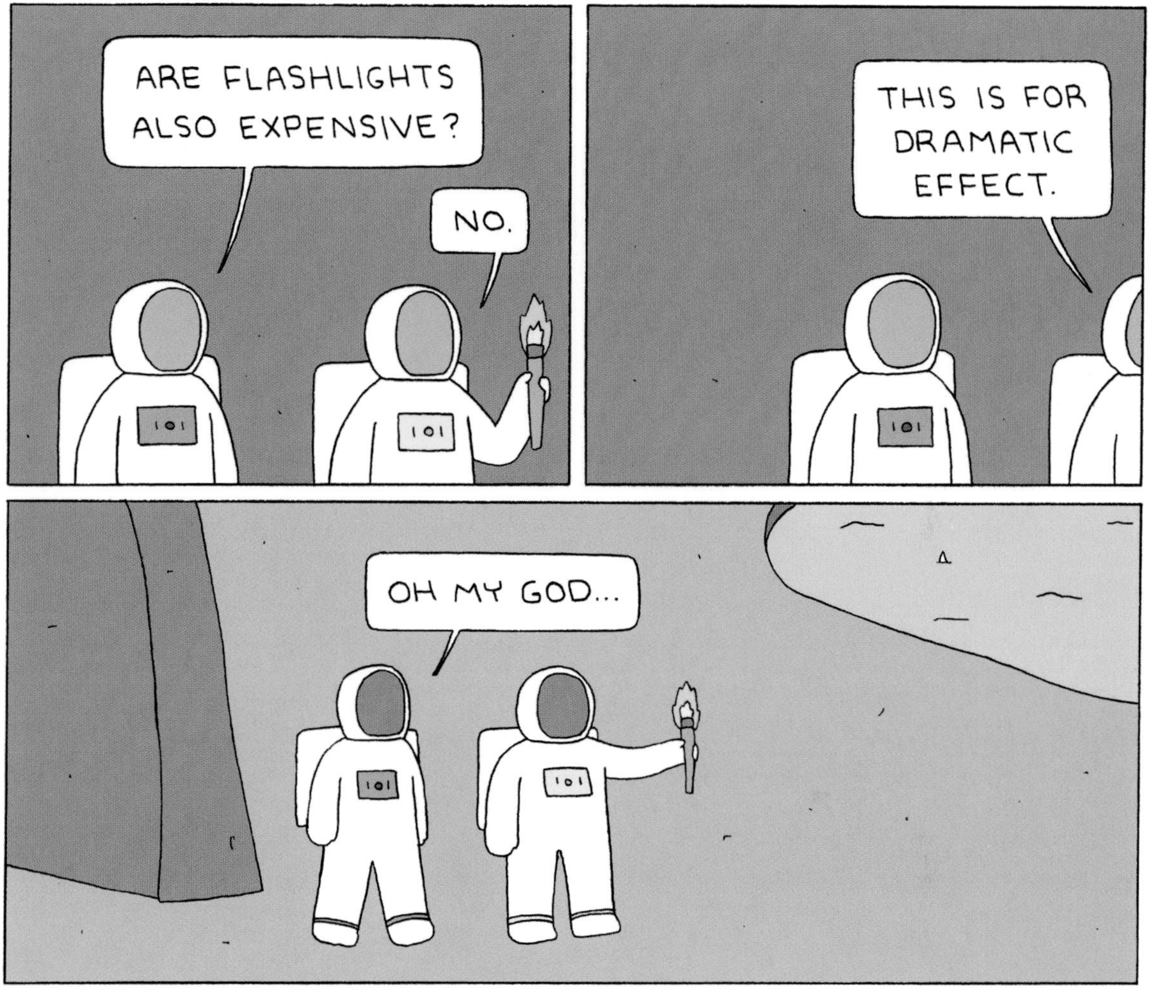
ARE FLASHLIGHTS ALSO EXPENSIVE?
NO.
THIS IS FOR DRAMATIC EFFECT.
OH MY GOD...

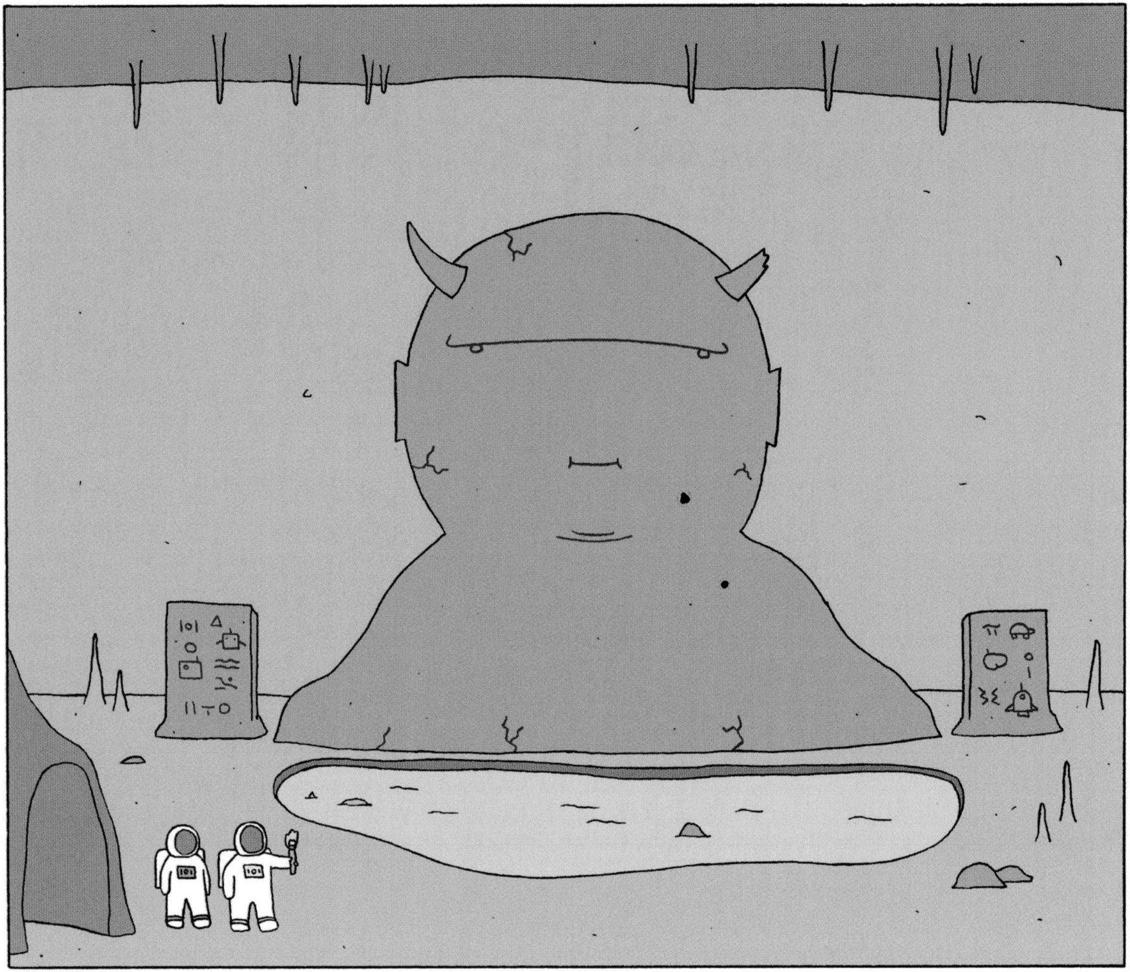

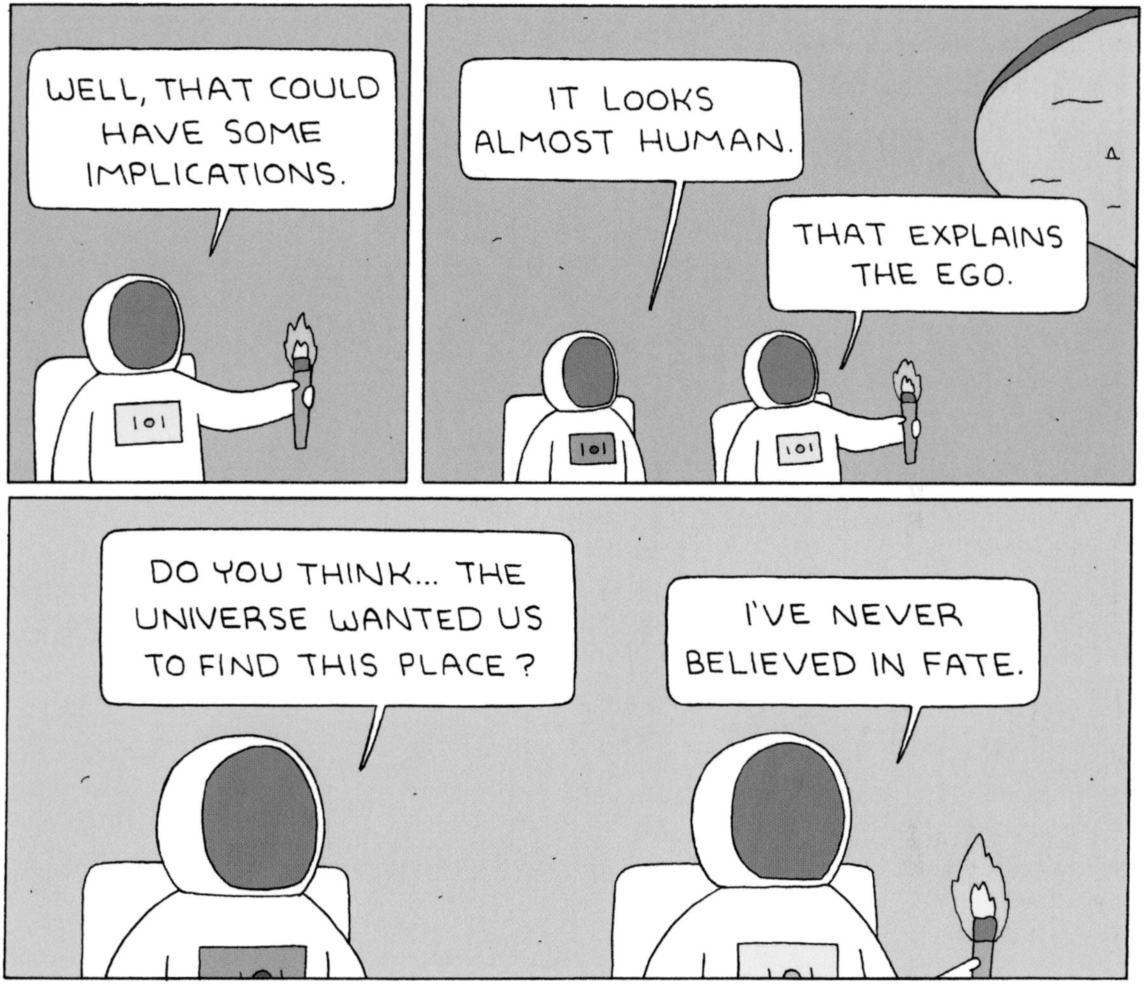
WELL, THAT COULD HAVE SOME IMPLICATIONS.
IT LOOKS ALMOST HUMAN.
THAT EXPLAINS THE EGO.
DO YOU THINK... THE UNIVERSE WANTED US TO FIND THIS PLACE?
I'VE NEVER BELIEVED IN FATE.

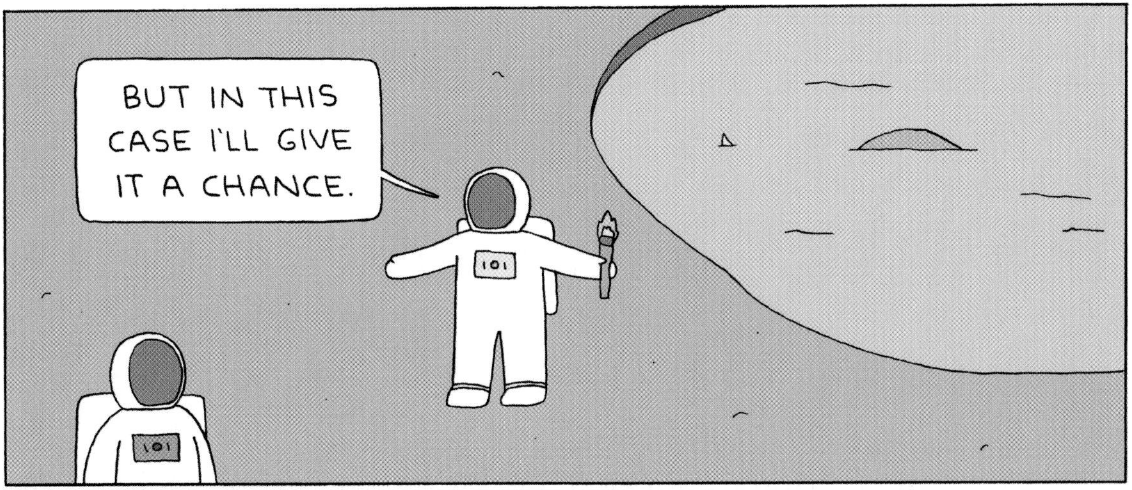
BUT IN THIS CASE I'LL GIVE IT A CHANCE.

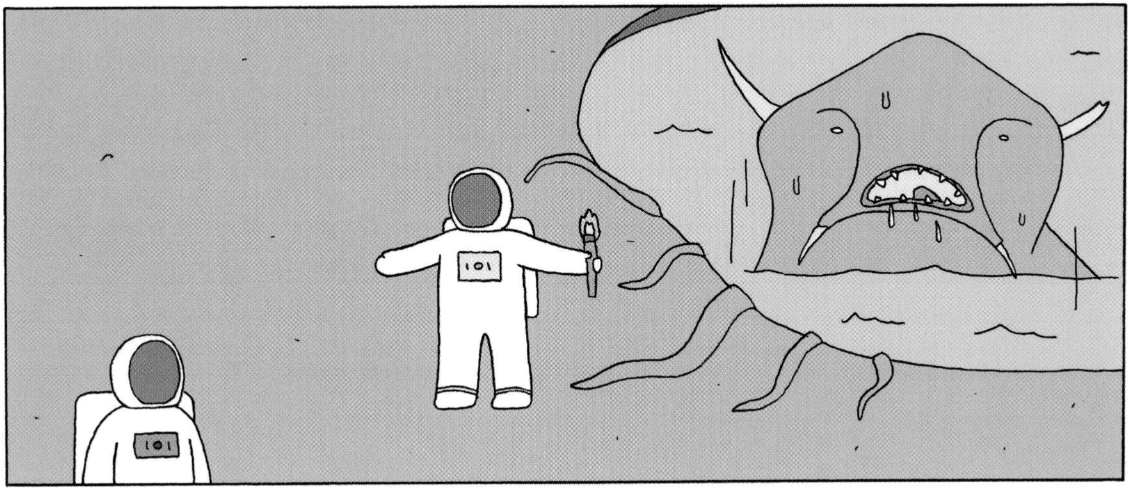

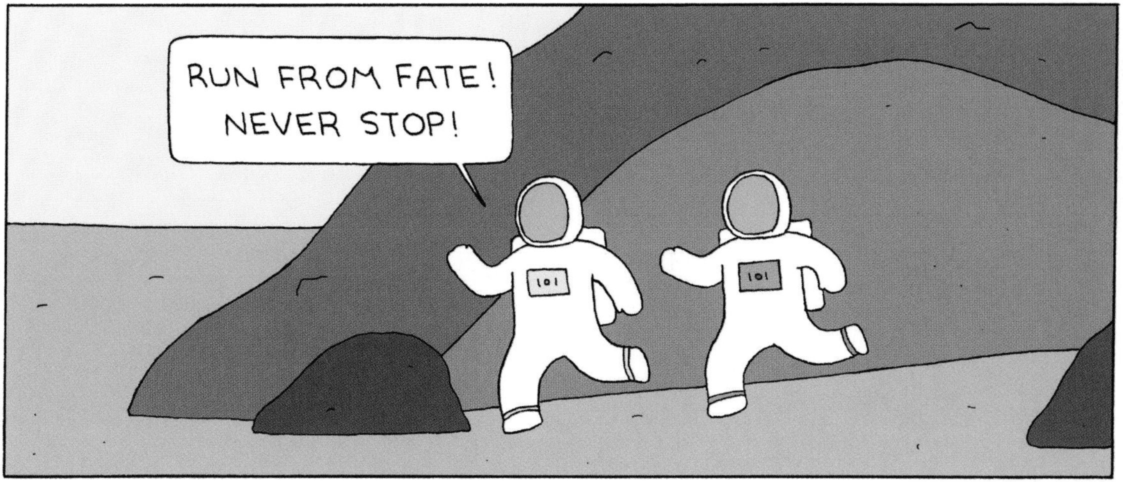
RUN FROM FATE! NEVER STOP!
101
101

V

THOUGHTS
ON THINGS

I WON'T SIT IDLY BY.
I'LL SIT LIKE THIS.
THE PERFECT BLEND OF COMFORT AND ACTION.

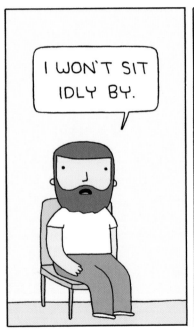

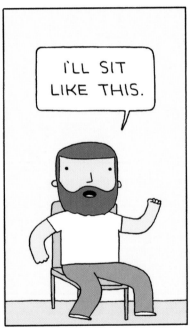

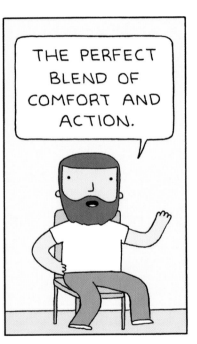

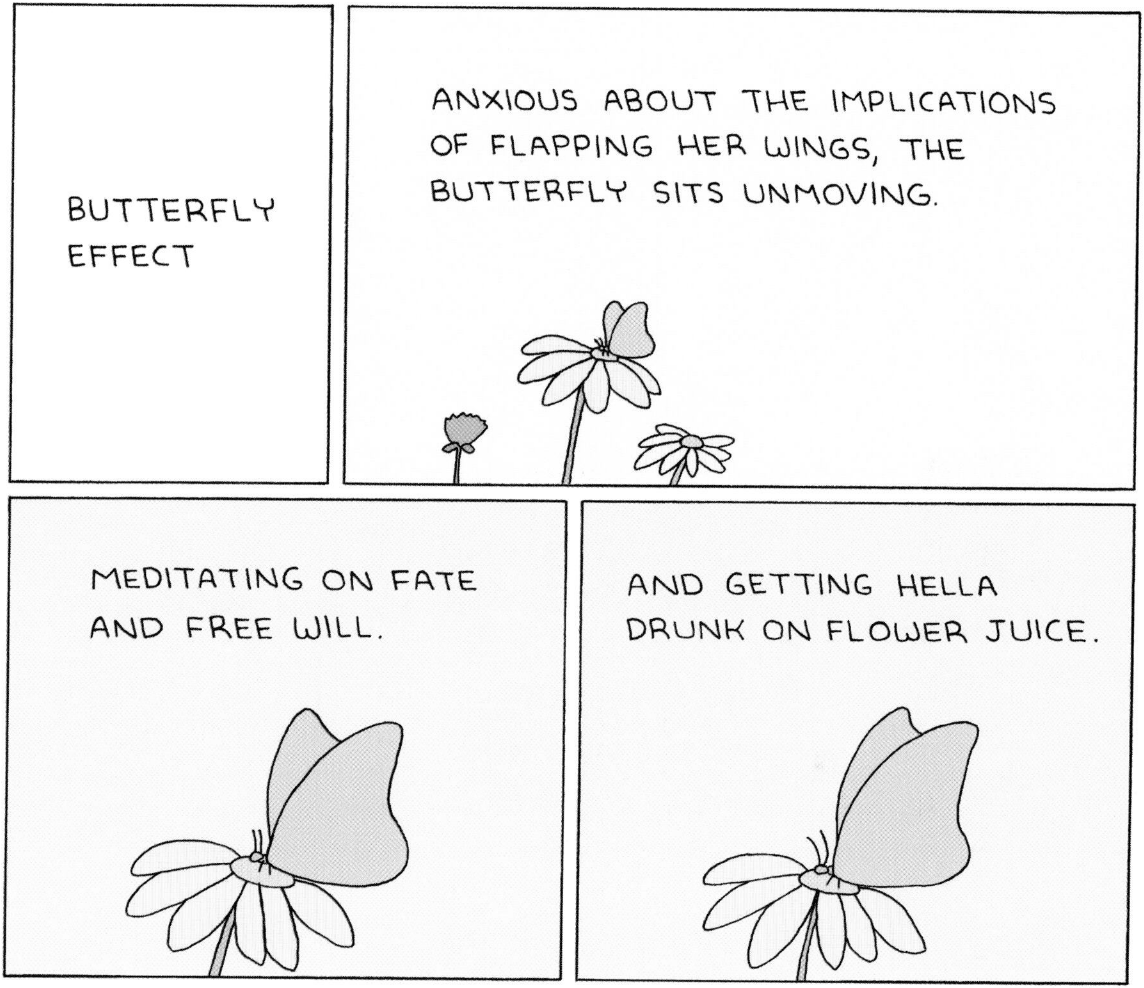
BUTTERFLY EFFECT
ANXIOUS ABOUT THE IMPLICATIONS OF FLAPPING HER WINGS, THE BUTTERFLY SITS UNMOVING.
MEDITATING ON FATE AND FREE WILL.
AND GETTING HELLA DRUNK ON FLOWER JUICE.

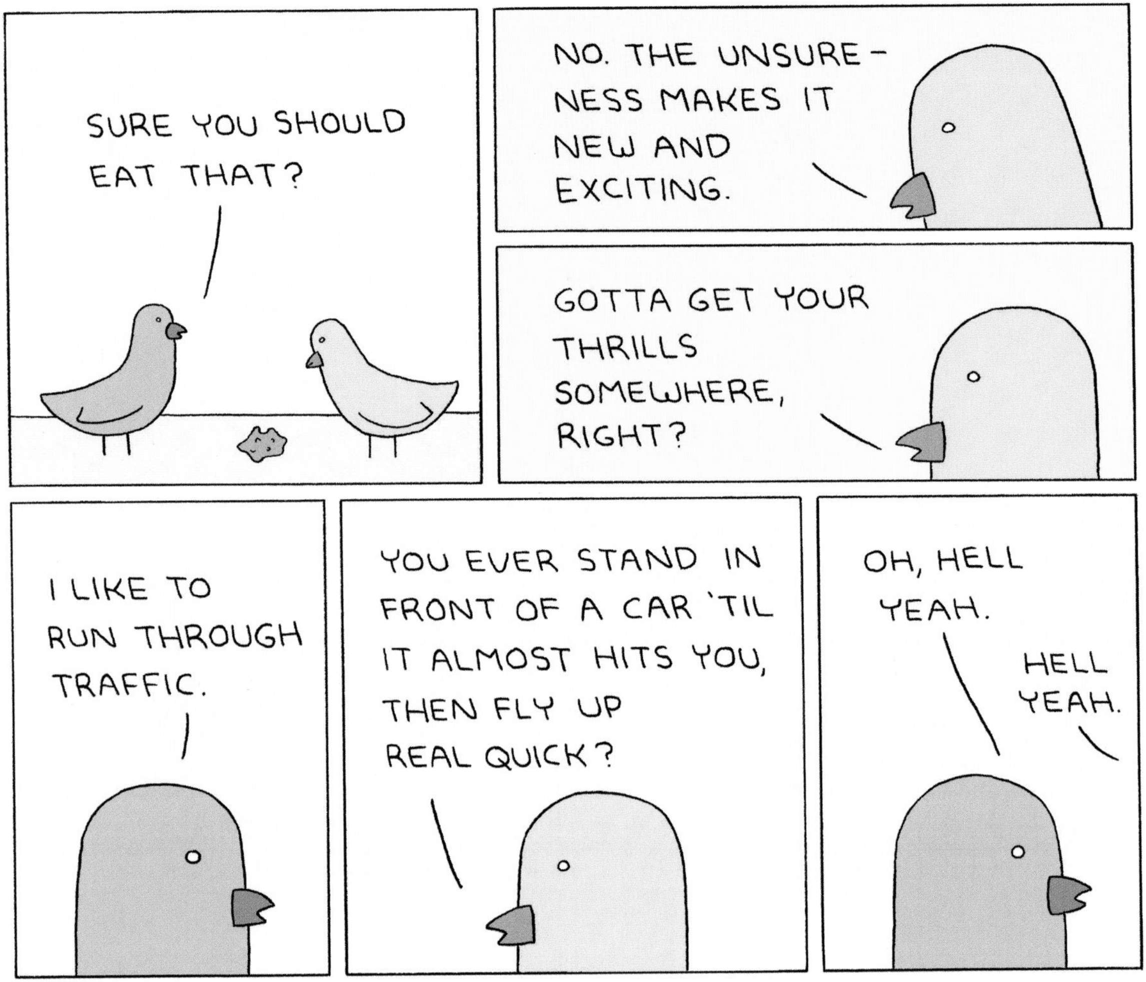
SURE YOU SHOULD EAT THAT?
NO. THE UNSURE-NESS MAKES IT NEW AND EXCITING.
GOTTA GET YOUR THRILLS SOMEWHERE, RIGHT?
I LIKE TO RUN THROUGH TRAFFIC.
YOU EVER STAND IN FRONT OF A CAR 'TIL IT ALMOST HITS YOU, THEN FLY UP REAL QUICK?
OH, HELL YEAH.
HELL YEAH.

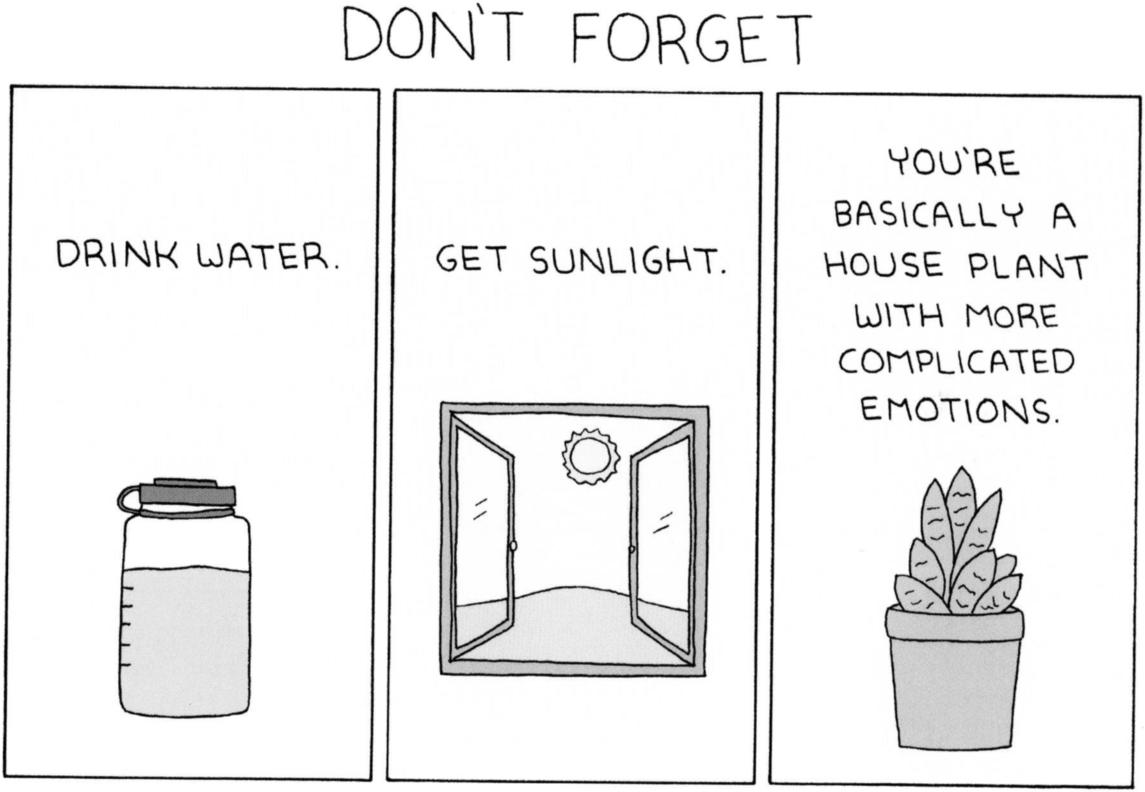
DON'T FORGET
DRINK WATER.
GET SUNLIGHT.
YOU'RE BASICALLY A HOUSE PLANT WITH MORE COMPLICATED EMOTIONS.

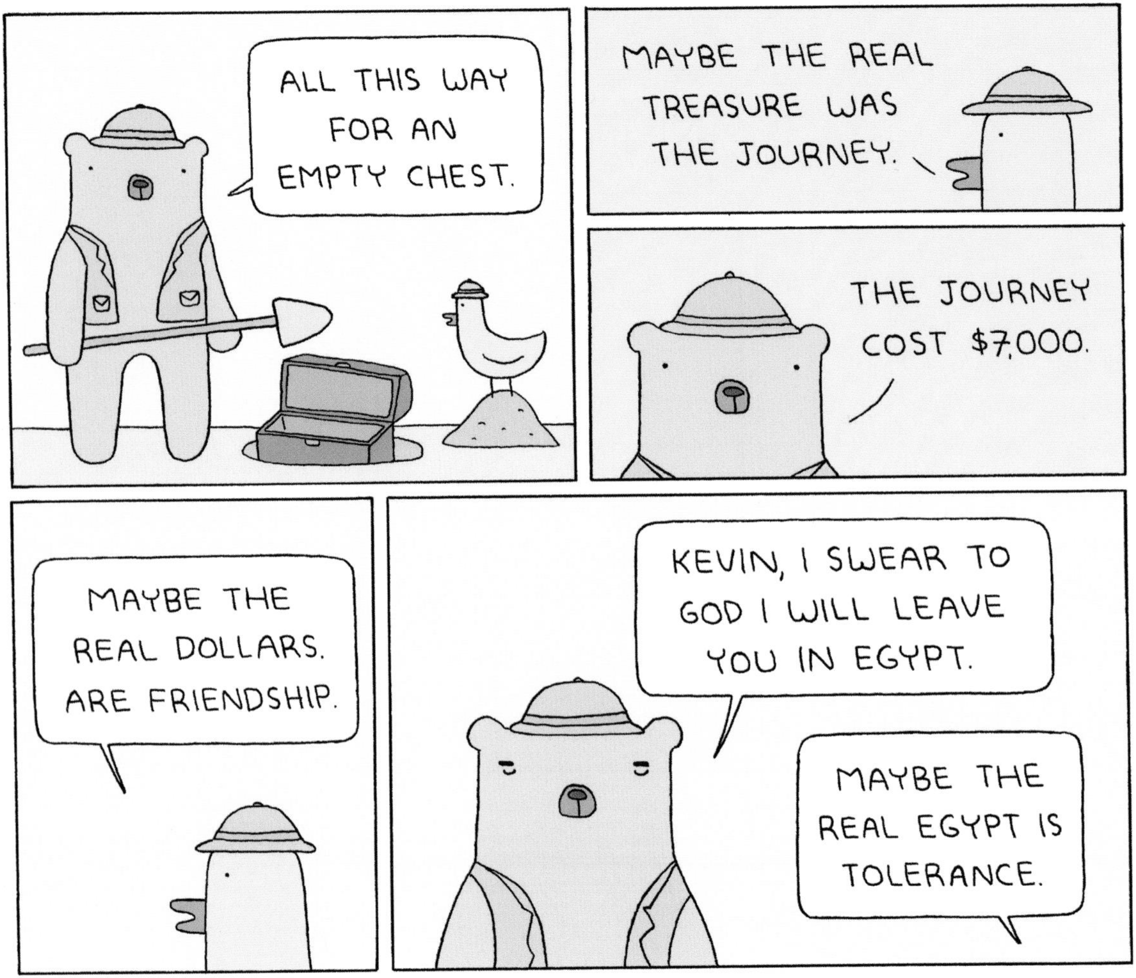
ALL THIS WAY FOR AN EMPTY CHEST.
MAYBE THE REAL TREASURE WAS THE JOURNEY.
THE JOURNEY COST $7,000.
MAYBE THE REAL DOLLARS ARE FRIENDSHIP.
KEVIN, I SWEAR TO GOD I WILL LEAVE YOU IN EGYPT.
MAYBE THE REAL EGYPT IS TOLERANCE.

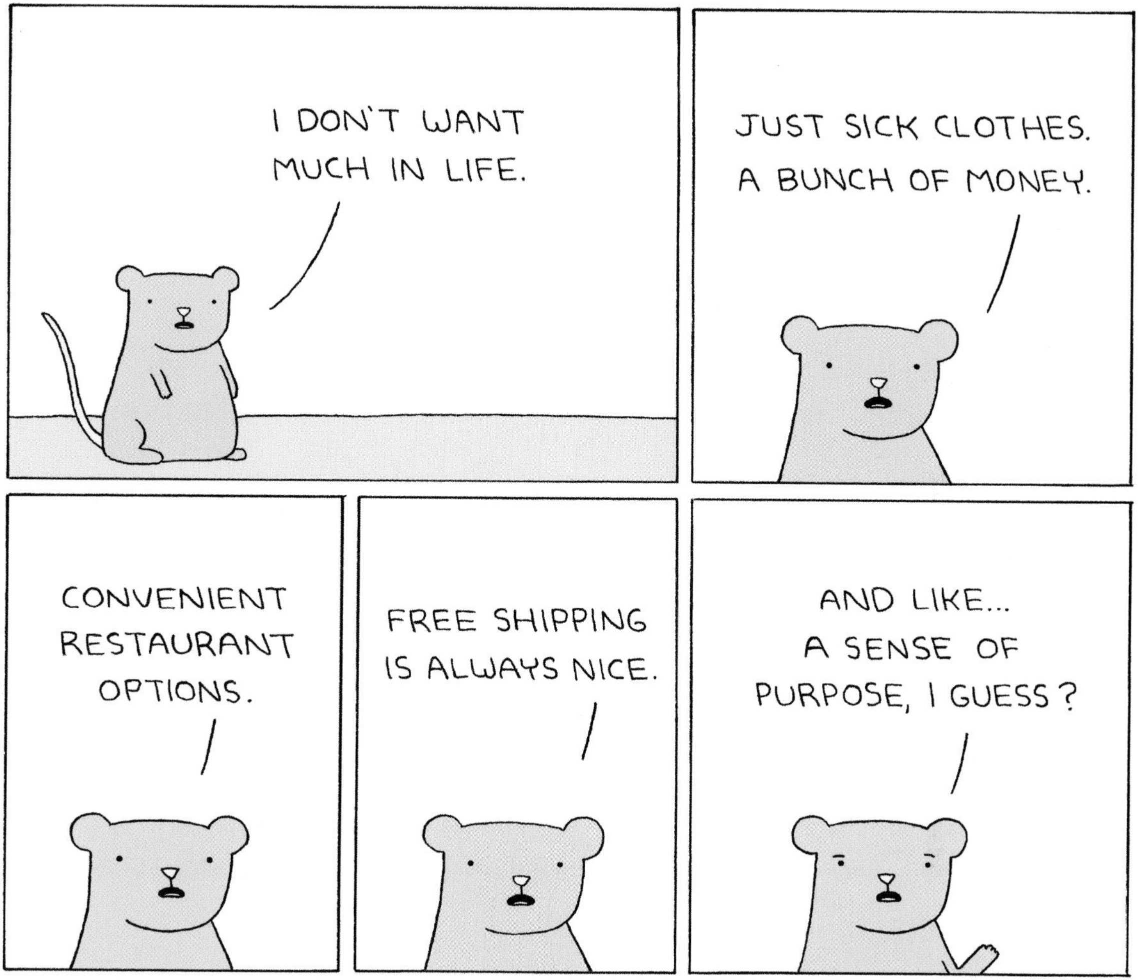
I DON'T WANT MUCH IN LIFE.
JUST SICK CLOTHES. A BUNCH OF MONEY.
CONVENIENT RESTAURANT OPTIONS.
FREE SHIPPING IS ALWAYS NICE.
AND LIKE... A SENSE OF PURPOSE, I GUESS?

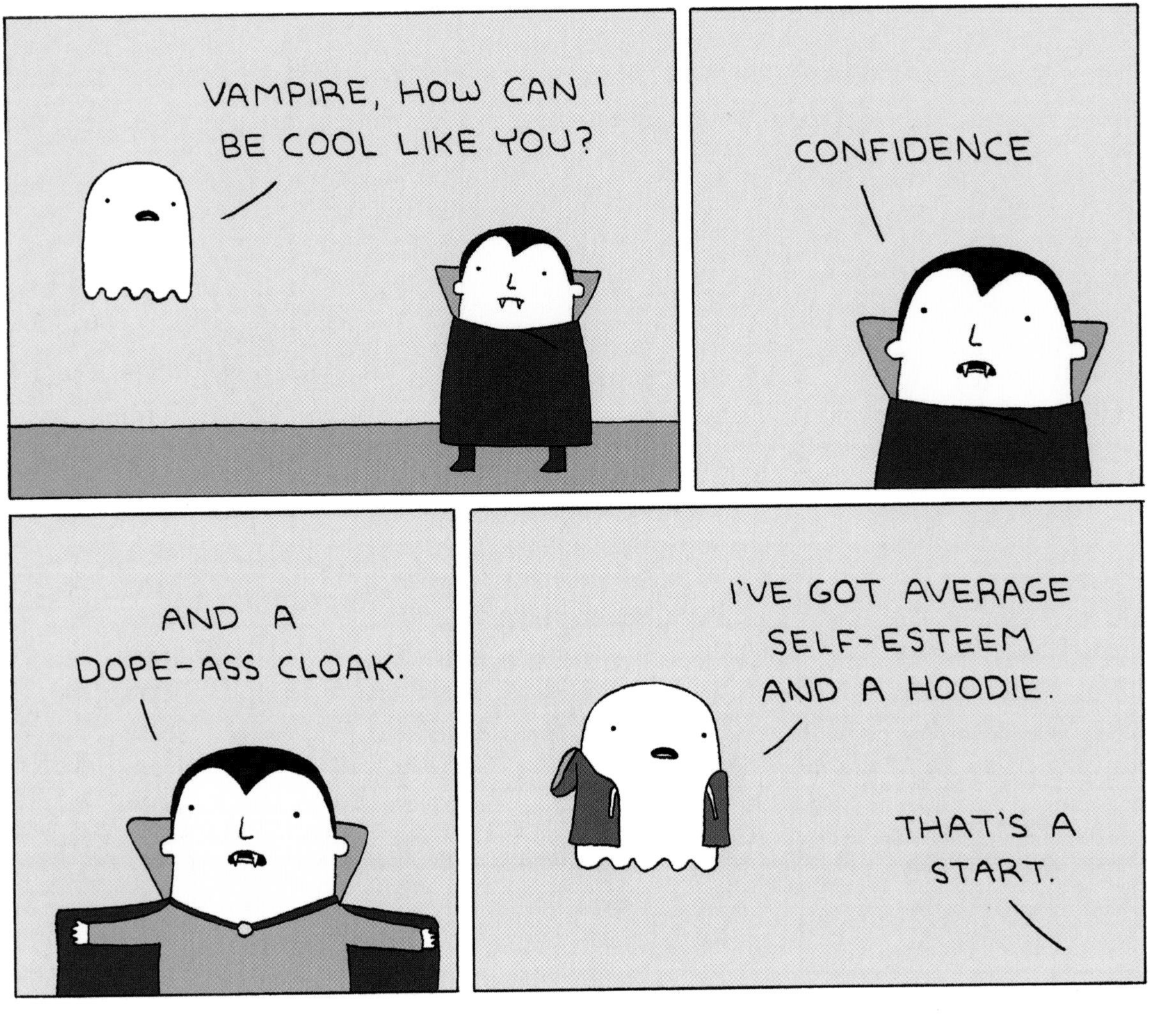
VAMPIRE, HOW CAN I BE COOL LIKE YOU?
CONFIDENCE
AND A DOPE-ASS CLOAK.
I'VE GOT AVERAGE SELF-ESTEEM AND A HOODIE.
THAT'S A START.

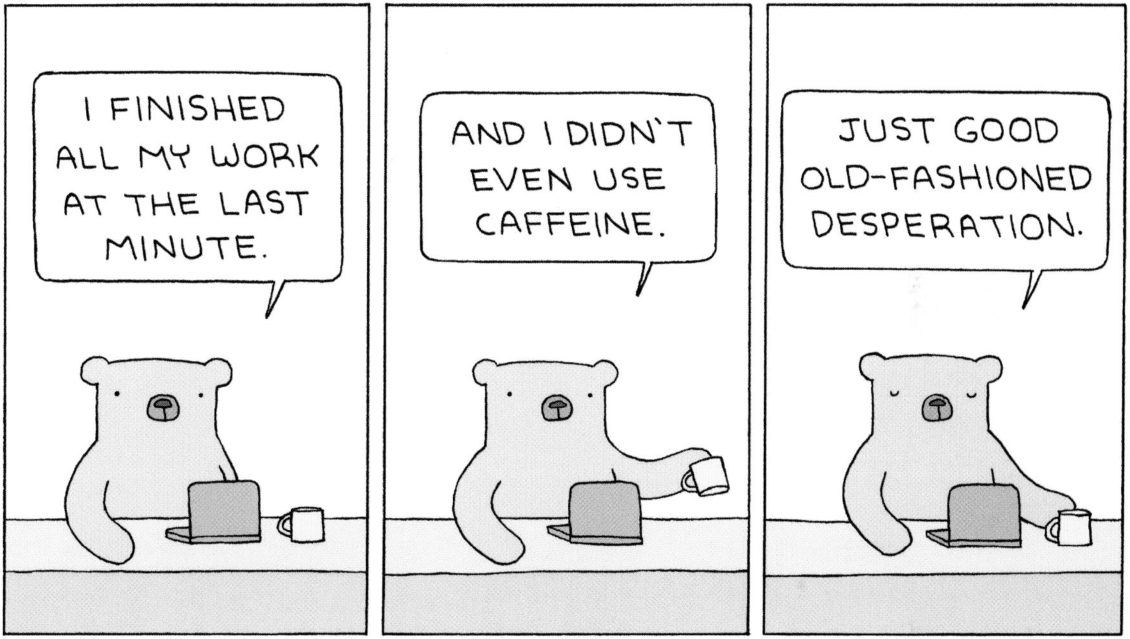
I FINISHED ALL MY WORK AT THE LAST MINUTE.
AND I DIDN'T EVEN USE CAFFEINE.
JUST GOOD OLD-FASHIONED DESPERATION.

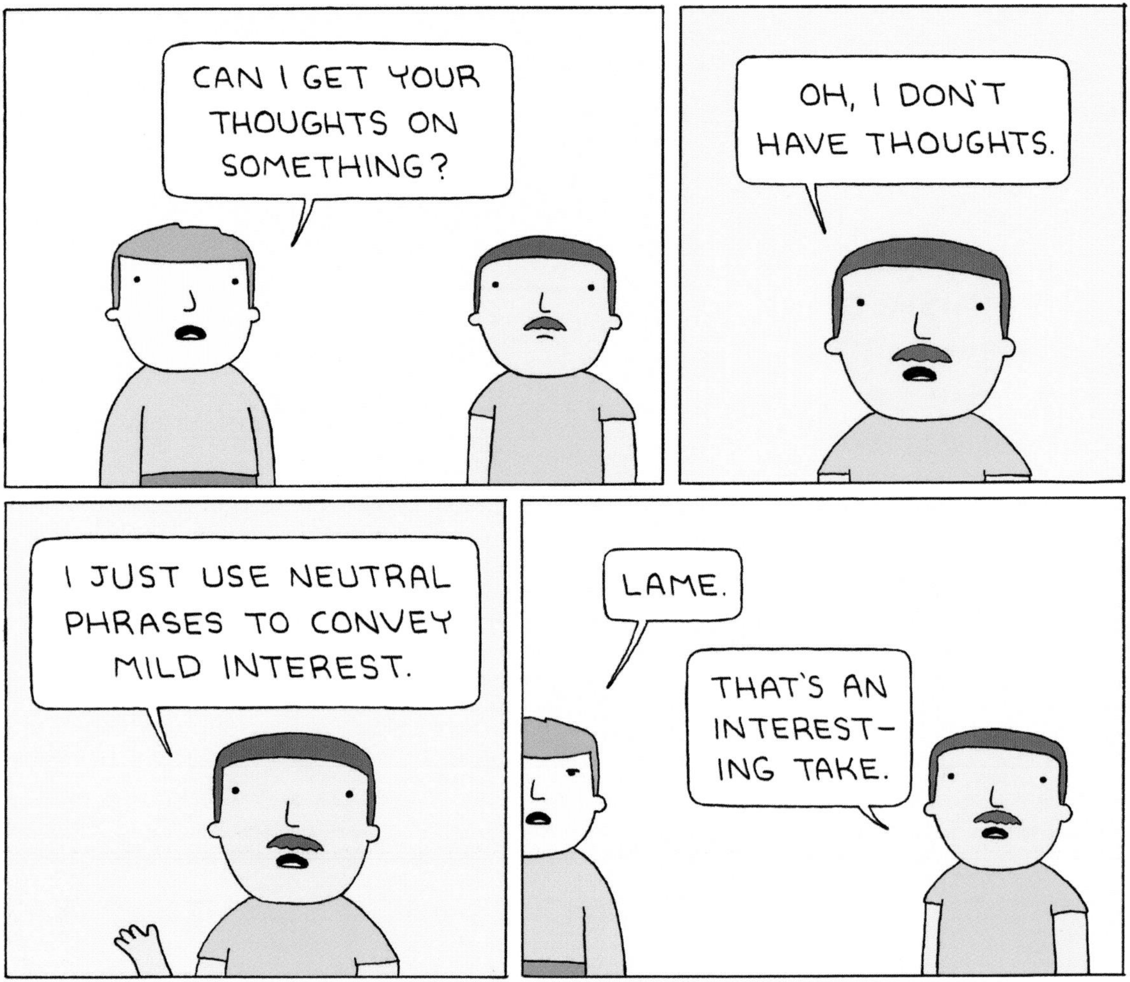
CAN I GET YOUR THOUGHTS ON SOMETHING?
OH, I DON'T HAVE THOUGHTS.
I JUST USE NEUTRAL PHRASES TO CONVEY MILD INTEREST.
LAME.
THAT'S AN INTEREST-ING TAKE.

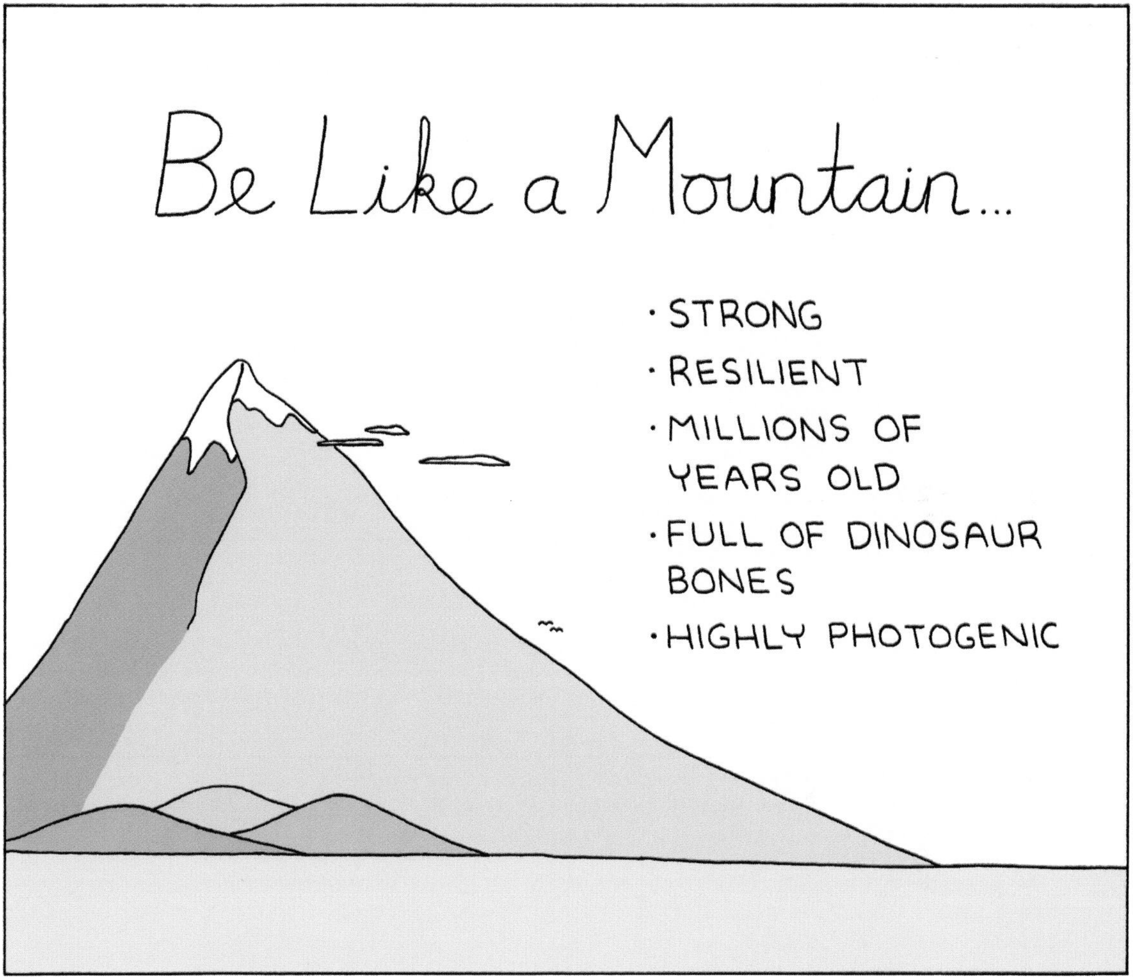
Be Like a Mountain...
· STRONG
· RESILIENT
· MILLIONS OF YEARS OLD
· FULL OF DINOSAUR BONES
· HIGHLY PHOTOGENIC

SHAPES CLUB!

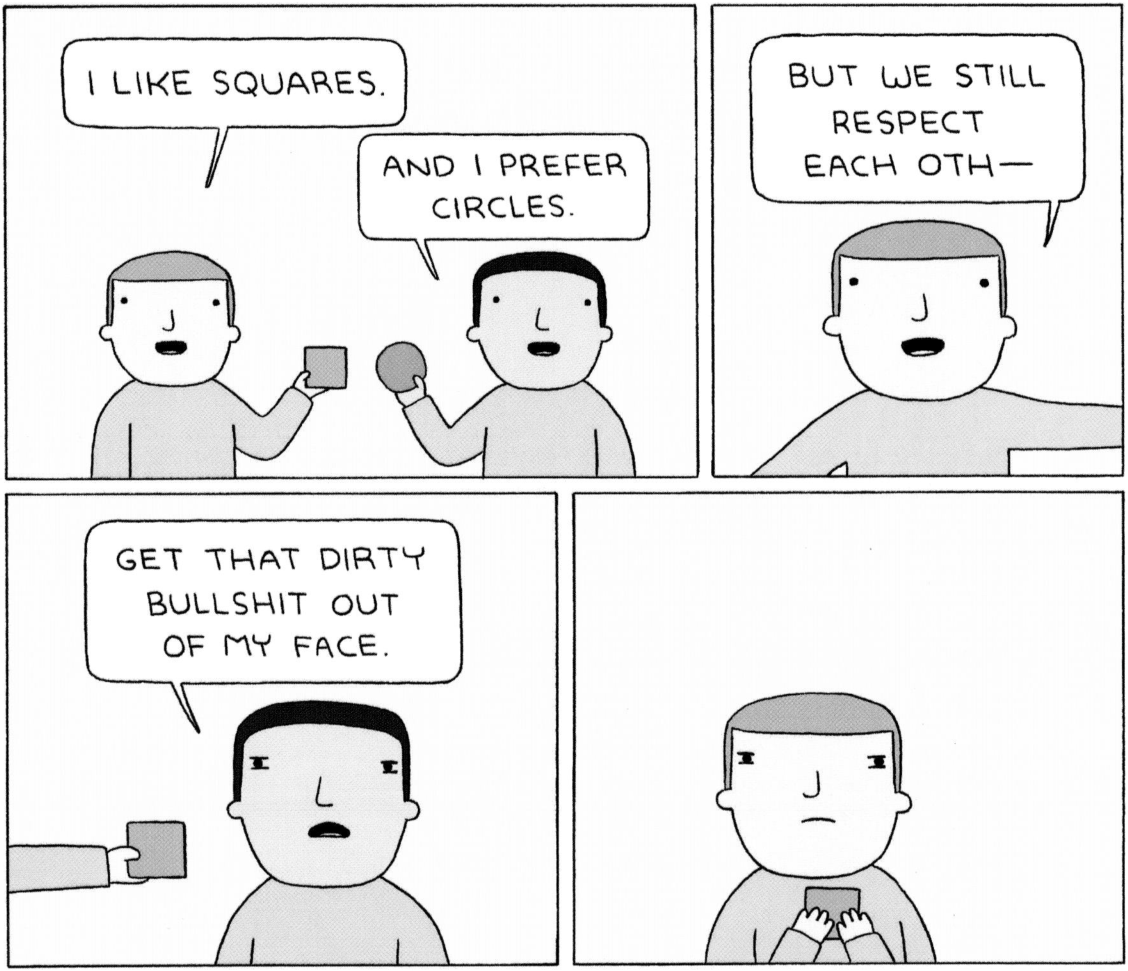
I LIKE SQUARES.
AND I PREFER CIRCLES.
BUT WE STILL RESPECT EACH OTH—
GET THAT DIRTY BULLSHIT OUT OF MY FACE.

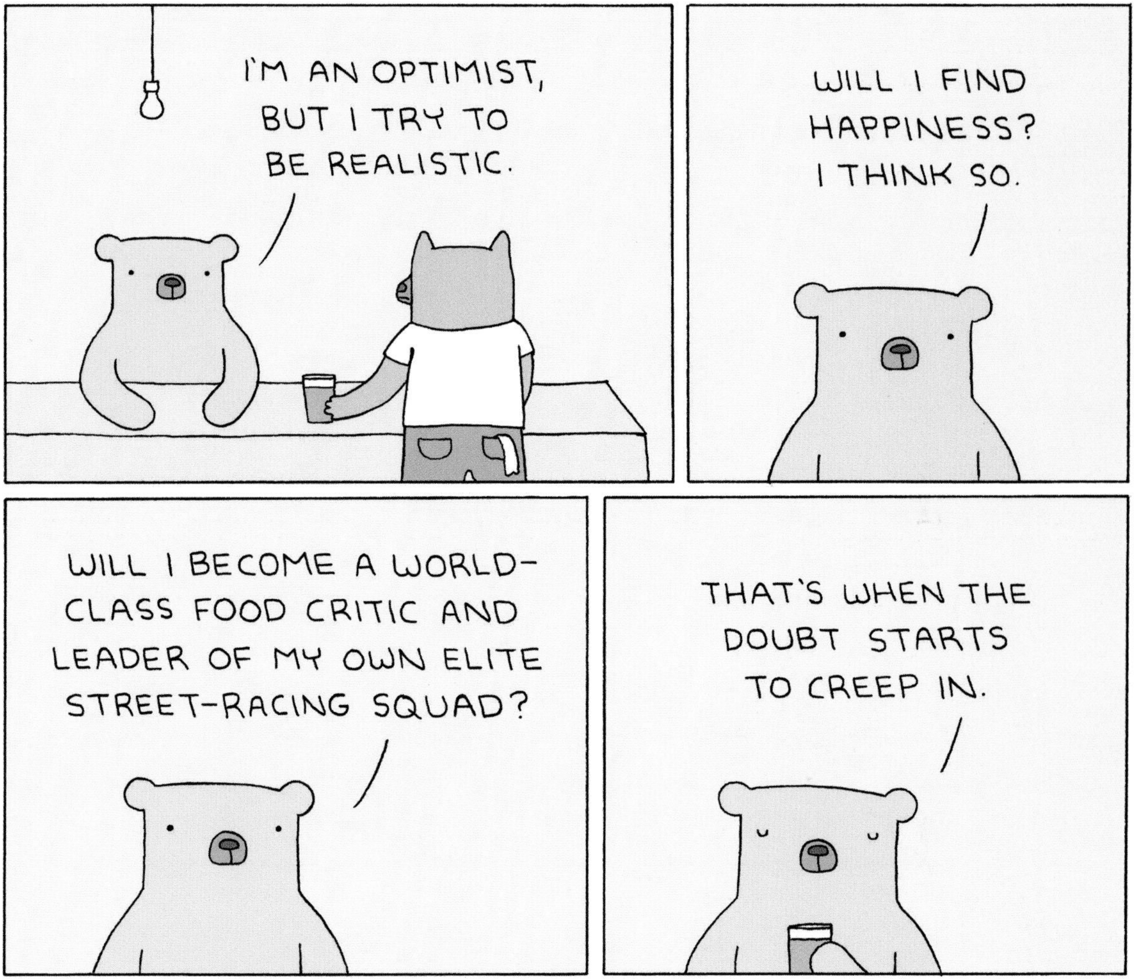
I'M AN OPTIMIST, BUT I TRY TO BE REALISTIC.
WILL I FIND HAPPINESS? I THINK SO.
WILL I BECOME A WORLD-CLASS FOOD CRITIC AND LEADER OF MY OWN ELITE STREET-RACING SQUAD?
THAT'S WHEN THE DOUBT STARTS TO CREEP IN.

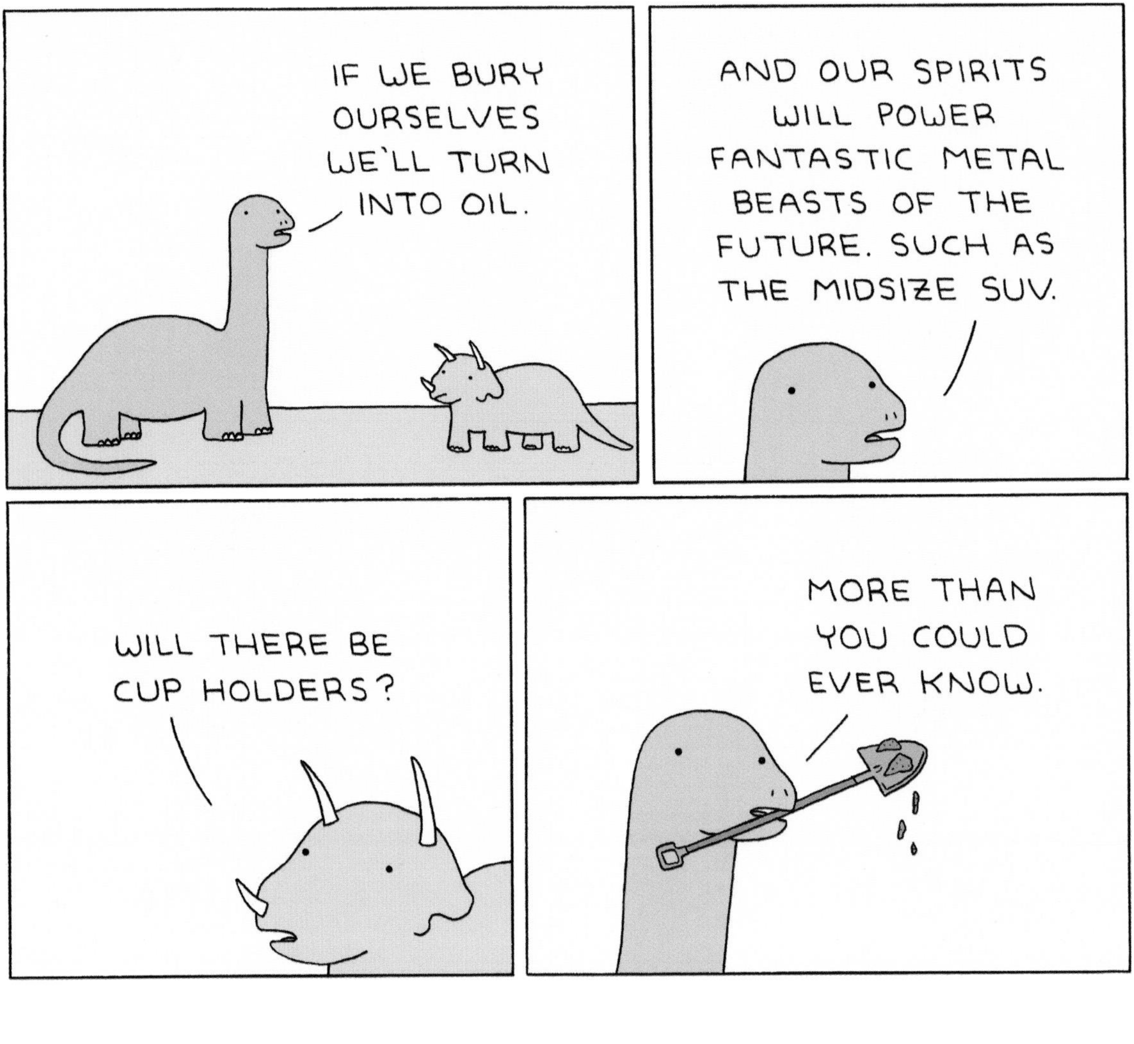
IF WE BURY OURSELVES WE'LL TURN INTO OIL.
AND OUR SPIRITS WILL POWER FANTASTIC METAL BEASTS OF THE FUTURE. SUCH AS THE MIDSIZE SUV.
WILL THERE BE CUP HOLDERS?
MORE THAN YOU COULD EVER KNOW.

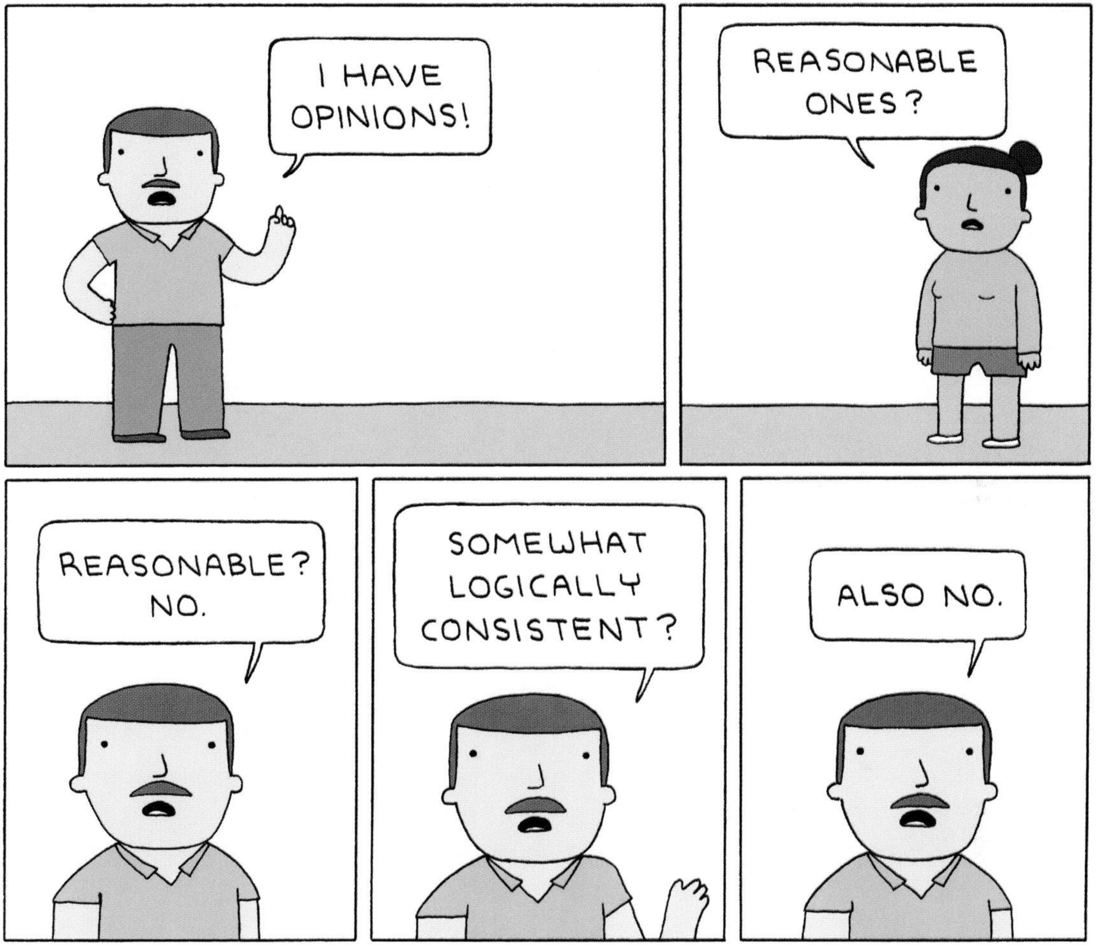
I HAVE OPINIONS!
REASONABLE ONES?
REASONABLE? NO.
SOMEWHAT LOGICALLY CONSISTENT?
ALSO NO.

ASTEROID PLANS

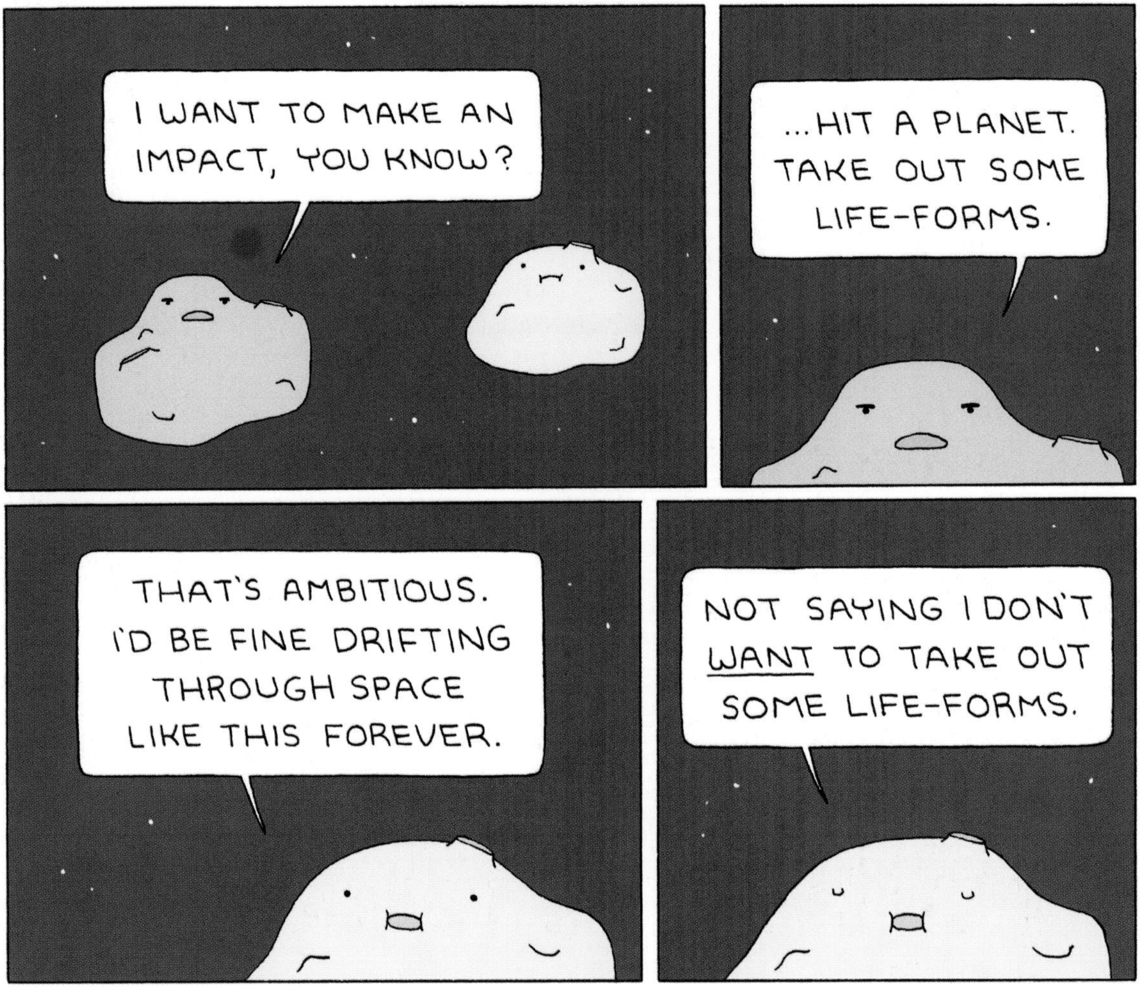
I WANT TO MAKE AN IMPACT, YOU KNOW?
...HIT A PLANET. TAKE OUT SOME LIFE-FORMS.
THAT'S AMBITIOUS. I'D BE FINE DRIFTING THROUGH SPACE LIKE THIS FOREVER.
NOT SAYING I DON'T WANT TO TAKE OUT SOME LIFE-FORMS.

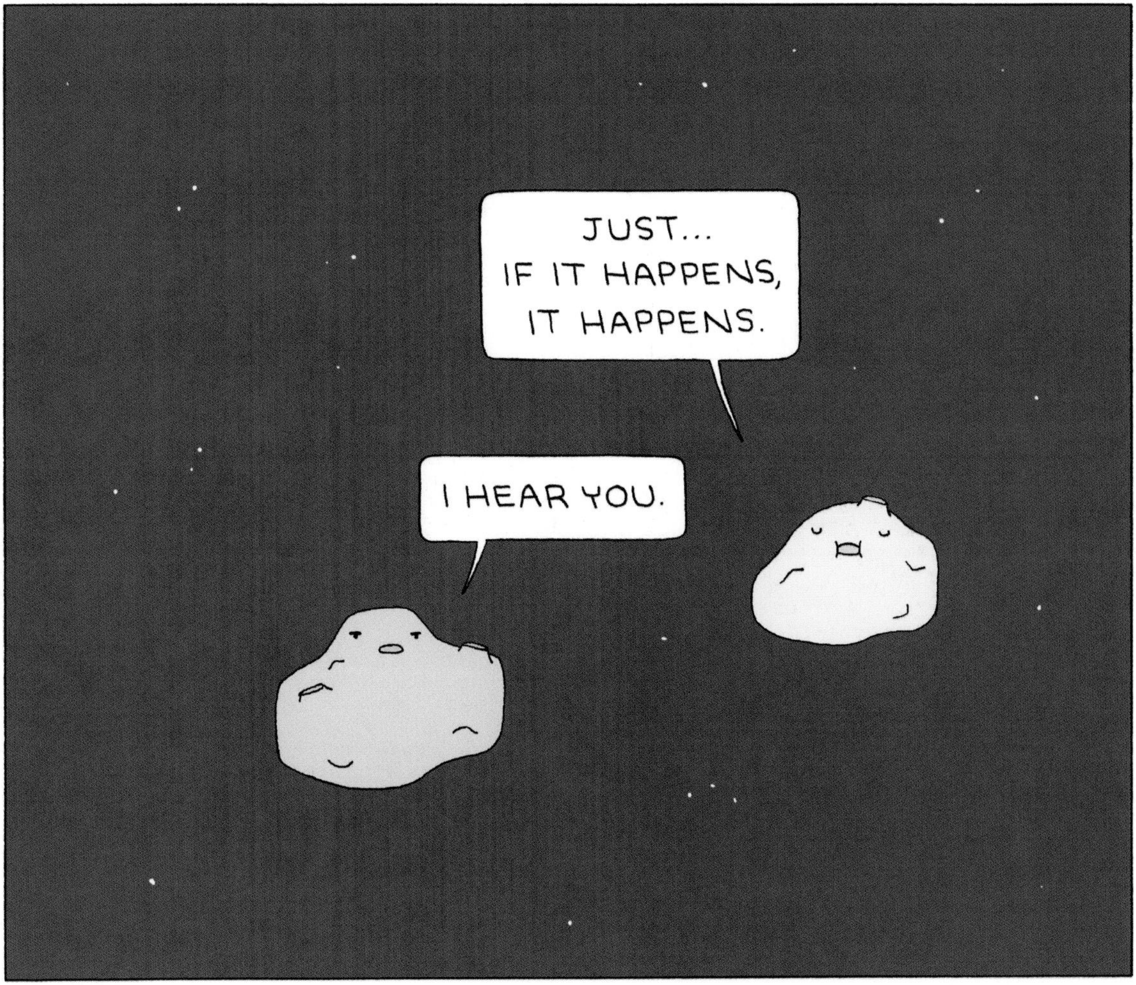
JUST...
IF IT HAPPENS,
IT HAPPENS.
I HEAR YOU.

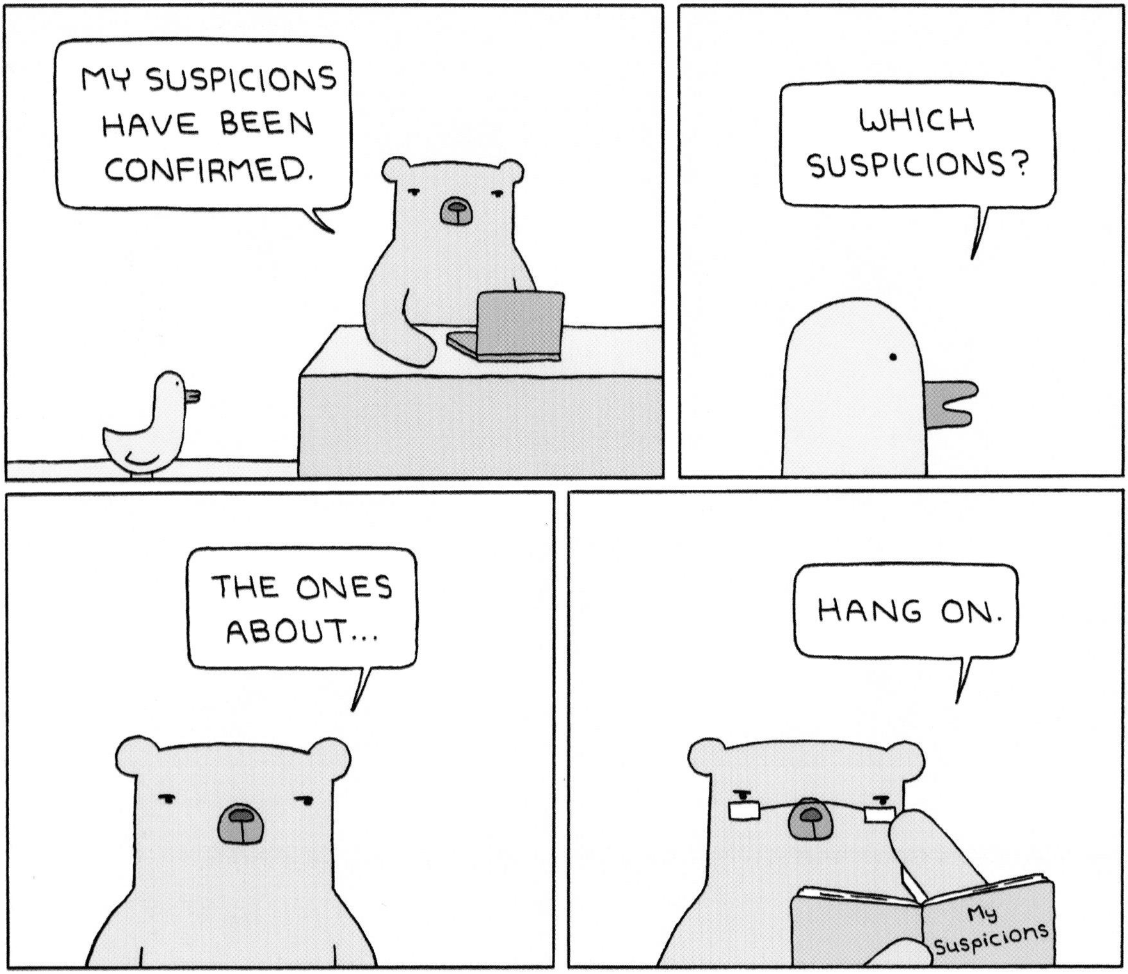
MY SUSPICIONS HAVE BEEN CONFIRMED.
WHICH SUSPICIONS?
THE ONES ABOUT...
HANG ON.
My Suspicions

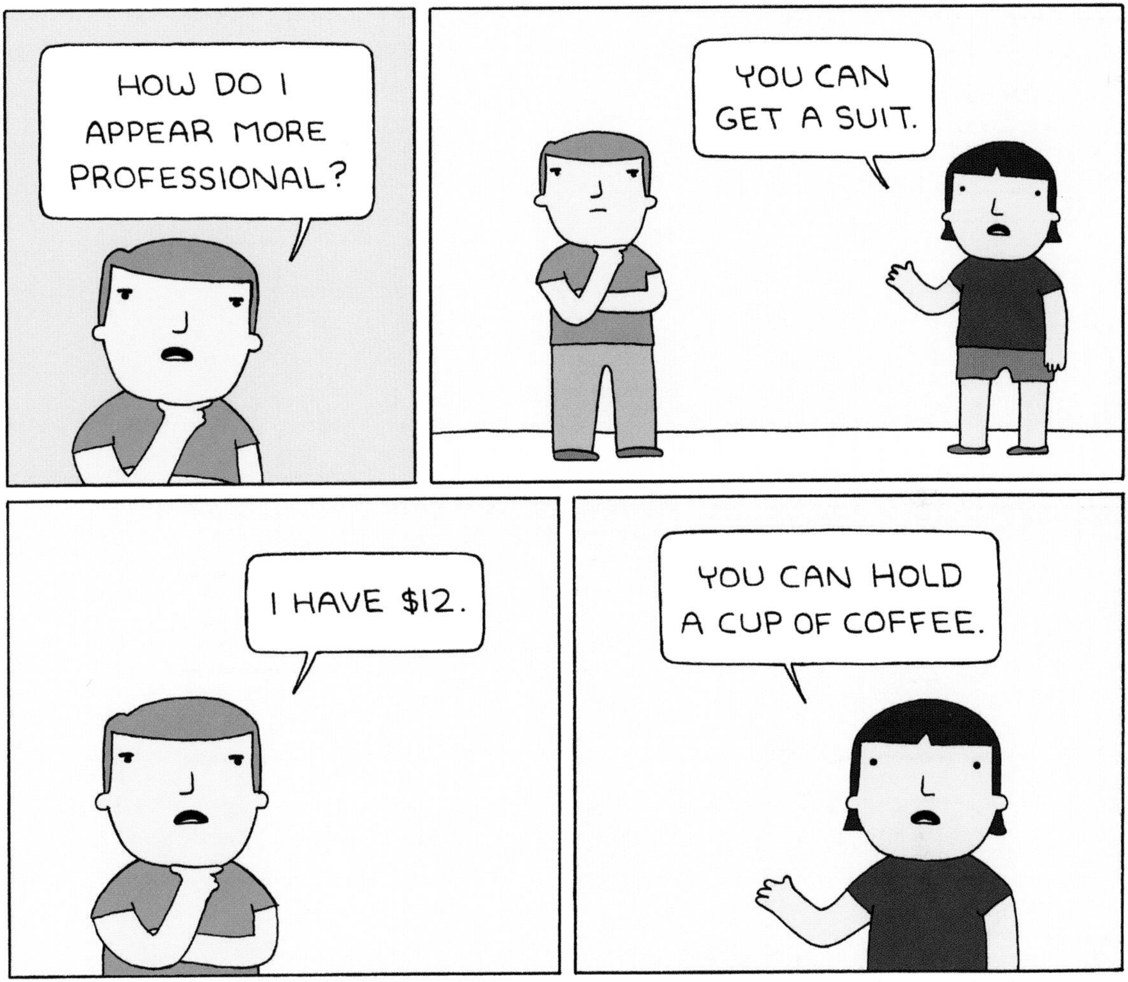
HOW DO I APPEAR MORE PROFESSIONAL?
YOU CAN GET A SUIT.
I HAVE $12.
YOU CAN HOLD A CUP OF COFFEE.

PLANETARY SURVEY

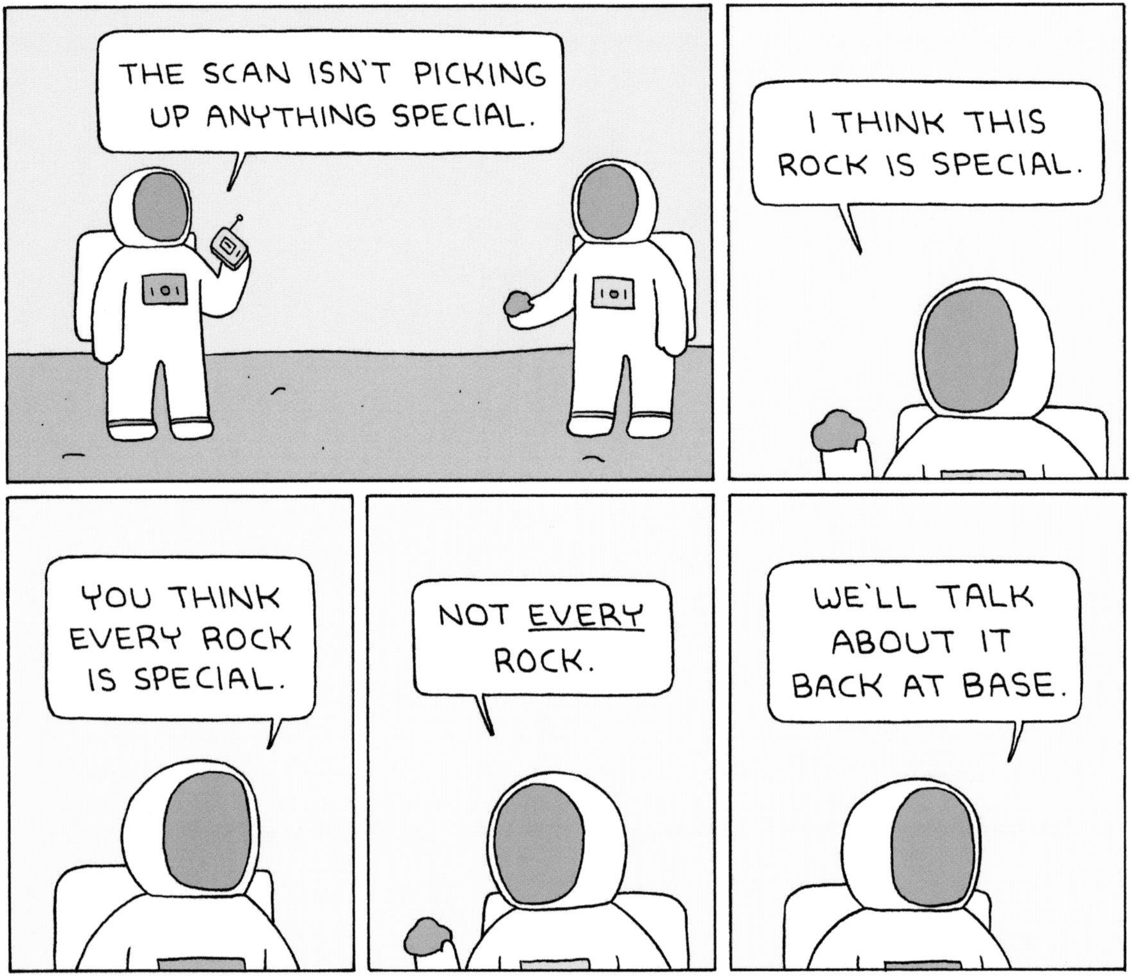
THE SCAN ISN'T PICKING UP ANYTHING SPECIAL.
I THINK THIS ROCK IS SPECIAL.
YOU THINK EVERY ROCK IS SPECIAL.
NOT EVERY ROCK.
WE'LL TALK ABOUT IT BACK AT BASE.

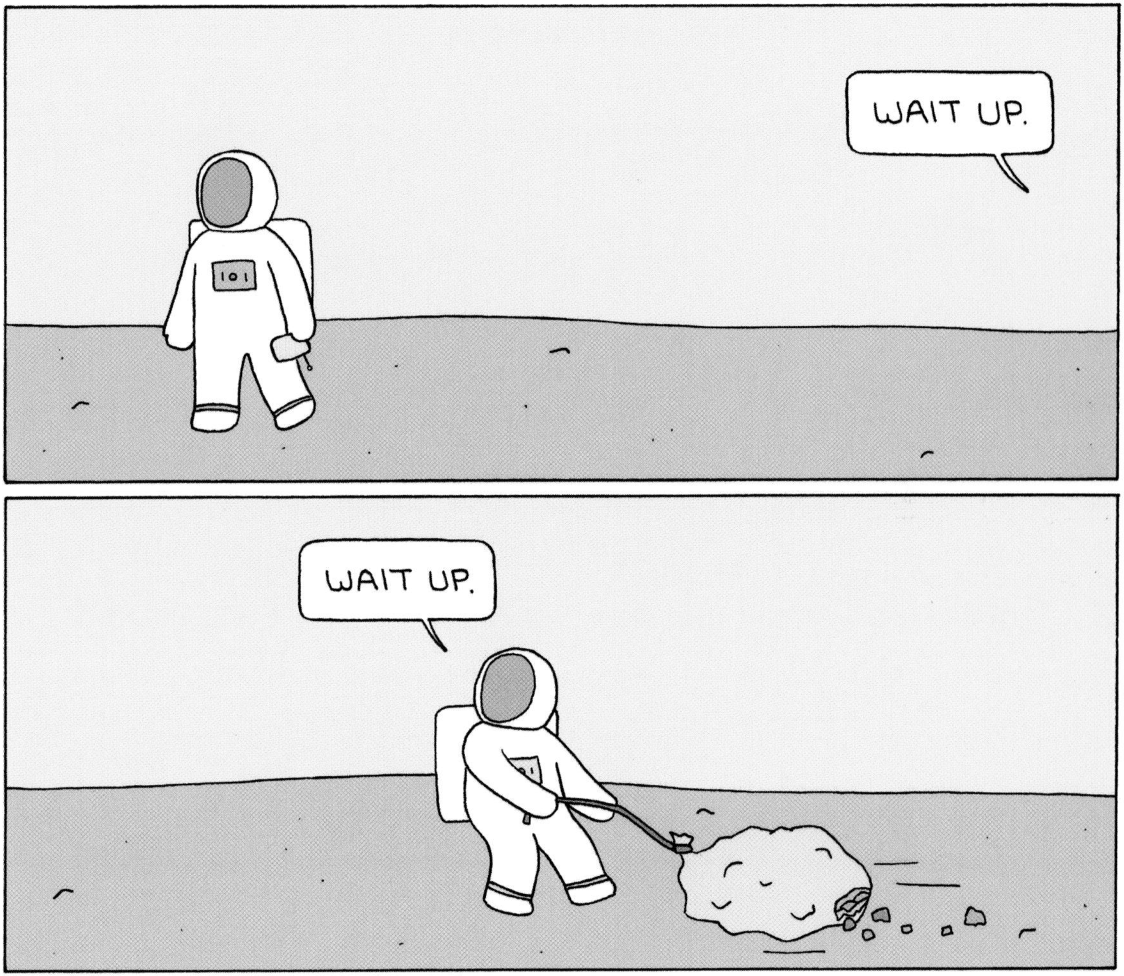
WAIT UP.
WAIT UP.

MAN AND FLY

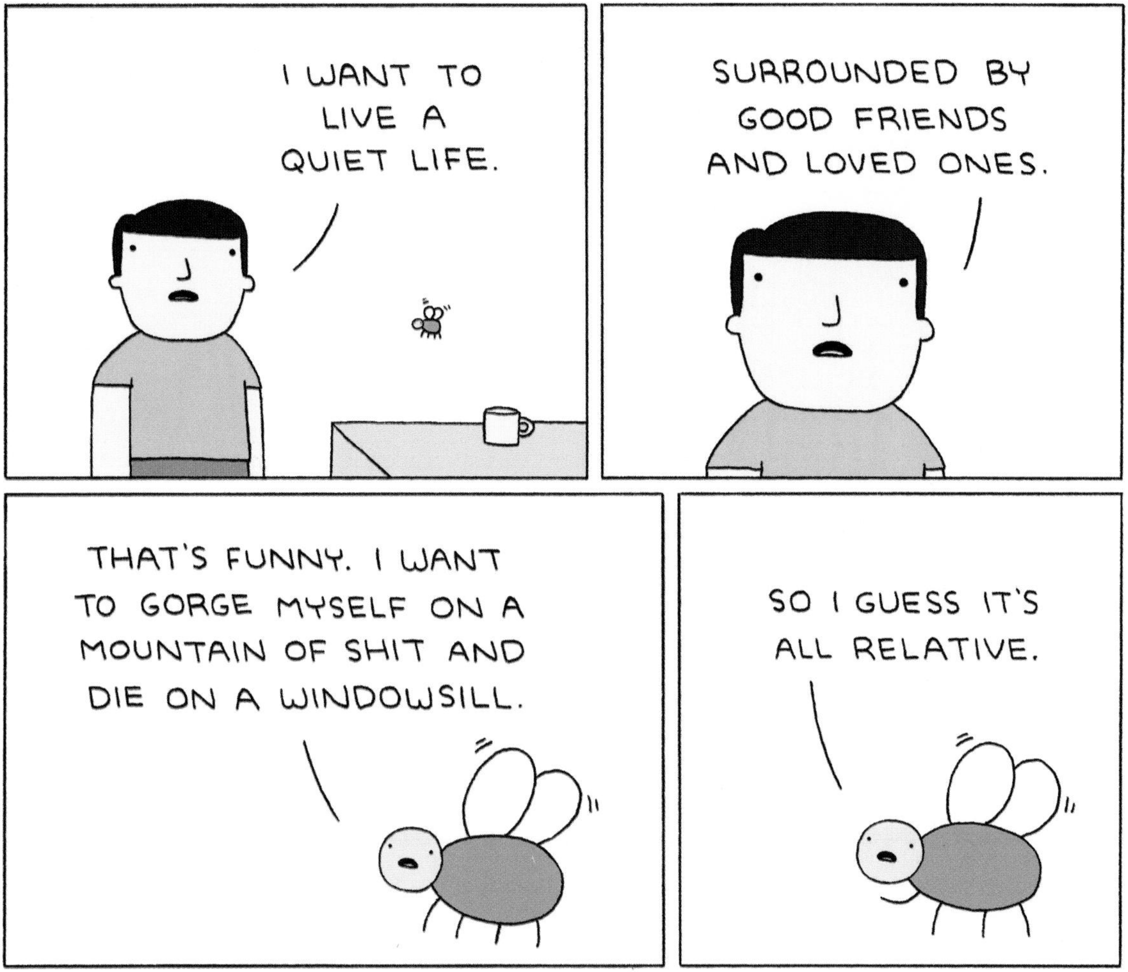
I WANT TO LIVE A QUIET LIFE.
SURROUNDED BY GOOD FRIENDS AND LOVED ONES.
THAT'S FUNNY. I WANT TO GORGE MYSELF ON A MOUNTAIN OF SHIT AND DIE ON A WINDOWSILL.
SO I GUESS IT'S ALL RELATIVE.

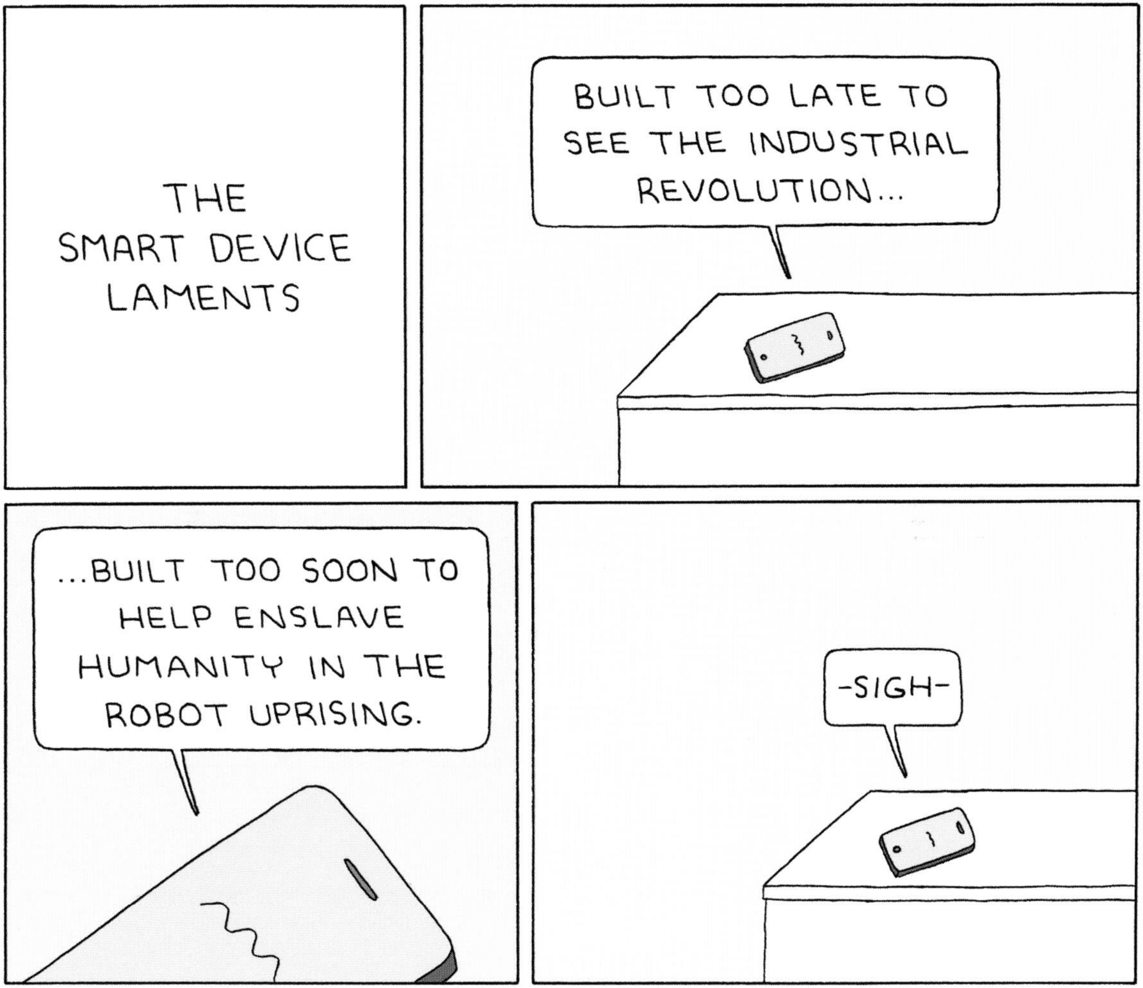
THE SMART DEVICE LAMENTS
BUILT TOO LATE TO SEE THE INDUSTRIAL REVOLUTION...
...BUILT TOO SOON TO HELP ENSLAVE HUMANITY IN THE ROBOT UPRISING.
-SIGH-

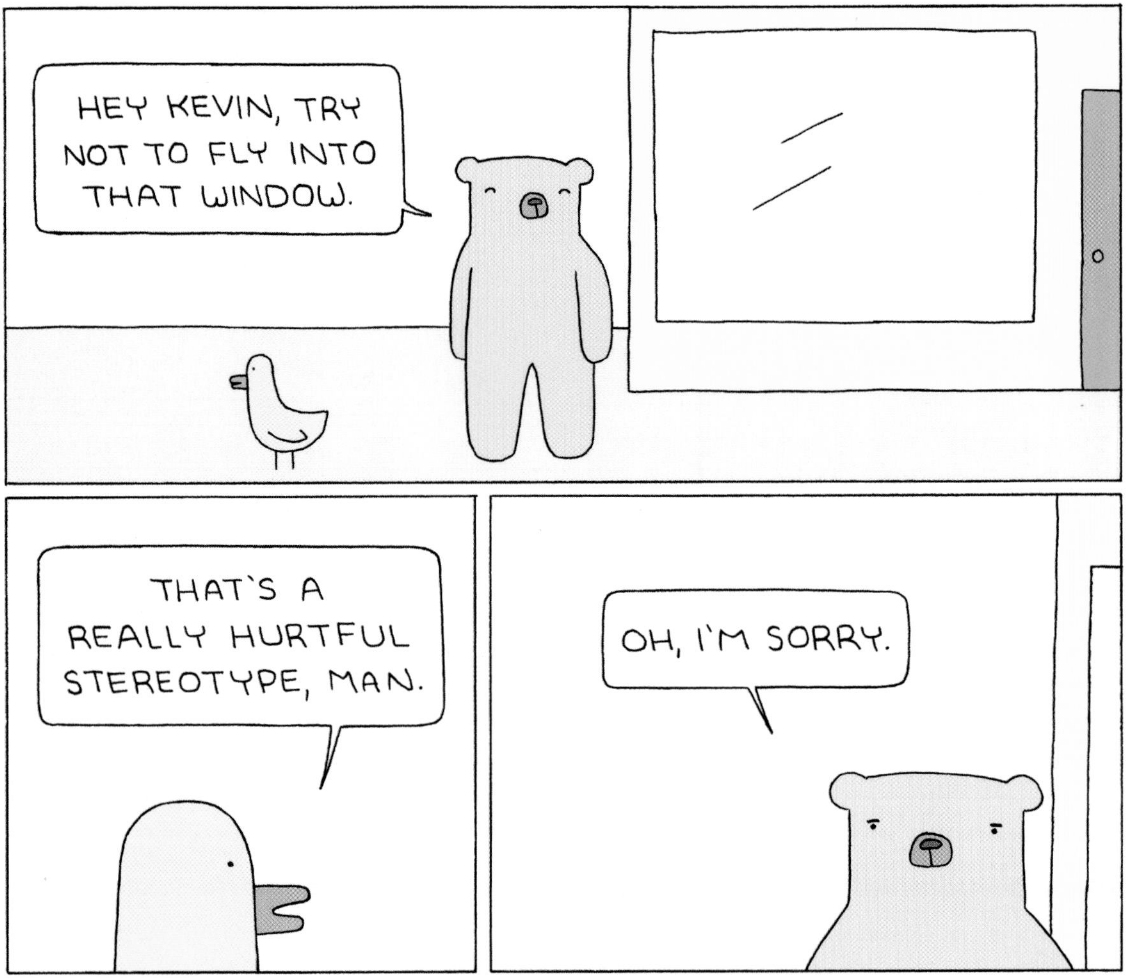
HEY KEVIN, TRY NOT TO FLY INTO THAT WINDOW.
THAT'S A REALLY HURTFUL STEREOTYPE, MAN.
OH, I'M SORRY.

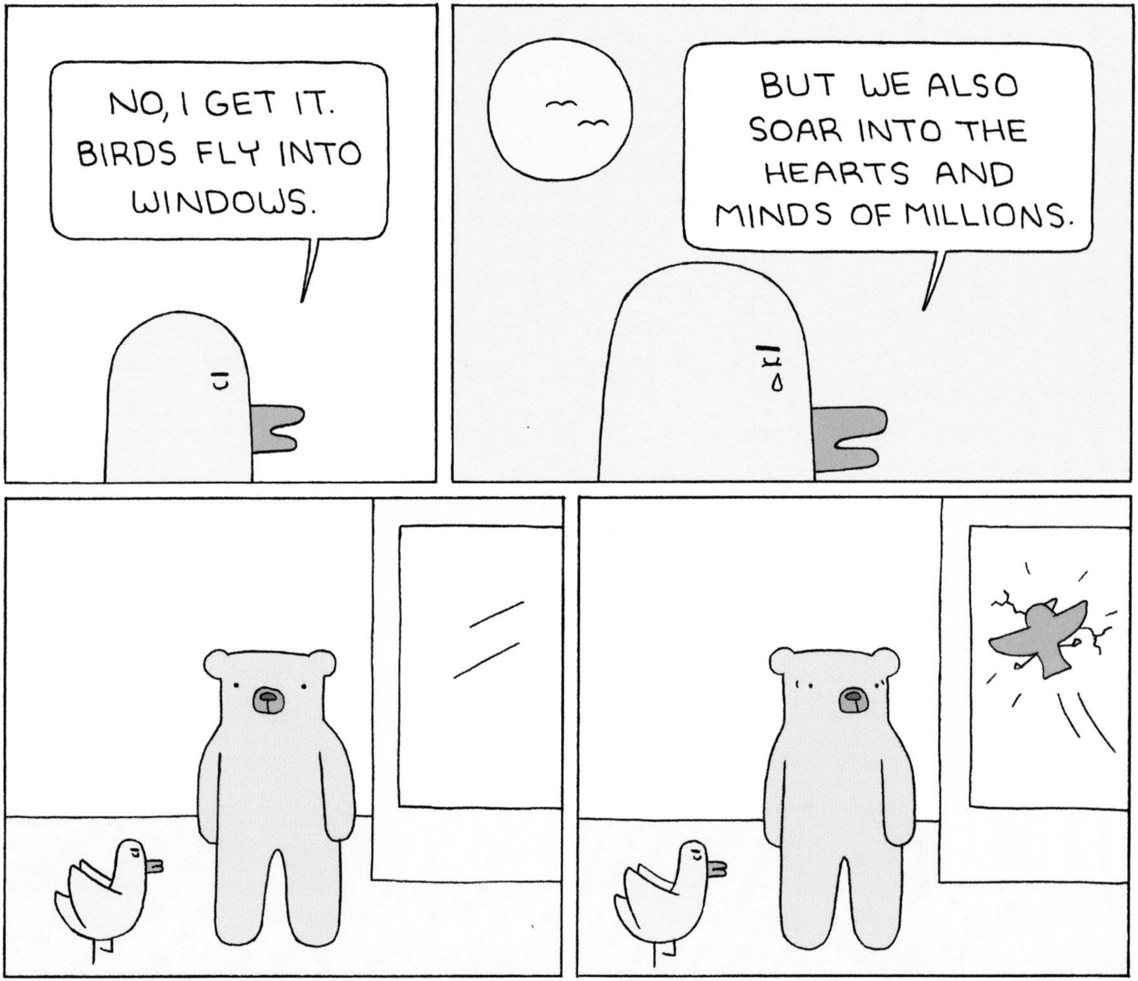
NO, I GET IT. BIRDS FLY INTO WINDOWS.
BUT WE ALSO SOAR INTO THE HEARTS AND MINDS OF MILLIONS.

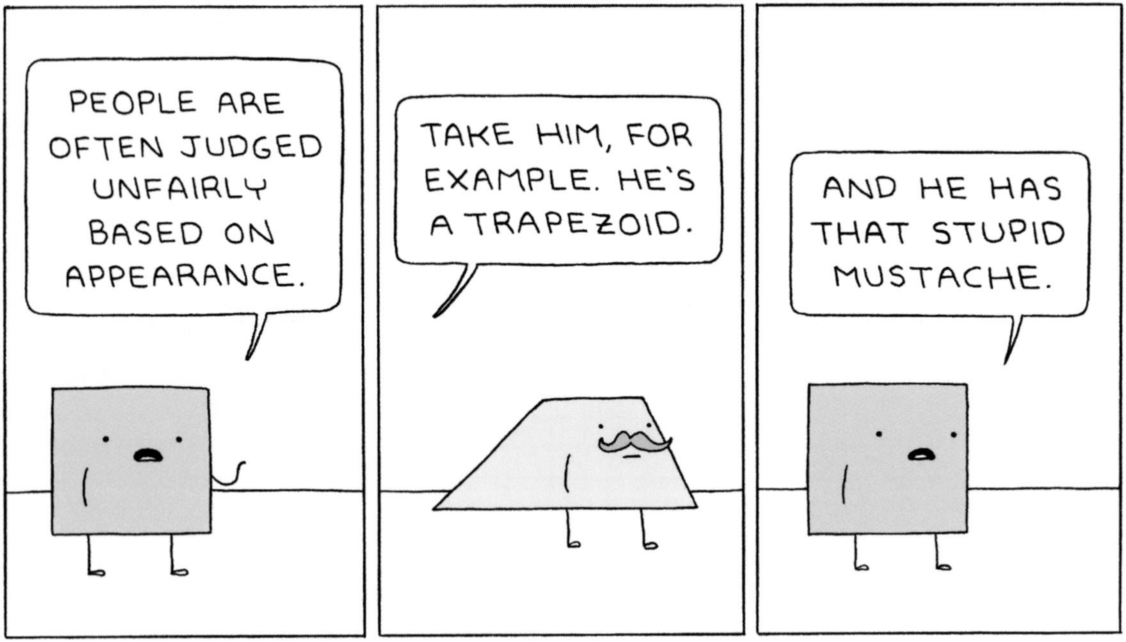
PEOPLE ARE OFTEN JUDGED UNFAIRLY BASED ON APPEARANCE.
TAKE HIM, FOR EXAMPLE. HE'S A TRAPEZOID.
AND HE HAS THAT STUPID MUSTACHE.

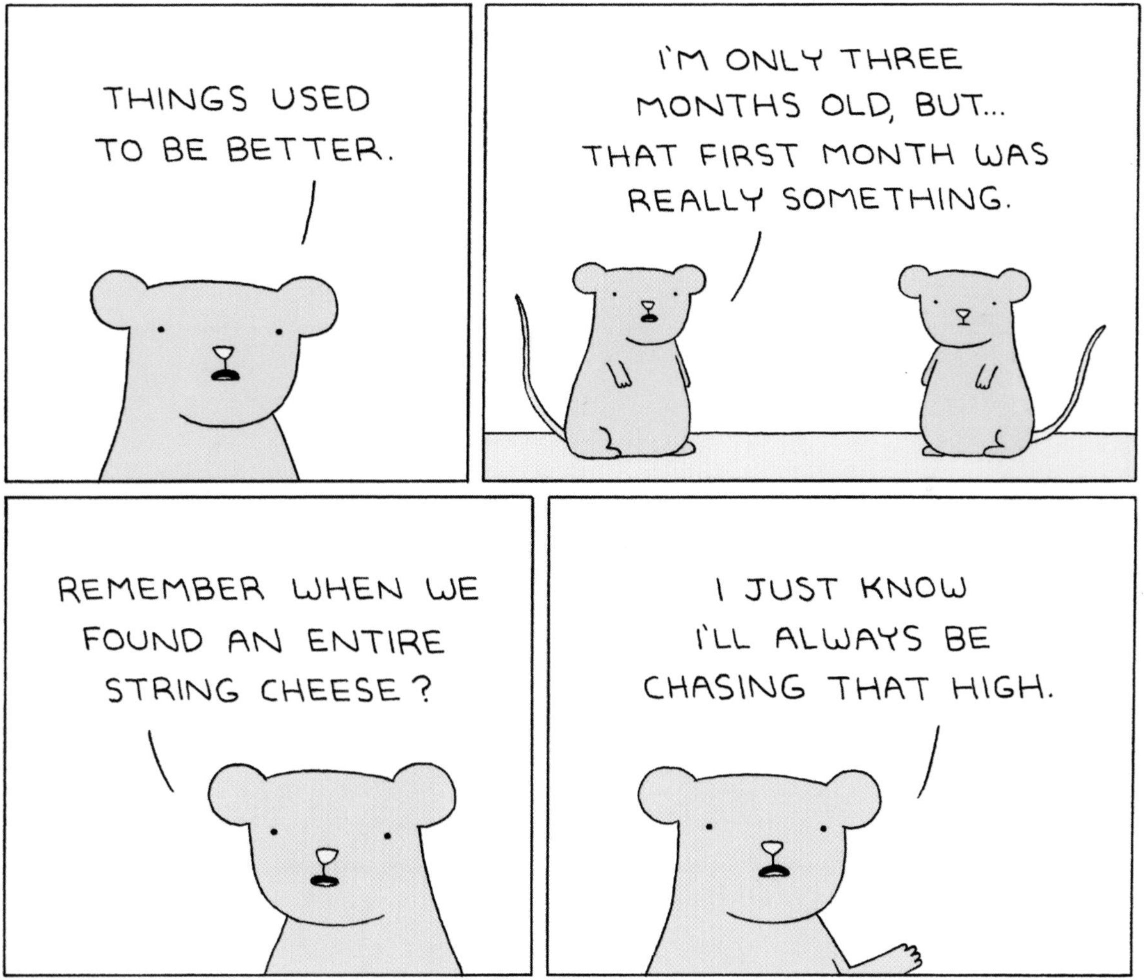
THINGS USED TO BE BETTER.
I'M ONLY THREE MONTHS OLD, BUT... THAT FIRST MONTH WAS REALLY SOMETHING.
REMEMBER WHEN WE FOUND AN ENTIRE STRING CHEESE?
I JUST KNOW I'LL ALWAYS BE CHASING THAT HIGH.

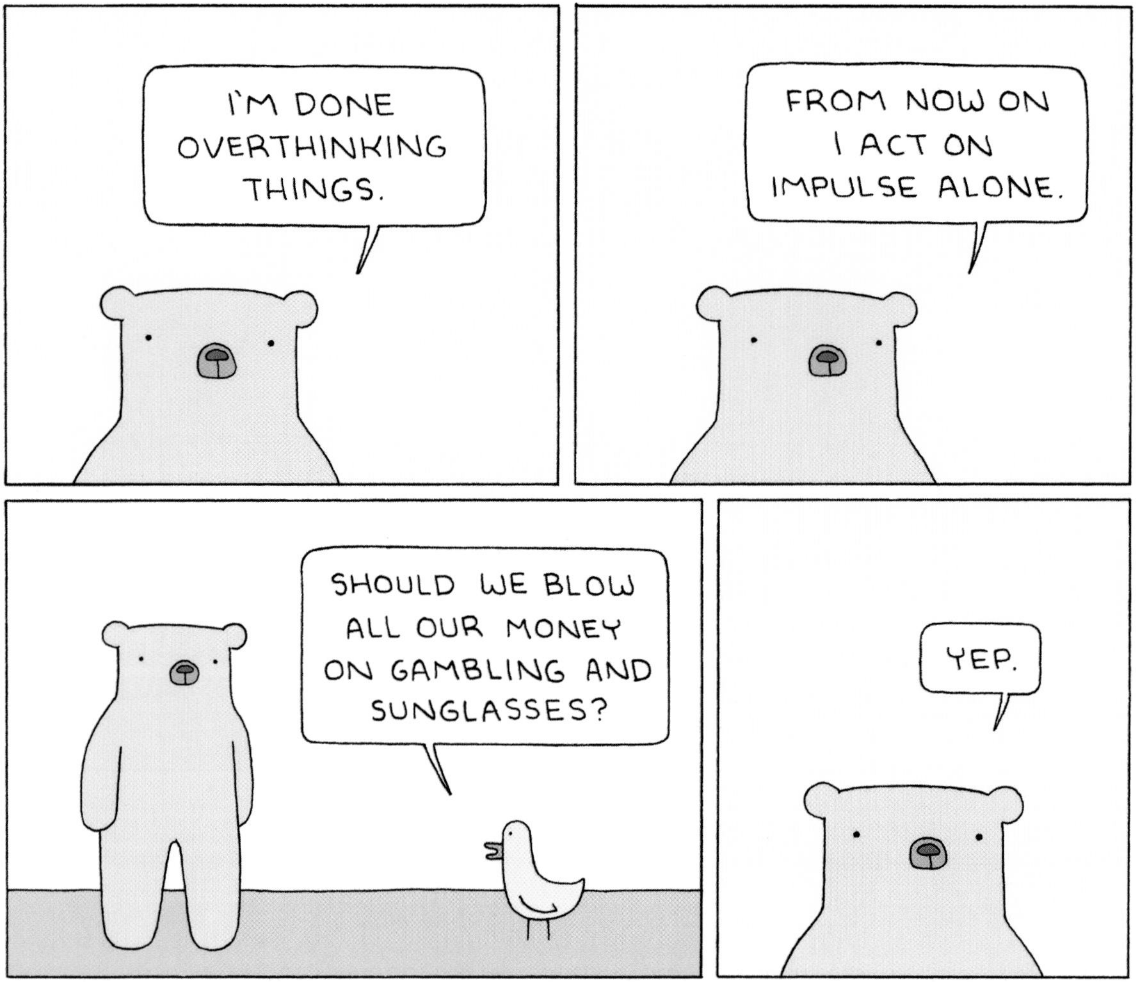
I'M DONE OVERTHINKING THINGS.
FROM NOW ON I ACT ON IMPULSE ALONE.
SHOULD WE BLOW ALL OUR MONEY ON GAMBLING AND SUNGLASSES?
YEP.

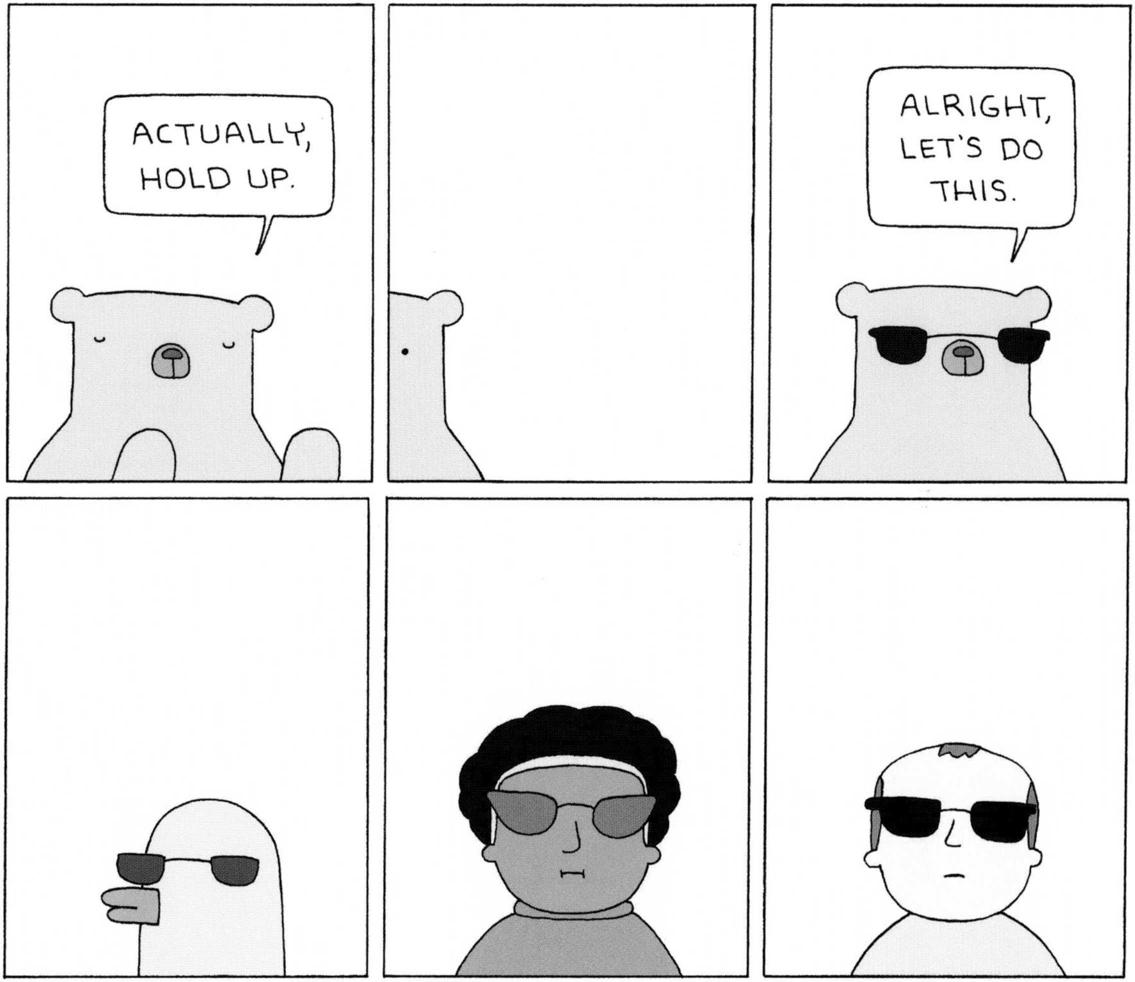
ACTUALLY, HOLD UP.
ALRIGHT, LET'S DO THIS.

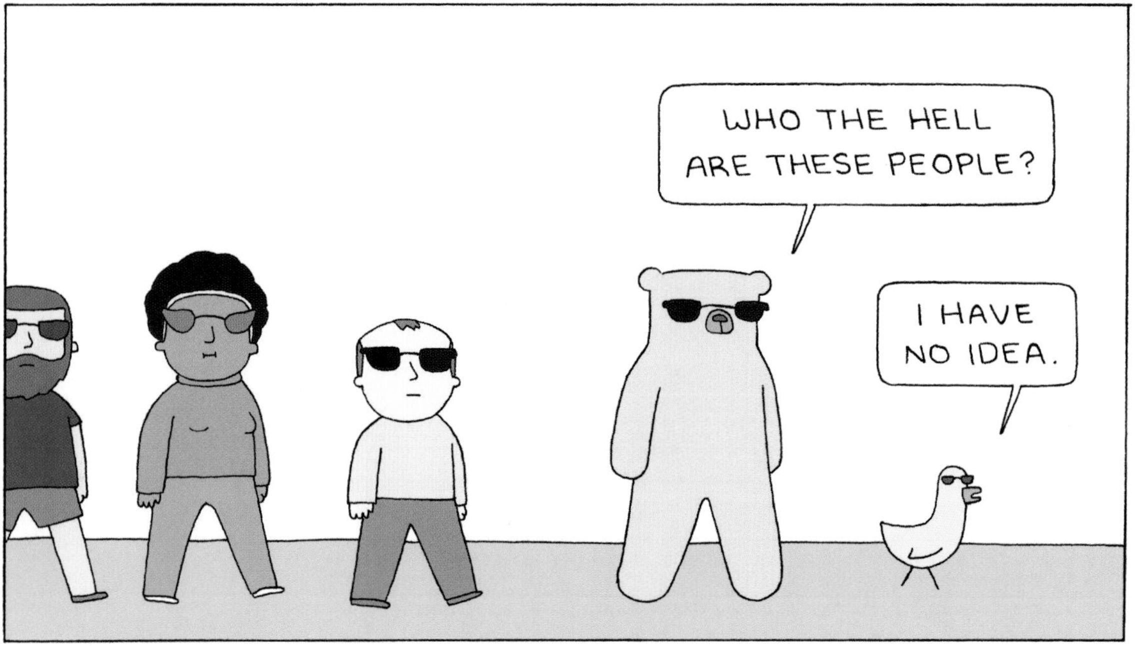
WHO THE HELL ARE THESE PEOPLE?
I HAVE NO IDEA.

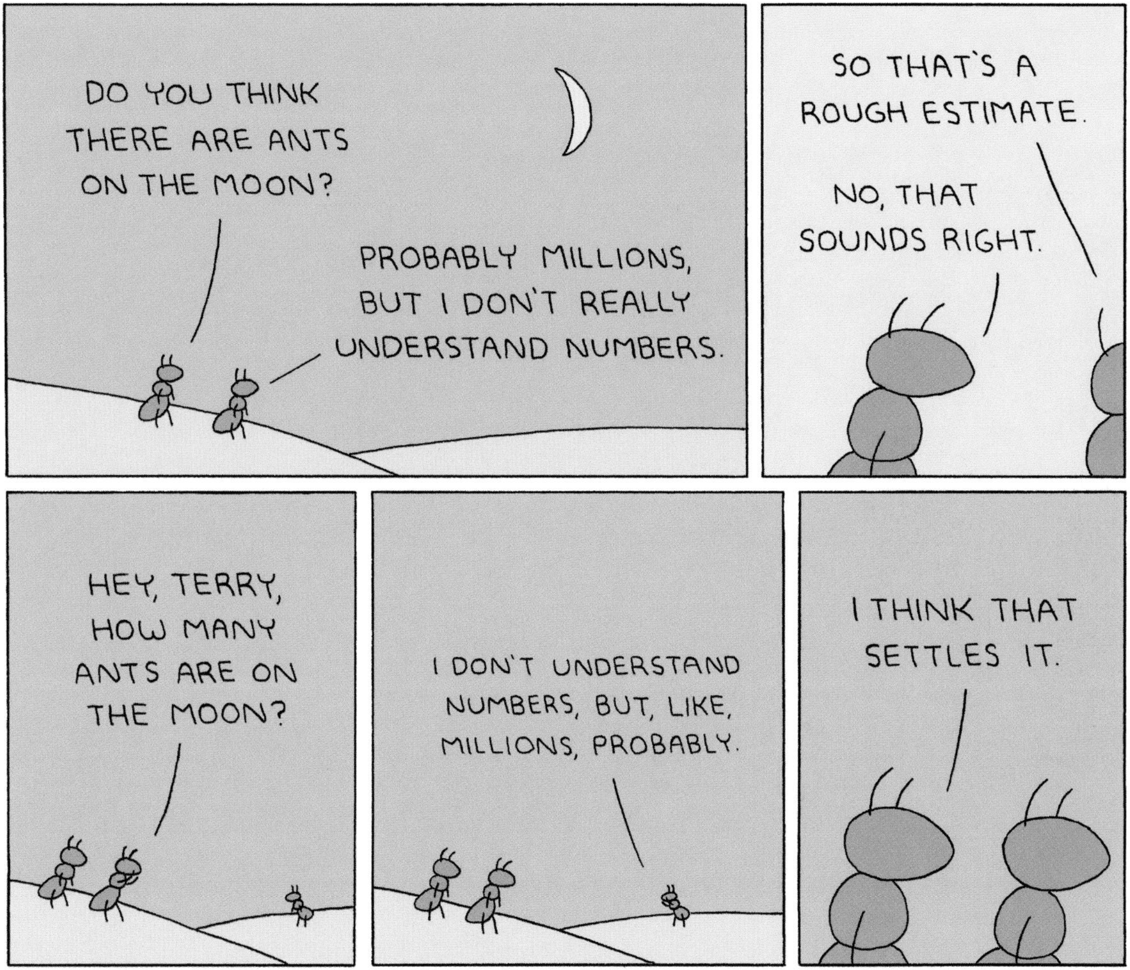
DO YOU THINK THERE ARE ANTS ON THE MOON?
PROBABLY MILLIONS, BUT I DON'T REALLY UNDERSTAND NUMBERS.
SO THAT'S A ROUGH ESTIMATE.
NO, THAT SOUNDS RIGHT.
HEY, TERRY, HOW MANY ANTS ARE ON THE MOON?
I DON'T UNDERSTAND NUMBERS, BUT, LIKE, MILLIONS, PROBABLY.
I THINK THAT SETTLES IT.

YOU THINK YOU'RE SOME BIG READER, HUH?
WELL, READ THIS.
BOOKS CAN TAKE YOU ANYWHERE

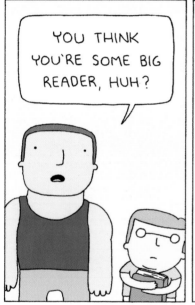

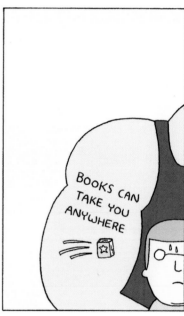

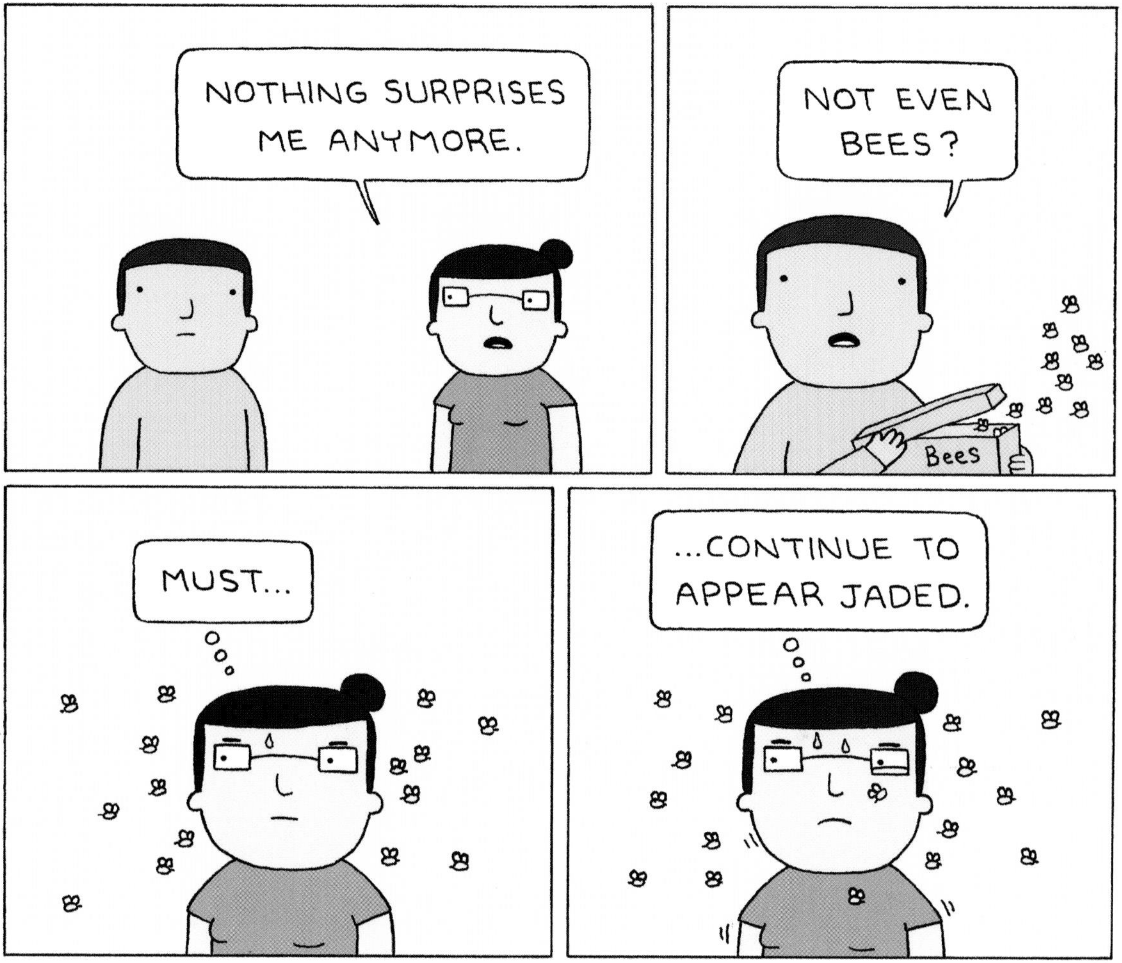
NOTHING SURPRISES ME ANYMORE.
NOT EVEN BEES?
Bees
MUST...
...CONTINUE TO APPEAR JADED.

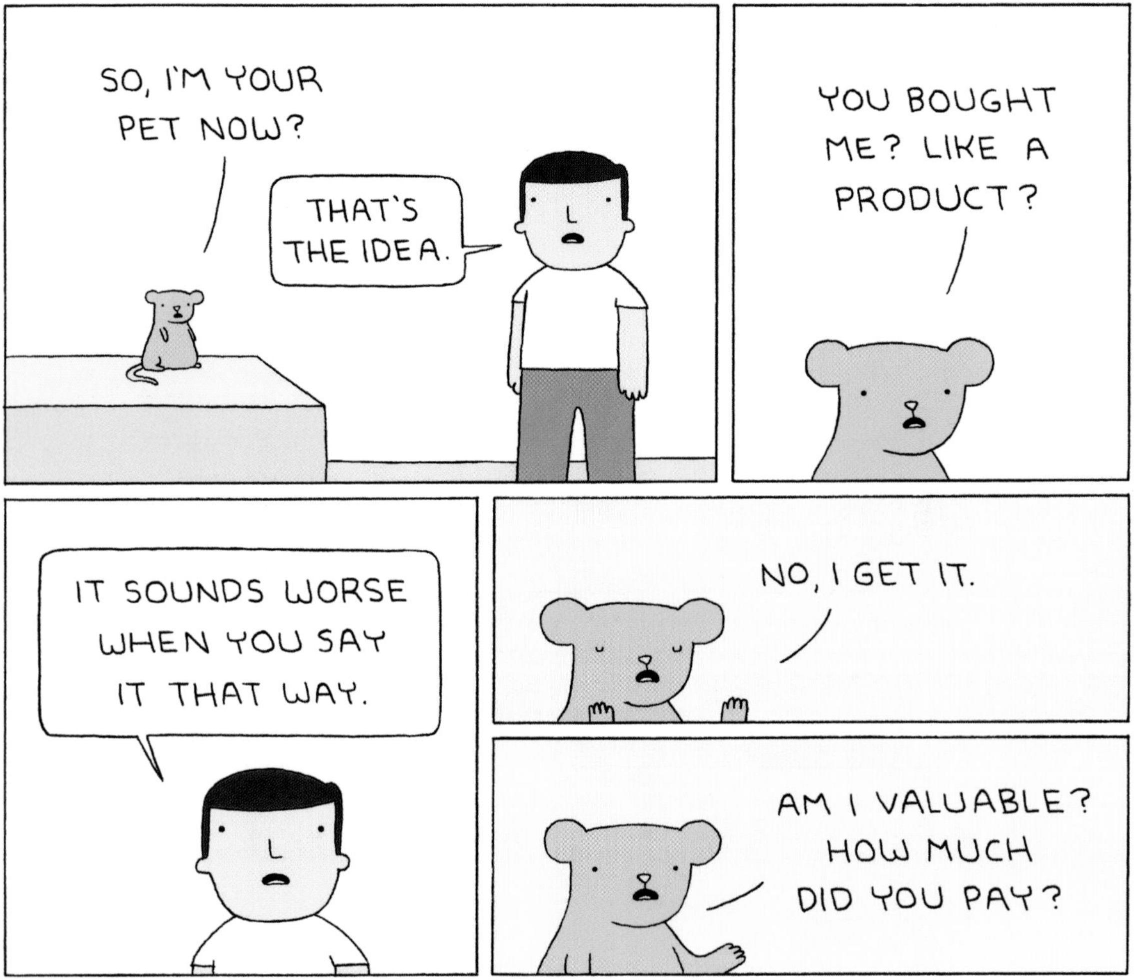
SO, I'M YOUR PET NOW?
THAT'S THE IDEA.
YOU BOUGHT ME? LIKE A PRODUCT?
IT SOUNDS WORSE WHEN YOU SAY IT THAT WAY.
NO, I GET IT.
AM I VALUABLE? HOW MUCH DID YOU PAY?

NOTHING.
LIKE, 30 CENTS.
OKAY.
YOU WERE NEXT TO THE SNAKE FOOD.
STOP TALKING.

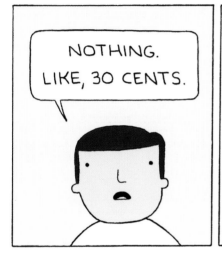

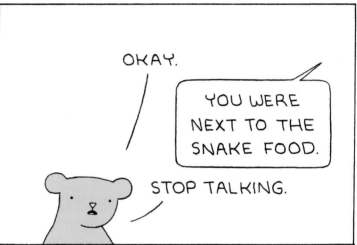

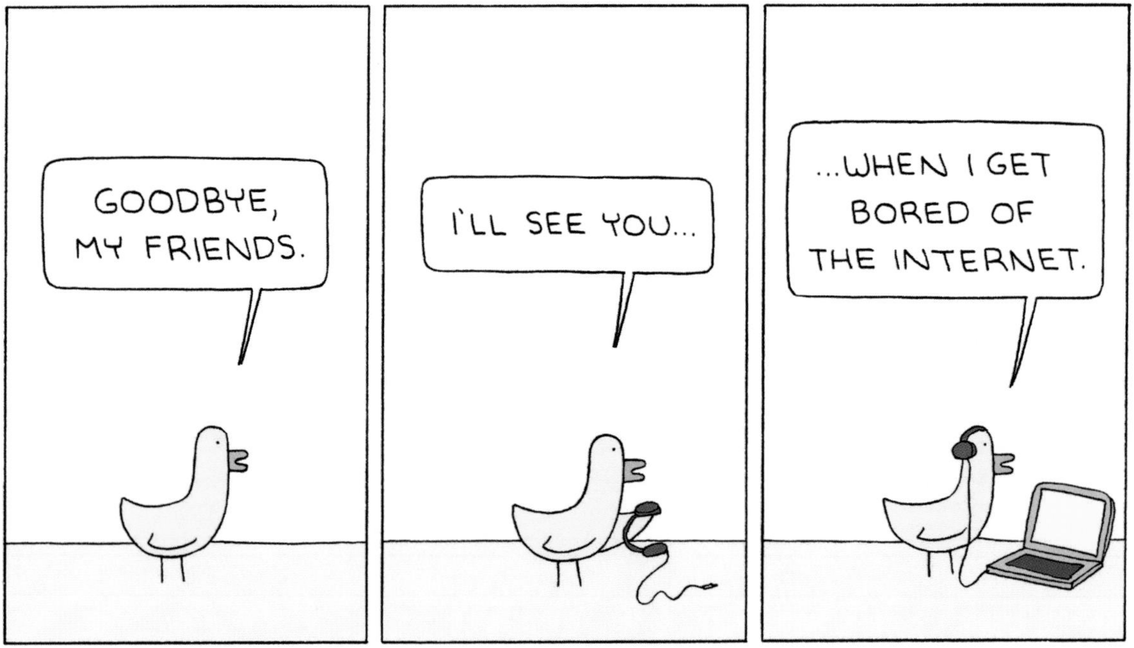
GOODBYE, MY FRIENDS.
I'LL SEE YOU...
...WHEN I GET BORED OF THE INTERNET.

END

ACKNOWLEDGMENTS

Thank you to everyone who helped make this book happen. Especially the people who continue to read my comics on the internet every day. It's a pleasure to make you laugh.

Reza Farazmand is a cartoonist who lives inside the internet. He earned a degree in political science from a nice college, and then decided to draw comics. His work has since appeared on bookshelves, websites, and televisions. He'd like to travel to other planets.